NUMBERING THE PEOPLE

'TAKING THE CENSUS.

JE UNIVERSIT

Numbering the people

The eighteenth-century population
controversy and the development
of census and vital statistics in Britain

D.V. Glass

SAXON HOUSE, FARNBOROUGH, HANTS

Published 1973 by D. C. Heath Ltd,
1 Westmead, Farnborough, Hants, England

0 347 00200 5

Designed and produced by Design for Print Ltd, London SW1
Text printed in Hungary by Franklin Nyomda, Budapest

Preface

Twice during the eighteenth century the population of England and Wales was the subject of debate. The question was not one of numbers increasing more rapidly than the means of subsistence – that was essentially a nineteenth-century concern – but of whether the population had fallen since the Glorious Revolution of 1688. The arguments put forward on both sides were faulty and the evidence drawn upon was often unreliable. But the controversy stimulated demographic inquiries and formed the background, though not the primary cause, of the development of regular censuses and civil vital registration in the nineteenth century.

The aim of this book is to examine the eighteenth-century controversy and the subsequent development of census and vital statistics in Britain. The main focus is on the earlier developments, less well known than those of the twentieth century. But to complete the account the story has been continued to the present day, though only in a very summary fashion. The scope of current British demographic statistics can be seen in the census volumes and in the annual publications of the Registrars General.

The book is designed to be self-contained. But it has been written in connection with the collective reprint of a large number of documents – books, pamphlets and official publications – brought together to illustrate developments from the eighteenth to the mid-nineteenth centuries. Many of the materials reprinted are now scarce and difficult of access. No library contains all the original materials, and few libraries possess even the larger part of them. In any case, bringing the documents together makes it far easier for students to use primary sources.

In writing this book, and in preparing the associated collective reprint, I have been helped by many institutions and individuals. The Library of the London School of Economics (the British Library of Political and Economic Science) bore patiently with my endless borrowings both from its own collection and, with its aid, from other libraries in Britain and abroad. I am also indebted to the Wellcome Institute of the History of Medicine; to the Library of the House of Commons; to the Institute of Actuaries; to the General Register Office for allowing me to use and reprint manuscripts in its possession; to Mr K. Smith, City Librarian, Carlisle Public Libraries, for enabling me to consult and reprint materials in the Heysham Collection; and to Dr J. Cassedy, of the National Library of Medicine, Bethesda, USA. Dr Cassedy's co-operation made it possible to form a complete collection of John Heysham's Bills of Mortality – the Bills on which Joshua Milne based his Carlisle life table, the first realistic English life table. Mr Robert MacLeod, Deputy Registrar General of Scotland, generously commented on developments in vital registration in Scotland in nineteenth century and undertook a special tabulation on my behalf. And Dr Michael Cullen gave me a copy of a chapter of his study of the development of social statistics in Britain in the early nineteenth century.

Miss G. Charing spent much time in locating and obtaining copies of various publications drawn upon in writing this book. I am especially grateful to Miss Pat Weaver, who was responsible for typing a difficult manuscript, and to Mrs Phyllis Scutt for her invaluable help in correcting the proofs.

DAVID GLASS   March 1972

For R U T H

Contents

Publisher's note

Many of the documents and works cited by Professor D. V. Glass in this book are reprinted in full in *The Population Controversy* and *The Development of Population Statistics*, two collections of contemporary materials published by Gregg International Publishers Ltd, Westmead, Farnborough, Hants, England.

Illustrations

Annual Bill of Mortality for London, 1665   page 22

This was the year of the Great Plague. It is by no means certain that the 1665 outbreak was the worst. Dr Ian Sutherland makes out a case for a still higher mortality
in 1563 as well as in 1603 and 1625 (Ian Sutherland 'When was the Great Plague',
in *Population and Social Change*, ed. D. V. Glass & R. Revelle, London 1972). Even
so, the recorded burials in London in 1665 (the City, Liberties, Out-parishes and
Distant Parishes) amounted to 97,306 (as compared with 18,297 in 1664), of
which 68,596 were attributed to plague. The total deaths were certainly understated and, as John Graunt showed, it is very likely that sizeable numbers of deaths
from plague were attributed to other causes. The total population of London
before the 1665 plague outbreak was perhaps between 5-600,000, so that probably
a fifth of the population died during the plague year. After 1665, plague was
rapidly eliminated. The last plague deaths recorded in the London Bills of Mortality were 2 in 1679 (1 death in 1708 and another in 1710 were attributed to 'plague
in the guts', but that was evidently not bubonic plague). (Source: Wellcome
Library.)

Schedule for a seventeenth-century demographic inquiry   page 52

A proposal for a survey of the population and the births, burials and marriages
in parishes of 'about an hundred families'. The proposal was found in a collection
of tracts in the British Museum Library (816m. 6/80). The source is not known
and there is no evidence that the survey was ever carried out. The illustration
is included here because it suggests an early proposal to collect demographic
statistics (the years cited suggest that the proposal was earlier than the work of
Gregory King). The data specified includes age, sex and marital status. The
censuses of Britain did not provide age statistics until 1821 (on a voluntary basis –
the provision did not become compulsory and regular until 1841), or statistics
on marital status until 1851.

William Wales's questionnaire   page 58

This questionnaire appears to have been circulated after the publication of Wales's
book, *An Inquiry into the Present State of Population in England and Wales*, London, 1781.
Correspondence with John Heysham suggests that Wales intended to write a
second book, or a new edition of his earlier book, based upon a much wider range
of statistics. But the work was not published and the only completed questionnaires
I have seen are those collected for William Wales by Dr John Heysham. (Source:
Heysham Collection, Carlisle City Library.)

Cartoon: Filling up the census paper   page 92

Although this cartoon refers to the 1851 census, details on the household were
specified from 1841 onwards. The 1841 census was the first truly 'modern'
British census. It broke away from the tradition established by John Rickman,
of returns – usually recorded only in summary form in the localities – digested
locally and sent in a digested state to London. Instead, from 1841 onwards a

separate schedule was provided for each householder, and the names and required characteristics of every individual in the household were listed. The full returns were then sent to London for analysis at the General Register Office. The question of who is the householder is important because, among other reasons, the kin links of all other members of the household are specified by their relationship to him (or her). (Source: *Punch*, Vol.XX, 1851, p.152.)

Two cartoons of 1851 : 'Taking the Census' (frontispiece) *and 'Overpopulation'* page 102
By 1851, the interests of vital statisticians and sanitary reformers had begun to overshadow the earlier concern of economists with Malthusian theory. Chadwick and Farr had drawn attention to the heavy burden of premature death. At the same time Britain had become more prosperous. The 1851 exhibition was in part a demonstration of self-confidence and satisfaction with progress in Britain. Cruik-shank, perhaps the best-known cartoonist of the day, could thus afford to look at the humorous side of large families and substantial population growth. (Source: Cruikshank's *Comic Almanack*, 1851.)

Northampton Bill of Mortality   page 122
Apart from the entries in the registers of individual parishes, several towns main-tained collected returns of the marriages, baptisms and burials in their areas. But relatively few towns had regular series of published returns. Northampton and Liverpool are examples of towns for which there were regular Bills of Mortality, on lines similar to those for London. Some towns in continental Europe also published Bills – those for Paris are said to have been inspired by John Graunt's *Natural and Political Observations*, which appeared in 1662. (Source: Wellcome Library.)

Registration warning   page 128
Civil vital registration was accepted quite quickly by the bulk of the population. But there was some opposition and it was necessary to warn people and to engage in exemplary prosecutions to demonstrate that the law had teeth. Some of the opponents of the new system claimed that it resulted in marriages which were unacceptable to the church and which would not have been permitted had parochial registration remained in force. One such case, reported in *The Times* of 3 November 1838 and 7 March 1839, concerned a man of 20 who married his grandmother, and she under age! The girl in question, also aged 20, was not, of course, his 'natural' grandmother. The local clergyman protested and entered a *caveat* – 'because William Taylor is the illegitimate son of Benjamin Paine, the son of William Paine, the deceased husband of the said Anne Paine'. But the view of the Registrar General was that 'however objectionable the marriage to which you allude may be in a moral point of view, yet the *caveat* does not contain any grounds on which the solemnization of the marriage can be legally prevented'. (Source: General Register Office Collection.)

CHAPTER 1

The population controversy in eighteenth-century England[1]

THE BACKGROUND

In evaluating the work of earlier writers on population statistics, it is not always easy to make a fair judgement. To see the faults of those writers, without appreciating the difficulties inherent in the situation or period in which they wrote, is one danger. But there is an equal danger of expanding their merits beyond any real worth, and of finding in their writings views in advance not only of their period but also of their own intentions. On the participants in the population controversy, which began in the 1750s and had not ended when the Bill for taking the 1801 census was being discussed, the comments of subsequent writers have tended far more to disparagement than to excessive praise. McCulloch, for example, writing when regular censuses were already an established fact and when civil registration of births, deaths and marriages had been initiated, regarded almost the whole statistical literature of the previous hundred and fifty years as of little interest to the serious statistician. In the preface to *A Descriptive and Statistical Account of the British Empire*, he claimed that, 'during the long interval between Sir William Petty and Dr Beeke, statistical science could hardly be said to exist'.[2] It is a little difficult to see why Dr Beeke should be regarded as marking the end of a period so little worthy of consideration,[3] but for the rest there is obviously much to be said for McCulloch's view. Especially so far as the population controversy is concerned, the writers of the period were hampered both by the lack of reliable statistics and by their own, personal, limitations. As Gonner put it, 'the many inquiries on this subject [the course of the population since the end of the seventeenth century] made in the eighteenth century have achieved results which fall far short of accuracy. The best of them is but an approximation, while the worst bears no relation whatever to the truth.'[4]

Yet it is not simply a question of the accuracy of the results which is of interest. The population controversy – the debate on whether the population of England and Wales had increased since the Glorious Revolution – is part of the history of British demography. In one sense the controversy ended when the results of the 1801 census, the first of the regular censuses, were made known. In another sense, the controversy remains unresolved to the present day, in spite of the work of Rickman, Farr, Brownlee, Griffith and subsequent writers. We are still very uncertain as to the absolute figures of population growth before 1801; and though there have been new and much more informed studies in recent years, the course of fertility and mortality during the eighteenth century remains in doubt.[5] But whether or not the controversy has been ended, what is still of interest today is the background of the problem, the way in which the several main participants approached it, and the pioneer work which they and lesser known writers undertook in the field of practical demography. The present study is not designed to give a definitive account of the course of the population of England and Wales in the eighteenth century – it is unlikely, with the materials at present available, that any account could be definitive – but to outline the background of the controversy, to comment on the main contributions to it, and to draw attention to its direct and indirect impact upon the subsequent development of census and vital statistics in Britain.

The controversy itself falls into two stages. The first stage began in the pages of the *Philosophical Transactions of the Royal Society*, in 1755, with a paper by the Rev. William Brakenridge, Rector of St Michael Bassishaw, London, arguing that the population of London had fallen since the earlier part of the century. Subsequent papers extended his remarks to the whole kingdom. Brakenridge was attacked for his pessimism and his erroneous calculations by the Rev. Richard Forster, Rector of Great Shefford, Berkshire, also in the columns of the *Philosophical Transactions*. But the debate was not successfully terminated because, perhaps on the grounds that 'this correspondence must now cease', a long paper by Forster was not accepted for publication, and is available only in the Birch MSS in the British Museum. Chalmers said of this: 'the algebraical sophisms of Brakenridge were printed in the foreign gazettes: the true philosophy of Forster, by *experiment*, and *fact*, was buried in the rubbish of the Royal Society.'[6]

The second stage of the controversy attracted far more attention, at least partly because it was initiated by Dr Richard Price, one of the better known writers of the eighteenth century. The argument began relatively quietly in the various editions of his *Observations on Reversionary Payments*,[7] and in the *Appeal to the Public on the subject of the National Debt*.[8] Price's views were then attacked by Arthur Young in *Political Arithmetic* (Part I, London 1774). But the real incentive to the attack came with the publication of Price's *Essay on the Population of England and Wales*, first as an appendix to William Morgan's *The Doctrine of Annuities and Assurances on Lives and Survivorships* (London 1779) and later (1780) as a separate book. Almost immediately (1780) a criticism of Price was included by William Eden in the new edition of his *Four Letters to the Earl of Carlisle*, and shortly afterwards (1781) the two most outstanding replies to Price were published – William Wales's *An Inquiry into the Present State of Population in England and Wales*, and the Rev. John Howlett's *An Examination of Dr Price's Essay...* Thereafter the argument was rather desultory. But the two works of Beeke, already referred to, and Sir F. M. Eden's *An Estimate of the Number of Inhabitants in Great Britain and Ireland* (1800), all containing material designed to refute Price's contentions, were published shortly before the first census was actually taken.[9]

It is, of course, evident that a lengthy debate on the absolute growth or decline of the population of England and Wales could be maintained only because of the inadequacy of contemporary population statistics. England was not singular in this respect. It is true that a number of countries had made great progress in the collection of population statistics by the middle of the eighteenth century. In Iceland, for example, a complete census was taken in 1703, largely because, with the extreme degradation of that country at the time, it was considered essential to obtain a detailed account of the extent of poverty and of the need for economic assistance and relief. But there was no comprehensive analysis of the results of the census, and the subsequent censuses in 1762, 1769 and 1785 were less satisfactory.[10] In Sweden, primarily in response to the mortality and depopulation associated with, or resulting from, the Great Northern War (1700-21), attempts were made in the 1740s to ascertain the numbers of inhabitants of the country, and these resulted in the establishment, by an Act of 1748, of national registration, on a parochial basis, of population and vital statistics. With various modifications, the system thus created has continued to provide the demographic statistics of Sweden. Even in its early beginnings, in the 1760s, the system supplied, through the work of Wargentin and Runeberg, the outstanding demographic statistics of the eighteenth century.[11] In Austria, too, under the impact of the population policy of Maria Theresa, which in turn was a response partly to the effects of the Turkish wars and partly to the general influence of mercantilism, censuses were initiated in 1754.[12] There was a census in Norway in 1769 and censuses in Denmark in 1769 and 1787. But even for these countries, with the exception of Iceland, the data began with the middle of the eighteenth century, and the position in the earlier part of the century was relatively obscure. For most other countries, census statistics were far less satisfactory. In the German states there was a long history of local enumerations, and this was also the case for Italy.[13] But early enumerations covering large territories were lacking or else substantially defective. Demographic statistics for France were also unsatisfactory. France was, through Colbert, one of the first countries to initiate a mercantilist population policy, in 1666, but as in so many other countries, statistics lagged far behind policy.[14]

Modern statisticians and demographers, fitting together the various sets of statistics dating from early periods, can sometimes produce a coherent and reliable account of the size and trend of populations in the seventeenth and eighteenth centuries. But to do so requires not only a knowledge of more advanced techniques of demographic analysis than were available in the eighteenth century, but also the background of experience which comes from having and using, over a long period, reliable and comprehensive population data. Moreover, it should be remembered that many of the earlier data were not available to contemporary writers, either because there was no effective central organization for collecting and collating local results or because, under the impact of mercantilism, population statistics were considered too valuable to statesmen to be made public. The original results of the Austrian census of 1754 were assumed to have disappeared. Treated as confidential materials, they lay buried in the archives until they were rediscovered in the present century.[15] Even in Sweden, which was more free than most other European countries from this obsession of secrecy, the data collected in the early years of the new system of national registration were kept unpublished. It was not immediately apparent that, if full use was to be made of census and vital statistics, they should be published, and it was in the 1760s that, for example, reports on, and analysis of, these statistics by Runeberg and Wargentin first appeared in the proceedings of the Swedish Academy of Science.[16]

In England and Wales both population and vital statistics were highly defective until the nineteenth century. There were various estimates of the total population and some estimates of the populations of a number of cities and regions, but these were very largely based upon statistics collected for quite different purposes, usually in connection with taxes of various kinds. In modern times, many more of such estimates have been made. But an indication of the range of estimates available when the population controversy was taking place may be seen from the pages of Chalmers's well-known study.[17] Thus Chalmers gives an estimate for the year 1377, based upon the returns of the poll tax levied on all lay persons, save beggars, aged fourteen years and over. Taking the number of persons in respect of whom the tax was paid (1,367,239), and adding allowances for tax evasion, for the clergy and for the omission of Wales, Chester and Durham, a total figure of about 2·09 millions is reached. Chalmers does not complete the calculation, but mentions that persons under fourteen years of age would amount to a good deal less than one-third of the total population, according to Halley's life table for Breslau and Price's life table for Norwich.[18] Hence the total population would amount to almost 3 millions. A second estimate for the years 1575 to 1583, based on the figures given by Harrison and Raleigh for the fighting men, or men capable of bearing arms, takes the initial number of 1·172 millions and multiplies by four to reach a 'total population' of 4·688 millions.[19] Chalmers argues that this result is supported by a third estimate, for the year 1603, based upon the returns by the bishops of the numbers of communicants and recusants (the data related, apparently, to persons aged sixteen years and over) in their dioceses. The 2·065 million persons shown would, according to Chalmers, imply a total population of nearer 5 than 4 millions, and this would fit in well with the previous figure.[20]

Apart from computations based upon the returns of the window tax, which computations form part of the population controversy itself, the latest estimate given by Chalmers is that derived from Gregory King, who had given a figure for 1695 of almost 1·3 million houses and about 5·5 million persons in England and Wales. Chalmers regarded King's multiplier (the estimated number of persons per house) as too low, and thought that the total population might have been as high as 6·5 or even nearly 7 millions. For his purposes, however, even King's lower figure sufficed to show that the population of the nation had increased between the period of the Reformation and that of the Glorious Revolution.[21] Whether King's multiplier was too low and whether, in addition, his estimate of the number of houses was even approximately correct, are questions which have been discussed elsewhere. It is probable that King's estimate was nearer the truth for this period than any of the earlier estimates given by Chalmers are for theirs, even though Chalmers in referring to the data for 1377, says: 'We can now build upon a rock; having before us proof almost equal in certainty to actual enumerations.'[22] But that this was not fully realized at the time of the controversy is fairly evident. Nor is it surprising, for King's work, which was peculiarly inexplicit both as regards the sources of the data used and the methods of estimation, was in any case available to most writers only in the summary and somewhat mutilated form in which it was abstracted by Davenant.[23] Chalmers himself examined a complete copy of the original estimates – the *Natural and Political Observations* – and saw Harley's queries and comments regarding them, but he did not publish the full version of King's contribution until 1802.[24] Nevertheless, King's main results were widely referred to by eighteenth-century writers and often used as the starting point for discussions of the subsequent course of the population. Their relatively detailed nature, even in Davenant's 'mutilated' abstract, must have appeared impressive, and Davenant's praise would have helped to establish their reputation.

It is clear then, that at the time of the population controversy, knowledge of the absolute size of the population of England and Wales, and of its past growth, was very inadequate. It is not surprising that widely differing estimates continued to be put forward up to the time when the 1801 census results became available, their magnitude in part reflecting the attitude of the writer to the population controversy. Thus William Black, a well-known medical writer, suggested a population of 9 millions for Great Britain and Ireland.[25] And in 1798 Henry Beeke, referred to earlier, put the figure for England and Wales at not less than 11 millions.[26] The position was in some ways worse than for Scotland, for the work of the Rev. Alexander Webster, based in part upon inquiries conducted for him by the Society for Propagating Christian Knowledge in the Highlands and Islands, had resulted in a reasonably well-founded estimate of the population of Scotland at 1·265 millions in 1755.[27]

Nor could vital statistics be of much assistance, though they were plentiful and had a long history. In the first place, their utility was much reduced because of the absence of basic population data. Secondly, though they were plentiful, they were not easily available. In essence they were parochial records, the responsibility of the local clergy of the Church of England since Thomas Cromwell's injunction of 1538.[28] Attempts to provide a central index of the data had failed. Thus in 1590 Lord Burghley, the Lord Treasurer, had sent to the Archbishop of Canterbury a proposal for a general register office, one of the advantages of which was stated to be: 'There shall be also yearly delivered unto your honour, and unto every lord treasurer, for the time being, a summary of the whole. Whereby it shall appear unto you and them, how many christenings, weddings, and burials be every year in England and Wales, and every County particularly by itself, and how many men-children and women-children in either of them, severally set down by themselves'.[29] Nothing came of the proposal as such. Instead, it was ordered in 1597 that annual transcripts of the parish registers be sent to the bishop of the diocese, and this was repeated in a further Church order of 1603. But the transcripts were far from complete,[30] and even if they had been complete, they would still not have been a really effective substitute for a central office of registration. Finally, the original parish data were themselves defective. For, except during two relatively short periods, the responsibility of the local minister of the Church of England was not to register the births and deaths occurring in his district, but to record the baptisms, burials and marriages of members of his congregation.[31] Dissenters and members of other faiths were thus very largely excluded from the records, and so, too, were many adherents of the established Church who did not wish, or could not afford, to pay the fees associated with ecclesiastical registration. And as Dissent grew, and industrial expansion gave rise to new urban development, it is not unlikely that the parish registers decreased in completeness. An additional factor regarding the exclusion of Dissenters from the registers in the late eighteenth century was the Act of 1785, which extended the stamp duty on parish registration (levied by an Act of 1783) 'to all his Majesty's Protestant subjects dissenting from the Church of England'. This stamp duty gave Dissenters the mistaken idea that their own, non-parochial registers would henceforth have equal validity with the parish registers. This was not the case, but at least until the Act was repealed in 1794 there may have been a still greater omission of Dissenters from the parish registers.

The incompleteness characteristic of parish registers applied no less to the Bills of Mortality published for various towns, and especially for London.[32] The Bills were drawn up and published by a civil organization – in London, by the Company of Parish Clerks – and were often much more ample in the scope of their information that the entries in the parish registers. Thus in London, in the eighteenth century, they gave the ages of the persons who died (apparently from 1728 onwards) as well as lists of deaths by cause, though the account by John Graunt of the method of ascertainment of causes does not inspire too much confidence in the results. But the Bills of Mortality, like the parish registers, were primarily records of baptisms and burials of members of the established Church. Many deaths were omitted, and still more births, and this must have been especially the case in London. Heberden drew attention to the various defects of the London Bills and emphasized that the registration of births was much more defective than that of deaths, largely because of the exclusion of Dissenters. He wrote: 'the burials of some few papists, and of more dissenters, but the births of none in either persuasion, are registered there.'[33] Maitland, who undertook a special inquiry in 1729, estimated that the numbers of deaths omitted within the area of the Bills of Mortality in that year amounted to 3038, allowing for burials in non-parochial cemeteries of the Church of England (for example, St Paul's Cathedral, Westminster Abbey, Temple Church, St Peter's ad Vincula) and in hospital burial grounds, but not taking into account sailors who died in London or persons dying in London but buried in the country.

It was because of these omissions that Maitland believed 'the Bill of Mortality of the City of *London* is certainly one of the most defective of its kind. . .'[34] Corbyn Morris wrote on the desirability of improving the Bills from the point of view of demographic analysis, as well as from that of completeness.[35] Dr John Fothergill[36] added his voice and so did Dr William Black.[37] Attempts were made to improve the accuracy and comprehensiveness of the Bills. For example, in 1735 and 1736 the Company of Parish Clerks petitioned Parliament for authority to register deaths instead of burials, but without avail. In 1751 they drafted a Bill to make it compulsory for parents to notify the birth of a child, and for undertakers and other persons to notify deaths before putting the body in a coffin or removing it. This Bill, which was objected to by the clergy, reached its second reading, but was then withdrawn in favour of Mr Potter's abortive National Registration Bill. Again, in 1789 the Clerks tried unsuccessfully to obtain an Act authorizing the returns to cover births and deaths, instead of baptisms and burials.[38]

It was only rarely that local efforts to collect comprehensive and accurate vital statistics appeared to be successful.[39] The outstanding example is that of Carlisle at the end of the eighteenth century, on the initiative of Dr John Heysham. It was on the basis of Heysham's data, including the results of an enumeration undertaken by him in 1780 and of Heysham's 'corrected' version of a further enumeration taken in 1787, that Joshua Milne constructed his famous Carlisle life table, the first table, based on English data, to give a realistic view of mortality.[40] But the Carlisle Bills of Mortality related only to the end of the eighteenth century, and in any case found no real emulators.

These defects in the population and vital statistics were known to contemporary writers, or at least there were ample contemporary references to them. And, indeed, there were many recommendations and, in addition to the efforts of the

Company of Parish Clerks, two other specific attempts to improve English demographic statistics. Recommendations came, for example, from the participants in the population controversy. Thus Forster wrote, in 1757: 'I cannot conclude this long scroll without recommending it strongly to the members of the Royal Society, who have many of them seats in parliament, and most of them interest in those that have, to get an Act passed for perfecting registers. The trouble is trifling; the expence nothing. It would be of great service likewise to number the people: and this might be done with great ease.'[41] Arthur Young argued strongly in favour of a quinquennial census, a proposal not adopted until the Census Act of 1920 and not actually implemented until 1966.[42] Nor did he want the census simply to give total numbers, but also to provide data on houses and families, by counties, towns and cities, to classify every man or family by business or profession, to subdivide the landlords, and to distinguish regular and occasional parish poor and vagrants.[43] Young was not worried, as was William Wales, about the need for secrecy regarding the size of the population. Wales was theoretically in favour of a census; he felt that Young's proposal 'would certainly be very agreeable to every speculative mind, intent on the inquiry after truth, in any branch of natural knowledge; and, perhaps, at some future time, such a project may be put in execution without any fear of bad consequences ...' At that particular time, however, he feared that, should a census show a smaller population than 'our enemies' had estimated to obtain in England, they might take fresh courage and believe us to be weaker than we really were.[44] Young, on the other hand, thought that our enemies already knew much more important facts about us – for example, the sums of money raised each year and the amounts borrowed. 'Hence we find', he concluded, 'that each nation knows of the other, all that imports it to know; facts of real consequence cannot be hid; in such a case we should not be surprised, if some persons thought the shadow of more consequence than the substance.' In fairness to Wales it should be added that, while stating that a census taken at the time would 'determine nothing with respect to our number at any former time', he contemplated going somewhat further than Young in the scope of a census should one be considered advisable. He cited the views of the clergy of 'some of the most extensive parishes in England, who think it might be done, even in their parishes, with ease and certainty, in two months; with the addition of age, situation and profession of each individual'. But that there was also substantial opposition to the idea of censuses and comprehensive vital registration is only too evident from the treatment of the two Bills introduced in Parliament to that end – Mr Potter's Bill of 1753 and another Bill of 1758.

The discussion in Parliament of the 1753 Bill is well known, largely because of the contemporary publicity evoked by William Thornton's attack. Considerable space was given to the debate in *The Gentleman's Magazine*,[45] but in the main the arguments in favour of the proposal were only briefly summarized, while the tirade of Thornton was reported at length. At the same time the actual details of the proposal are not stated in the contemporary reports, and it is thus of some interest to give the main outlines of the Bill itself.

The proposal was entitled 'An Act for Taking and Registering an Annual Account of the Total Number of People and the Total Number of Marriages, Births and Deaths; and also the Total Number of Poor receiving Alms from every

Parish and Extraparochial Place in Great Britain'.[46] It provided that, on 24 June 1754, and on the same day of each subsequent year, the Overseers of the Poor should go from house to house in their parishes, recording the numbers of persons actually dwelling in each house during the twelve preceeding hours, distinguishing separately for males and females the numbers under twenty years of age, those aged twenty and under sixty years, and those aged sixty years and over. The total number of married persons was also to be noted, and the numbers of poor in receipt of alms during the previous year. Further, as from the following 24 June provision was made for the complete and compulsory registration of births and deaths. For births it was prescribed that 'when any child shall be born and shall in Baptism or otherwise receive a Christian or other additional name the parent or other person whether they be of the Church of England or not having the care or custody of the child shall within 14 days or on the 1st Sunday next after the expiration thereof on which Divine Service shall be performed deliver... to the officiating minister of the Parish or place a notice in writing of the birth, giving day of birth, sex and name or names of father and mother of the child...'[47] Death notification was to be on a similar basis, with day of death, sex, age[48] and disease to be recorded. Special register books, with printed headings for the appropriate columns, were to be provided by each parish at its own expense, and the information on births and deaths was to be entered, without charge, in these books by the responsible minister.[49] Duplicates were to be given to the local Overseer of the Poor and an abstract made. These duplicates and abstracts were then to be handed once a year (by 10 August) to the Chief Constable of the Hundred or Division, who was to pass them to the Clerk of the Peace. In turn the latter was to keep the duplicates for the country properly arranged, while transmitting the abstracts within one month to the Commissioners for Trade and Plantations. The Commissioners were really the responsible authorities, and it was their duty to compile an abstract for the whole of Britain and to present it each year to Parliament. Due precautions were also taken to ensure that all the people concerned complied with the provisions. Obstruction, refusal or neglect as regards notification was to be met by a fine of up to 40s. Officials refusing or neglecting to do their duty were to be liable to a fine of up to £5 for each offence, and any Clerk of the Peace neglecting to transmit the data to the Commissioners was to be fined not less than £10 or more than £20.[50]

As a proposal for collecting accurate population and vital statistics, the Bill had considerable merit. It is doubtful if the Overseers of the Poor were the most appropriate civil officers for the task of enumerating the population, though in fact they carried out that duty reasonably well at the censuses of 1801-31. Some doubt may also be raised as to the success of a registration system based upon the parish clergy. But, apart from clerical opposition at the time to any project to remove registration from the hands of the clergy,[51] Swedish registration has successfully made use of the local clergy for 200 years.

It was perhaps unfortunate that the Bill should have been introduced by Thomas Potter who, though a son of the late Archbishop of Canterbury, was apparently known as 'one of the profligate twelve who called themselves Franciscans, and held their orgies at Medmenham Abbey'.[52] At any rate he seems to have behaved rather arrogantly in the House. Nevertheless, he was sound in arguing that 'no gentleman who has sat any time in this House can be insensible of the utility of the law proposed; for seldom a session passes over but something happens in which it would be of singular advantage to the public, and a great satisfaction to ourselves, to have upon our table such authentic accounts as are proposed by this Bill to be laid yearly before parliament'.[53] So, too, was Grenville, in stating, in favour of the enumeration section of the Bill, that '... a few years will bring our knowledge of the whole number to a very great nicety, which never can be acquired from the register of births and deaths, were it to be exactly kept for many ages; because the very groundwork of all calculations from thence, is founded upon a supposition, that such a certain proportion of those that are alive die every year'. But for the rest, the supporters of the Bill were not very incisive in their arguments. The advantages they listed, according to *The Gentleman's Magazine* for November 1753, were to show the total numbers and their distribution; offer a basis for deciding whether a general naturalization was desirable; make it possible to estimate how large an army could be raised in time of need; provide evidence as to the desirability of emigration to the colonies; give a much firmer basis for local government; and for the first time show correctly the burden of the poor to the kingdom, and enable new inquiries about, and proper provision for, them to be made. These are not arguments which would nowadays be used to support a proposal for comprehensive census and vital statistics in, say, a Middle East or African country. But that is at least partly because we have seen how demographic statistics are used in the formulation of social and economic policy. In 1753 it was largely a matter for speculation.

Against the advantages cited by the supporters of the Bill were the fears of the population as reported, for example, by Matthew Ridley who, though in favour of registering births and deaths and ascertaining the numbers of the poor, was against a general census. He could see no point to it, and at the same time the superstition of the country was being aroused. He had received letters from various parts of the country, telling him 'that the people everywhere look upon it in this light [the light of superstition], which has not only filled them with imaginary terrors, but has raised such a violent spirit of opposition to this Bill, that if it be passed into a law, there is great reason to fear, they will in many places oppose the execution of it in a riotous manner; and that if it should be accidentally followed by any epidemical distemper, or by a public misfortune of any other kind, it may raise such a popular flame as will endanger the peace, if not the existence of our present government'. The traditional fear of divine anger if the people were to be numbered was obviously powerful. The supporters of the Bill dealt with Ridley's objections by arguing that much of the public antagonism, if indeed it really existed, was meaningless, and that people would cease to object once the Bill had been passed and they had seen how little inconvenience was actually involved. But these comments were no reply to William Thornton's attack. He spoke as the last defender of British freedom. For him there were only too obviously ulterior and unexpressed reasons for bringing in the Bill. He could not believe that the reasons given by the proposers were valid or even true. 'I cannot believe', he said in his widely quoted attack, 'that the motives which they [the proposers] are pleased to assign are those from which they act; the hope of some advantage to themselves can only urge them to perpetrate such evil to others; for, not to set any value upon the reputation or peace which they risk, it can never be imagined that they would molest and perplex every single family in the Kingdom merely to set a beggar to work, or determine any questions in political arithmetic.' He could find no advantage in knowing our numbers. 'Can it be pretended, that by the knowledge of our number, or our wealth, either can be increased?' He thus inferred that the results of the project would be increased tyranny at home, and he found nothing but ill in the whole proposal. It was 'totally subversive of the last remains of English liberty'. If it became law, he would oppose its execution, and if any official came to collect information regarding the 'number and circumstances of my family, I would refuse it; and, if he persisted in the affront, I would order my servants to give him the discipline of the horse pond...' If necessary, he would spend his remaining days in some other country rather than be a spectator of the ruin he could not prevent. These statements have a peculiarly timeless quality; similar views are occasionally expressed today.[54] Thornton did not, however, succeed in defeating the Bill, though he swelled the opposition at each successive division. Defeat came through the House of Lords, and very simply. At its second reading, on 23 May 1753, the Bill was ordered to be referred to a Committee of the whole House a month from that day. But since that was after the end of the parliamentary session, the Bill lapsed and it was not brought up again.[55]

So much for a project which, had it not miscarried, would have given us demographic statistics almost as comprehensive as those of Sweden, and beginning almost as early. This would not have been the case with the second attempt to improve the demographic statistics of England and Wales, presented to Parliament in 1758, though from the point of view of vital registration it was in one particular more interesting that the 1753 Bill. The 1758 proposal was entitled 'A Bill for Obliging all Parishes in this Kingdom to Keep Proper Registers of Births, Deaths, and Marriages: and for Raising therefrom a Fund towards the Support of the Hospital for the Maintenance and Education of Exposed and Deserted Young Children'.[56] The objective was thus mixed – to improve vital registration in England and Wales (no census was envisaged) and, at the same time, to provide funds for the Foundling Hospital by charging a registration fee, part of which would go to the hospital. The details to be recorded in the proposed 'regular and exact Registers of all Births, Deaths and Marriages' were similar to those provided for in the 1753 Bill, though it seems that there would be no compulsion to register the births of illegitimate children. For deaths the entries would show the name and profession of the deceased and of his parents, his residence, the time of death and an 'Account of the Distemper or Cause of the Death of the Deceased'. But the interesting part of the Bill is the provision for duplicates of the entries to be made, to be compared once a year with the original entries, and to be sent, via the local collector of the land tax and the county Receiver General, to a General Register Office to be set up under the direction of a 'Register General'. Thus the Bill envisaged a central registration office comparable with that finally established under the Act of 1836.

The Bill was not passed. It went through its second reading in the House of Commons and was reported on by Committee. But this was at the end of the session (June 1758); it then lapsed and was not again introduced. The exact nature of the opposition is not known, for the *Parliamentary History* gives no record of the debate. Perhaps the criticisms were similar to those emanating from the author of a pamphlet on the subject,[57] though he rather convicted himself of ignorance by saying 'it does not appear that any complaints have ever been made, that the present Method of registering Births, Deaths and Marriages, has been found liable to great Inconveniences, though, perhaps, in some Particulars, there might be Alterations and Amendments made, by which those of Births and Burials might be rendered more exact and useful...'[58] His general conclusion was that, 'having gone through the several Clauses, I leave it to every unprejudiced Man, who considers the whole tenor of the Bill, whether it does not appear, that thereby a fresh train of Embarrassments, Difficulties and Discouragements, will be heaped on the Sacerdotal Order; that a Tax is, in effect, to be laid on Baptism, which, as a Sacrament, ought certainly to be liable to none; and by that on Funerals, the Grief of Persons in low Life, on the Loss of their chief Support, by the Death of a Parent, is, at least, very unreasonably aggravated; and the Difficulties on Marriages greatly increased'. No further proposal of this magnitude was again presented to Parliament during the rest of the century.

Against such a background as has been depicted, the population controversy could only too easily flourish, unrestrained by hard facts. Nor is it surprising that writers should have come forward to expound or support the thesis that the population was declining. In any age, it is not difficult to become obsessed with the vices of the time and, like writers of letters to the press, believing that even the summers were better in their youth, to see only the stigmata of decadence.[59] And so far as the growth or decline of the population was in question, this attitude was encouraged by a persistent tendency to exaggerate the glories of antiquity – a tendency induced by too literal an acceptance of the 'statistics' of the classical historians and of the Bible – and by the evident existence, in continental European countries, of developments which might have *tended* to cause depopulation, though whether they actually did so is a different question.

The view that the population of particular countries, and of the world as a whole, had fallen since ancient times, was widespread in the seventeenth and eighteenth centuries. According to Mombert, the contemporary impulse in spreading this view may have come from Justus Lipsius, who reckoned the population of the city of Rome at 4 millions during the imperial epoch and gave comparably large figures for other cities in that period.[60] At any rate Lipsius was cited with approval by Isaac Vossius, an English writer who had a substantial influence upon his contemporaries and who believed that the world of antiquity was much more densely peopled than that of his day.[61] In France this view was perhaps most clearly expressed by Montesquieu. In his *Lettres Persanes* he argued that the population of the world was scarcely a tenth of what it had been in ancient times,[62] and even in *De l'Esprit des Lois* he still maintained that, in general, the countries of Europe had had larger populations in Charlemagne's days than in the mid-eighteenth century.[63] Montesquieu's views were carried over into discussions of the trend of population in France itself, and the later political arithmeticians, Messance and Moheau, found themselves in a distinct minority in attacking the belief that the population of France had been declining during the eighteenth century.[64] Similar attitudes to population trends in general, and to the decline of population (or the absence of increase) in the particular countries, were evident in Spain, Germany and Italy, being part of the argument used by many of the pro-natalists of the

A generall Bill for this prefent year,

ending the 19 of *December* 1665. according to the Report made to the KINGS moſt Excellent Majeſty.

By the Company of Pariſh Clerks of *London*, &c.

	Buried	Pla.		Buried	Pla.		Buried	Pla.		Burie	Pla.
St A'bans Woodſtreet	200	121	St Clements Eaſtcheap	38	20	St Margaret Moſes	28	25	St Michael Cornhill	104	52
St Alhallowes Barking	514	330	St Dionis Back-church	78	27	St Margaret Newfiſhſt	114	66	St Michael Crookedla	179	133
St Alhallowes Breadſt	35	16	St Dunſtans Eaſt	265	150	St Margaret Pattons	49	24	St Michael Queenhit	203	122
St Alhallowes Great	455	426	St Edmunds Lumbard	70	30	St Mary Abchurch	99	54	St Michael Que ne	44	18
St Alhallowes Honila	10	5	St Ethelborough	195	106	St Mary Aldermanbury	181	109	St Michael Royall	152	116
St Alhallowes Leſſe	239	175	St Faiths	104	70	St Mary Aldermary	105	75	St Michael Woodſtreet	122	62
St Alhall. Lumbardſtr.	90	52	St Foſters	144	105	St Mary le Bow	64	36	St Mildred Breadſtreet	52	26
St Alhallowes Staining	185	112	St Gabriel Fen-church	69	39	St Mary Bothaw	55	30	St Mildred Poultrey	68	46
St Alhallowes the Wall	500	356	St George Botolphlane	41	27	St Mary Colechurch	17	6	St Nicholas Acons	46	28
St Alphage	271	115	St Gregories by Pauls	375	232	St Mary Hill	94	64	St Nicholas Coleabby	125	91
St Andrew Hubbard	71	15	St Hexens	108	75	St Mary Mounthaw	56	37	St Nicholas Olaves	90	62
St Andrew Vnderſhaſt	174	189	St James Dukes place	262	190	St Mary Summerſet	342	262	St Olaves Hartſtreet	237	160
St Andrew Wardrobe	476	303	St James Garlickhithe	189	118	St Mary Stayning	27	17	St Olaves Iewry	54	32
St Anne Alderſgate	282	197	St John Baptiſt	138	83	St Mary Woolchurch	65	33	St Olaves Silverſtreet	250	132
St Anne Blacke-Friers	652	467	St John Euangeliſt	9		St Mary Woolnoth	75	38	St Pancras Soperlane	30	15
St Antholins Pariſh	58	33	St John Zacharie	85	54	St Martins Iremonger	21	11	St Peters Cheape	61	35
St Auſtins Pariſh	43	40	St Katherine Coleman	299	213	St Martins Ludgate	196	128	St Peters Cornehill	136	76
St Barthol. Exchange	73	17	St Katherine Creechu.	335	231	St Martins Orgars	110	71	St Peters Pauls Wharſe	114	86
St Bennet Fynch	47	22	St Lawrence Iewry	94	48	St Martins Outwich	60	34	St Peters Poore	79	47
St Benn. Grace-church	57	41	St Lawrence Pountney	214	140	St Martins Vintrey	417	349	St Stevens Colmanſtr	160	391
St Bennet Pauls Wharf	355	172	St Leonard Eaſtcheap	42	27	St Matthew Fridayſtr.	24	6	St Stevens Walbrooke	34	17
St Bennet Sherehog	11	1	St Leonard Foſterlane	335	255	St Maudlins Milkſtreet	44	22	St Swithins	93	56
St Botolph Billingſgate	83	50	St Magnus Pariſh	103	60	St Maudlins Oldfiſhſt	176	121	St Thomas Apoſtle	63	110
Chriſts Church	653	467	St Margaret Lothbury	100	66	St Michael Baſſiſhaw	253	164	Trinitie Pariſh	115	79
St Chriſtophers	60	17									

Buried in the 97 Pariſhes within the walls,——15207   *Whereof, of the Plague*——9887

	Buried	Pla.		Buried	Pla.		Buried	Pla.		Burie	Pla.
St Andrew Holborn	3958	3103	Bridewell Precinc	230	179	St Dunſtans Weſt	958	665	St Saviours Southwark	4235	3446
St Bartholmew Grea	493	344	St Botolph Alderſga	997	755	St George Southwark	1613	1260	St Sepulchres Pariſh	4509	2746
St Bartholmew Leſſe	193	139	St Botolph Alſgate	4926	4051	St Giles Cripplegate	8069	4838	St Thomas Southwark	475	371
St Bridget	2111	1427	St Botolph Biſhopſg	3464	2500	St Olaves Southwark	4793	2785	Trinity Minories	168	123
									At the Peſthouſe	159	156

Buried in the 16 Pariſhes without the walls,——41351   *Whereof, of the Plague*——28888

	Buried	Pla.		Buried	Pla.		Buried	Pla.
St Giles in the Fields	4457	3216	St Katherines Tower	956	601	St Magdalen Bermon	1943	1362
Hackney Pariſh	232	132	Lambeth Pariſh	798	537	St Mary Newington	1272	1004
St James Clarkenwel	1863	1377	St Leonard Shorditch	2669	1949	St Mary Iſlington	696	593
						St Mary Whitechappel	4766	3855
						Rotherhith Pariſh	304	210
						Stepney Pariſh	8598	6583

Buried in the 12 out-Pariſhes, in Middleſex and Surrey : 38554   *Whereof, of the Plague* 21420

	Buried	Pla.		Buried	Pla.
St Clement Danes	1969	1319	St Mary Savoy	303	198
St Paul Covent Garden	408	261	St Margaret Weſtminſt.	4710	3742
St Martins in the Fields	4804	2883	*bereof at the Peſthouſe*	156	

Buried in the 5 Pariſhes in the City and Liberties of Weſtminſter——12194
Whereof, of the Plague——8403

The Total of all the Chriſtnings	9967
The Total of all the Burials this year	97306
Whereof, of the Plague	68596

The Diſeaſes and Caſualties this year.

Abortive and Stilborne	617	Executed	21	Palſie	30
Aged	1545	Flox and Small Pox	655	Plague	68596
Ague and Feaver	5257	Found dead in ſtreets, fields, &c.	20	Planner	6
Appoplex and Suddenly	116	French Pox	86	Pluriſie	15
Bedrid	10	Frighted	23	Poyſoned	
Blaſted	5	Gout and Sciatica	27	Quinſie	35
Bleeding	16	Grief	46	Rickets	557
Bloody Flux, Scowring & Flux	185	Griping in the Guts	1288	Riſing of the Lights	397
Burnt and Scalded	8	Hangd & made away themſelves	7	Rupture	34
Calenture	3	Headmouldſhot & Mouldfallen	14	Scurvy	105
Cancer, Gangrene and Fiſtula	56	Jaundies	110	Shingles and Swine pox	2
Canker, and Thruſh	111	Impoſtume	227	Sores, Ulcers, broken and bruiſed	
Childbed	625	Kild by ſeverall accidents	46	Limbs	82
Chriſomes and Infants	1258	Kings Evill	86	Spleen	14
Cold and Cough	68	Leproſie	2	Spotted Feaver and Purples	1929
Collick and Winde	134	Lethargy	14	Stopping of the ſtomack	332
Conſumption and Tiſſick	4808	Livergrown	20	Stone and Strangury	98
Convulſion and Mother	2036	Meagrom and Headach	12	Surfet	1251
Diſtracted	5	Meaſles	7	Teeth and Worms	2614
Dropſie and Timpany	1478	Murthered and Shot	9	Vomiting	51
Drowned	50	Overlaid & Starved	45	Wenn	8

Chriſtned	Males	5114	Buried	Males	48569	Of the Plague	68596
	Females	4853		Females	48737		
	In all	9967		In all	97306		

Increaſed in the Burials in the 130 Pariſhes and at the Peſt-houſe this year——79009
Increaſed of the Plague in the 130 Pariſhes and at the Peſt-houſe this year——68590

Annual Bill of Mortality for London, 1665

period. Though these views were attacked, and by such influential writers as Voltaire and Filangieri, they nevertheless long retained their mournful attractiveness.

In continental Europe there were at least more substantial grounds for the fears that populations were decreasing, for, as has been suggested above, developments tending to depopulation were visible in many countries. In addition to the toll of mortality, there were other, more specific, factors to impress contemporaries.[65] In Spain there had been the expulsion of the Moors in 1609-14 to add, as a factor in demographic and economic decline, to the earlier expulsion of the Jews.[66] In Catalonia the streams of immigrants from France, supplementing natural increase, had dried up by the 1630s.[67] Religious celibacy was another factor noted by contemporary writers as contributing to demographic stagnation.[68] Such circumstances help to explain the complaints of depopulation which were already being heard at the end of the sixteenth century, as well as the seventeenth-century concern at one and the same time with general urban and industrial decay and with the excessive size and influence of Madrid, Granada and Seville as centres of luxury. It was this concern which led to the *Capitulos de reformación* of 1623, a series of laws aiming to stimulate population and industry by encouraging marriage and the founding of large families, attracting immigrants and prohibiting emigration, and limiting luxury.[69] In France the process was reversed, for Colbert's Acts of 1666 and 1667, which gave tax exemptions and cash allowances to large Catholic families (provided that none of the children had become priests or nuns),[70] were followed by the revocation of the Edict of Nantes in 1685, which some historians believe cost France 250,000-300,000 of her more industrious inhabitants in the last fifteen years of the century.[71] In Germany the ravages of the Thirty Years' War left behind a feeling of disaster[72] and helped to underline the views of the Cameralists and the measures of colonization and pro-natalism current in the eighteenth century.[73] In Sweden there had been the mortality associated with the Great Northern War. The Austro-Hungarian domains had suffered from the Turkish wars, and even before these ended, as soon as Ofen (Buda) had been retaken in 1686, colonization of Hungary was begun. During the eighteenth century, under Maria Theresa and Joseph II, the drive for immigration was intensified, primarily for German immigrants. By mixing German colonists with the native population, one might aspire, it was believed, 'more easily to prevent revolts among the common people'.[74] Provisions for encouraging marriage and favouring families were added to the drive for immigrants.[75]

Depopulating factors as important as those found in continental Europe did not apply to England. The last major outbreak of the plague occurred in 1665 in London, and, though its effects upon that city were terrible enough, they were at least limited in scope.[76] During the eighteenth century much publicity was given to gin-drinking as a factor in increased mortality and, quite apart from the possible effects of alcoholism as such, it is not unlikely that the concomitant deprivation of food among those sections of the people who could not afford both to eat and drink, as well as the harmful nature of the ingredients used to prepare the so-called gin of the period, may well have had serious results.[77] But it is nevertheless most unlikely that the results were comparable with, or as visible as those produced by famine, epidemics, war and substantial migration in continental Europe. Moreover, what-

23

ever the course of population in England in the eighteenth century, the initiation, at least, of the argument of a higher population in the past derived far more from a desire to demonstrate the historial truth of the Bible, a nostalgia for a misconceived and over-glorified antiquity, and a distaste for the growing importance of manufacture and commerce.

Two writers who based themselves upon the Bible were William Whiston and Richard Cumberland. Whiston believed that population had grown at a geometrical rate before the deluge and that it was unfavourable circumstances which had caused the present population to be so markedly below its former size.[78] Cumberland argued for extremely large populations within 2000 years after the deluge and explained the much smaller numbers of his day in terms of war and famine.[79] More important than either of these, and less crude in his approach, was Robert Wallace, Moderator of the General Assembly of the Church of Scotland, whose well-known study appeared anonymously just on the eve of the population controversy.[80] Beginning, as was customary at the time, with a theoretical analysis of the potential rate of growth of mankind,[81] Wallace argued that 'we ought not from hence to conclude, that the earth is actually peopled in this manner; that mankind are always increasing, and are most numerous in the ages most distant from the beginning; or that they multiply regularly, according to any stated law; on the contrary, it is certain, that they multiply irregularly, and may have been more numerous in some preceding, and some subsequent ages; and that, thro' various causes, there has never been such a number of inhabitants on the earth at any one point of time, as might have been easily raised by the prolific virtue of mankind'.[82] Wallace then discussed the major factors which influenced population growth, listing excessive employment in manufacture as having a restrictive effect, and with this as background, analysed the writings of Greek and Roman writers for evidence of the size of the populations of various countries in antiquity. He did not agree with Vossius or Montesquieu, both of whom he regarded as exemplifying 'too great a prepossession in favour of antiquity'. Nevertheless, he concluded that there had been a time when at least Europe was more densely populated than it had ever been since, or 'shall ever be hereafter, unless some mighty revolution produces unforseen changes', and that the point of time in question lay somewhere between the siege of Troy and the conquests of Alexander – that is, before the domination of the world by Rome.[83]

Wallace did not go unchallenged. Indeed, his book was attacked even before it was published, by David Hume,[84] who had seen a copy of the argument as originally presented to the Philosophical Society of Edinburgh, and the latter half of Wallace's book consists of an appendix designed to refute Hume's attack. Hume was sceptical of any evidence drawn from the Greek and Roman historians. As he said, 'we know not exactly the numbers of any *European* kingdom, or even city, at present; How can we pretend to calculate those of ancient cities and states, where historians have left us such imperfect traces?' So far as the ancient world was concerned, slavery would not have encouraged population growth, there was wholesale murder and barbarism as well as unstable government, and trade and industry were not so flourishing as in the eighteenth century. Moreover, 'with regard to remote times, the numbers of people assign'd are often ridiculous, and lose all credit and authority'. Hume doubted if antiquity had anything to compare, in the way of riches and populousness, with the area bounded by a circle of two hundred miles radius taking either Dover or Calais as centre. Nevertheless, Wallace published his dissertation, attempting in the appendix to 'discover the latent fallacy of those pompous arguments [of Hume], which puzzled, but did not convince'.[85] In fact, a second edition was published posthumously in 1809, when the results of the first census of Great Britain were already well known and when the fear of falling numbers had been replaced by the Malthusian devil of overpopulation.[86]

Subsequently, in introducing the first of his *Various Prospects of Mankind*, published in 1761, Wallace once again stated his thesis that, in comparing ancient and modern times, several countries would be found to have been 'much more populous anciently than they are at present. It will even appear probable that Italy, Greece, Egypt, and other countries which are situated near the Mediterranean sea, contained thrice as many people in proportion to their extent as, after all our boasted improvements, England contains in our age.' He added a note, drawing attention to an essay, awarded a prize by Cambridge University in 1756, which expressed principles closely resembling those of the *Dissertation on the Numbers of Mankind*.[87] This essay was William Bell's *Dissertation on . . . What Causes principally contribute to render a Nation Populous*.[88] Bell did, indeed, begin by accepting the Wallace view that 'there seems great reason to think, that the most considerable part of the world has been much fuller of inhabitants in some former ages, than it is at present', but this was simply an introduction to his main subject.[89] For most of his essay he was concerned to discuss, at least in principle, how to increase the population of a country. He urged that this would be done by making it easier for men to obtain the necessary supports of life; by preserving a 'frugal simplicity of taste and manners'; increasing the general spirit of industry; and promoting a 'virtuous regularity' and restraining 'vice and debauchery'.[90] These tenets seem unexceptional, if not especially illuminating, but the detailed elaboration became confused on the subject of agriculture and the arts necessary to life, versus commerce and the arts of elegance and refinement. Bell argued that agriculture was the employment to be sponsored, with equal division of land to encourage it, and that commerce was deleterious unless introduced when agriculture had helped to produce a population so large that it could no longer be supported by agriculture alone. Moreover, he thought that commerce could not be carried on successfully until there was a large population. In view of this confusion it is not surprising that Bell was sharply dealt with by I—B—, reputed to be William Temple, a Trowbridge clothier, in a tract devoted to the praise of commerce.[91] Temple was as much in favour as Bell of populousness, but agriculture alone would not achieve that end. For one thing, 'if men were to labour no more than what is sufficient to procure them bare simple necessities [that is, Bell's frugal simplicity], this would be so little, that they would soon contract a habit of sloth, and from an idle life and a habit of sloth sink into barbarism'.[92] For another, he believed that plenty of provisions (and high wages) were incompatible with populousness, for they would result in profligacy, intemperance, insolence, contempt of order and all manner of debauchery, which would overspread the state and end in depopulation. The contrast with Bell and Wallace is evident.[93]

Shortly before the publication of Temple's reply, Wallace had been given further support by the Rev. John Brown, whose lament for his times achieved far more public attention than did either Bell or Temple.[94] In his main argument, Brown followed the well-trodden path – that commerce, in its most advanced stages, 'brings in Superfluity and vast Wealth; begets Avarice, gross Luxury, or effeminate Refinement among the higher Ranks, together with general Loss of Principle'.[95] 'Vanity and Effeminacy' reduce the desire for marriage; the 'lower Ranks' in the large cities are rendered partly impotent by 'Intemperance and Disease'; and 'this Debility is always attended with a Shortness of Life, both in the Parents and the Offspring; and therefore a still further Diminution of Numbers follows on the whole'. There is nothing new here. What is new is the specific suggestion that England was, on the whole, 'less populous than it was fifty Years ago', and the statement that 'it appears by the Registers of some *Country* Parishes, which I have looked into, that from the Year 1550 to 1710, the Number of Inhabitants increased gradually; the two extremes being to each other, as 57 to 72; and that from 1710 to the present Time, the Number has been at a Stand, if not rather diminished'.[96] But the population controversy had already begun, and Brown was reflecting its early course.

NOTES

1 This chapter is a revised and enlarged version of my paper in *Population Studies,* July 1952. The remaining chapters are new.

2 Preface to third edition, London 1847, p.vii.

3 H. Beeke BD was the author of *Observations on the Produce of the Income Tax...*, 2nd edn, London 1800, and reputed author of *Letter to a County Member on the Means of Securing a Safe and Honourable Peace*, London 1798.

4 E. C. K. Gonner, 'The population of England in the eighteenth century', *Journal of the Royal Statistical Society*, February 1913, pp.261-296. Gonner's own work did not produce more reliable estimates.

5 The conflicts in interpretation are illustrated by several of the contributions to D. V. Glass & D. E. C. Eversley (eds.), *Population in History*, London 1965 – including my own paper, 'Population and population movements in England and Wales, 1700 to 1850'. An objective and balanced survey of the present state of knowledge is given by M. W. Flinn, *British Population Growth, 1700-1850*, London 1970.

6 G. Chalmers, *An Estimate of the Comparative Strength of Great Britain*, London 1786, p.183n. That there must have been opposition to the publication of Forster's last reply to Brakenridge is made clear by Forster's letter to Birch on the subject (Birch MSS, 4440, No.189). Forster wrote, as of 4 December 1760: 'I am so great a Friend to ye Liberties of Mankind, that I can never be displeased at People for doing what they will with their own. The Transactions [i.e. the *Phil. Trans.*] are your own, & you may put what you please into them. Upon this footing, I cannot take ye rejection of my Paper etc. How it came to be kept so long afterward, I cannot imagine. I wish I could reconcile this with Philosophic Justice & Impartiality. If you were equally carefull in ye publication of all your Papers It would be more for your Honour. Be so good to present my Respects to your Committee, & tell them I desire They would appoint one of their Number (an Englishman) to attend to ye

Sense only...' I do not know what happened after that. Forster was not the only one to complain of the Royal Society, as may be seen from a letter from William Wales to John Heysham, dated 30 January 1784 (Heysham MSS, Carlisle). Wales wrote: 'You will not wonder that objections were made to your paper at the Royal Society when you learn how things are carried on there. It is, in a great measure become lately a *genteel* Society, rather than a *learned* one. No man of learning has lately had any chance of admission, unless he was at the same time a man of fortune; and these two Qualifications come but too seldom together. Would you believe that in the present *committee of papers* there are but three, out of 21, who have ever given a paper to the Society; & of those, two have given but one each – one on Anatomie, the other an account of the Romansh Language. The third is Sir William Hamilton, Bart. I believe there are not three others who are capable of giving a paper worth printing...' Wales was himself a Fellow of the Society, and it cannot be entirely ruled out that his comments were written to mitigate Heysham's disappointment.

7 First edn, London 1771.

8 First edn, London 1772.

9 There was also a pamphlet by an unknown author, surveying the whole controversy – *Uncertainty of the Present Population of the Kingdom...*, London 1781.

10 The results were not analysed in detail until the present century. See T. Thorsteinsson, 'The first census taken in Iceland in 1703', *25th Session of the International Statistical Institute*, Washington, DC, 1947, Vol.III, B, pp.614-623; and Iceland, Statistical Bureau, *Manntalid, 1703*, Reykjavík 1960 (English summary and table headings).

11 For Scandinavia in general see [H. Westergaard], *The Official Vital Statistics of the Scandinavian Countries and the Baltic Republics*, Geneva 1926, pp.8-18. For Sweden see in particular, E. Arosenius, 'The history and organisation of Swedish official statistics', in J. Koren, *The History of Statistics*, New York 1918, pp.537ff; and H. Gille, *Population Studies*, June 1949. On Norway see the papers by J. E. Backer in *Population Studies*, September 1947 & December 1948; and by Käre Ofstad in *Population Studies*, June 1949. See also M. Drake, *Population and Society in Norway 1753-1865*, Cambridge 1969.

12 See H. Grossmann, *Die Anfänge und geschichtliche Entwicklung der amtlichen Statistik in Österreich*, Brünn 1916; and S. Peller, 'Zur Kenntnis der städtischen Mortalität im 18 Jahrhundert...', *Zeitschrift für Hygiene und Infektionskrankheiten*, 1920, Vol.CX, pp.227-262, esp. pp.232-235. For the population policy of Maria Theresa, see especially K. Schünemann, *Bevölkerungspolitik unter Maria Theresia*, Vol.I (all published), Berlin (1935).

13 Many references to early censuses in the German States are given by E. Keyser, *Bevölkerungsgeschichte Deutschlands*, Leipzig 1938, pp.202-221 & 291-293. On Italy the most exhaustive collection of the early material is to be found in K. J. Beloch, *Bevölkerungsgeschichte Italiens*, Vols.I & II, Berlin & Leipzig 1937, 1939; Vol.III, Berlin 1961. But there are also many studies of particular communities, some of which are referred to in the contribution by C. M. Cipolla to Glass & Eversley, *op. cit.*

14 The classical studies of the historical demography of France are P. E. Levasseur, *La population française*, Vol.I, Paris 1889, and the various articles of A. Des Cilleuls, in the *Revue Générale d'Administration* (1885, 1893, 1895) and the *Réforme Sociale* (1892,

1900). But a much more cogent appreciation of the early data, and of the various estimates based upon them, is given by P. E. Vincent, 'French demography in the eighteenth century', *Population Studies*, June 1947. More recently there has been a renascence of demographic history in France, on far more solid foundations and with the application of new techniques of analysis. This largely has been the result of the stimulus and guidance of Louis Henry, whose initial studies (L. Henry, *Anciennes familles genevoises*, Paris 1965; E. Gautier & L. Henry, *La population de Crulai; paroisse normande*, Paris 1958) have served as a model for subsequent work, much of which has appeared in the *cahiers* of the Institut National d'Études Démographiques. French historians have also played a major part in these developments. See e.g. P. Goubert, *Beauvais et le Beauvaisis de 1600 à 1730*, Paris 1960; E. Leroy Ladurie, *Les Paysans de Languedoc*, Paris 1966; and the various issues of *Annales de Démographie Historique*.

15 See S. Peller, 'Mortality, Past and Future', *Population Studies*, March 1948, p.406.

16 P. W. Wargentin's famous report was 'Mortaliteten i Sverige, i anledning af Tabell-Verket', *KVA's Handlingar*, 1766, pp.1-25. An English edition, under the title of *Tables of Mortality based upon the Swedish Population prepared and presented in 1766 by Per Wilhelm Wargentin* (Stockholm 1930), was issued by the Thule Life Insurance Company for presentation to members of the Ninth International Congress of Actuaries. For a discussion of Wargentin's work on population see N. V. E. Nordenmark, *Pehr Wilhelm Wargentin*, Uppsala 1939, pp.232-269 & 377-381.

17 G. Chalmers, *An Estimate of the Comparative Strength of Great Britain*, London 1786. There were many editions (some published in Edinburgh, including one in 1812). An early edition is cited here to bring the references as near as possible in time to the population controversy. In addition to the estimate given in the discussion above, Chalmers also refers (1786 edn, p.4) to estimates of Hale (*The Primitive Origination of Mankind*, London 1677) and Gregory King of the population of England being 'somewhat above *two million*' at the time of the Norman invasion. Some idea of the range of modern estimates may be seen in M. Atsatt, *Population Estimates for England and Wales from the Eleventh to the Nineteenth Centuries* (unpublished, but microfilm copies are available from the Library of Congress, Washington, DC).

18 Chalmers, pp.12-13, citing R. Price, *Observations on Reversionary Payments*, Vol.II, pp.35-36, 39-40 (the references would appear to be to Price's 4th edition, London 1783). The nature and limitations of Price's life tables will be referred to subsequently.

19 *Op. cit.*, pp.33-34.

20 *Op. cit.*, p.35n.

21 *Op. cit.*, pp.44-50.

22 *Op. cit.*, p.13.

23 Davenant referred to King's work in more than one of his own books. The most extensive reference was, however, given in [C. Davenant], *An Essay upon the Probable Methods of Making a People Gainers in the Balance of Trade*, 1st edn, London 1699, pp.15-24, 41-44, 70-77. On King's estimates see my two papers in Glass & Eversley, *op. cit.*

24 Published as an appendix to his 1802 edition of *An Estimate of the Comparative*

Strength, &c. He subsequently published the *Observations* (together with a short life of King and King's table of the population of Gloucester, all of which had been included in the 1802 edition) as a separate small book in 1810.

25 W. Black, *Observations Medical and Political, on the Small-Pox,* London 1781, p.264.

26 [H. Beeke], *Letter to a County Member on the Means of Securing a Safe and Honourable Peace,* London 1798, pp.73-74. He put the population of Ireland at about 4 millions and that of Scotland at about 2½ millions, and reported his estimates as conservative (p.78). An example of the highly unsatisfactory basis of some of the estimates came to light in the course of correspondence with Professor William Kruskal, of the University of Chicago. Professor Kruskal was attempting to trace the origin of Thomas Paine's estimate (in *The Crisis,* No.X, October 1780, and again in *The Rights of Man,* London 1791, 1792) of a population of about 7 millions for England and Wales. After examining the contemporary literature, Professor Kruskal found what is most probably the source of the estimate, namely the 1755 edition of John Chamberlayne's *Magnae Britanniae Notitia,* which gives a figure of 7,055,706, based upon Houghton's figure of 1,175,951 houses and a multiplier of six persons per house.

The figure for houses is that of John Houghton (*A Collection of Letters for the Improvement of Husbandry and Trade,* No.26, 3 February 1692/3), and if it was based on the Hearth Tax returns it must relate to a year not later than 1689. But the Hearth Tax returns fluctuated substantially from year to year and cannot be regarded as reliable or necessarily indicative of houses. Further, no evidence is given of the validity of the multiplier of six. And finally the basic data relate to a time a hundred years earlier than that at which Paine was writing.

27 Webster's work – 'An Account of the Numbers of People in Scotland in the Year One Thousand Seven Hundred and Fifty-Five, by Alexander Webster, one of the Ministers of Edinburgh' – has been published in J. G. Kyd (ed.), *Scottish Population Statistics,* Edinburgh 1952. For an assessment of Webster's work see A. J. Youngson, 'Alexander Webster and his Account of the number of People in Scotland in the year 1755', *Population Studies,* November 1961.

28 For the history of parish registers and registration prior to the Act of 1836, the most useful general account is given by J. S. Burn, *Registrum Ecclesiae Parochialis: The History of Parish Registers in England,* 2nd edn, London 1862. See also A. M. Burke, *Key to the Ancient Parish Registers of England and Wales,* London 1908; J. C. Fox, *The Parish Registers of England,* 1910; and *Report from the Select Committee on Parochial Registration,* 1833 (B.P.P. 1833, XIV). An examination of the deficiencies of parochial registration, based upon a considerable amount of new research, will be found in J. T. Krause, 'The changing adequacy of English registration' (in Glass & Eversley, *op. cit.*). But see also, for a different assessment, the paper by P. E. Razzell, 'The Evaluation of Baptism as a Form of Birth Registration through Cross-Matching Census and Parish Register Data', *Population Studies,* March 1972.

29 Strype's *Annals,* Vol.IV, cited in J. S. Burn, *op. cit.,* pp.21-22. There was an earlier proposal in 1562-63.

30 J. S. Burn, *op. cit.,* pp.22-24 & 199ff. Similar provision was made in Rose's Act of 1812, for 'the better regulating and preserving Parish and other Registers of Births, Baptisms, Marriages, and Burials in England'.

31 The exceptional periods were those inaugurated by the Acts of 1653 and 1694. The first Act provided for *civil* registrars and for *civil* registration of births, marriages and deaths. But at the Restoration, registration was handed back to the clergy. The Act of 1694, originally passed for five years but later extended for another five years, aimed at covering *all* marriages, births and deaths in England and Wales, and supplementary legislation was passed in an endeavour to ensure that the parish registers (including the separate registers provided for unchristened children) would really be comprehensive. That the objects of the legislation were not completely achieved is evident from the fact that an Act of Indemnity was passed in 1706, protecting the clergy from the prospects of bankruptcy on account of liability to fines for not keeping absolutely complete and accurate registers. And tests show substantially incomplete registration. Nevertheless, it is possible that during the decade in which the legislation was in force, registration was more comprehensive than at any subsequent period prior to the introduction of civil vital registration in the nineteenth century. On the provisions and implementation of the 1694 Act, see my introduction to W. Kellaway (ed.), *London Inhabitants within the Walls 1695*, London Record Society, London 1966.

32 The term 'Bills of Mortality' is sometimes used to describe any published information on baptisms and burials – e.g. the lists occasionally published in newspapers or periodicals. What is meant here, however, is the regular and separate publication (at least annually) of the data by some institution which made the collection and publication of such material one of its normal responsibilities. The London Bills were of that kind and continued to be published until 1849. Comparable Bills were published during the eighteenth century for Northampton and Liverpool. By contrast, the 'Bill' for Newcastle upon Tyne appeared in the local press (*The Newcastle Magazine*), while that for Norwich was not printed, though it was drawn up regularly (and in the nineteenth century, at least, prepared on printed forms). Many of the eighteenth-century writers on population collected parish register data and presented them in summary form in their books.

33 [W. J. Heberden], *A Collection of the Yearly Bills of Mortality, from 1657 to 1758 inclusive*, London 1759, esp. pp.4-8. The attribution of authorship was given by Dr Heberden's son (see Joshua Milne's article, 'Bills of mortality', in the Supplement to the *Encyclopaedia Britannica*, 1824). Heberden's statement was a little sweeping. It is known that some people not belonging to the Church of England registered births, marriages and deaths in the parochial registers as providing the only legally admissible evidence of descent (see, for example, W. S. Samuel, 'Sources of Anglo-Jewish genealogy', *Journal of the Society of Genealogists*, December 1932). But it is probable that, in the main, the conclusion was correct.

34 W. Maitland (& others), *The History and Survey of London*, 2 vols, London 1756, Vol.II, pp.719-720, 740-744.

35 [Corbyn Morris], *Observations on the Past Growth and Present State of the City of London*, London 1751 (reprinted in Heberden, *op. cit.*). Among other things, Morris proposed that cause of death be given by age, that deaths be reported by year of birth as well as by age (though not in combination), and that infant deaths be reported for under 1 month, 1 to 3 months, and 3 months to one year. Morris's proposals were taken further by James Dodson (the originator of the 'mutual' basis of life assurance, adopted by the Equitable Company, and marking the change

from life assurance as a form of wager to a system based upon a realistic assessment of probabilities of survival) in 'A letter from Mr. James Dodson to Mr. John Robertson, F.R.S. concerning an Improvement of the Bills of Mortality', *Phil. Trans. Royal Soc.*, Vol.47, 1752, pp.333-340. Dodson wanted the Bills to record cause of death by sex, age (with a split between 40-44 and 45-49) and whether the individuals were born in London or elsewhere. He also proposed that an additional category of causes of death be specified, namely 'child-bed, miscarriages, and feminine disorders'.

36 John Fothergill contributed to *The Gentleman's Magazine*, December 1751, and wrote a letter to the Medical Society, 30 December 1768 (see John Fothergill MD, *Works*, 8vo edn, London 1783, Vol.I, pp.157 & 164-169; and *Works*, 4to edn, London 1784, pp.293-296).

37 W. Black MD, *Observations Medical and Political on the Small-Pox and the Advantages and Disadvantages of General Inoculation*, London 1781, pp.265-267 & 268-284.

38 J. Christie, *Some Account of Parish Clerks...*, London 1893, pp.142ff. Ralph Bigland, *Observations on Marriages, Baptisms, and Burials, as preserved in Parochial Registers*, London 1764, made a number of suggestions for improving parish registers and recommended that there should be a general register of all marriages in the Kingdom, with indexes giving the surnames of husbands and wives.

39 Local studies of mortality and population growth were undertaken by several doctors, but it is far from clear that these covered all births and deaths. See Dr J. Haygarth's studies of Chester in 1772, 1773 and 1774 (*Phil. Trans.*, Vol.64, 1774, pp.67-78; Vol.68, 1778, pp.131-154). There were similar studies of Manchester by Dr Thomas Percival (*Phil. Trans.*, Vol.64, 1774, pp.54-66; Vol.65, 1775, pp.322-335; Vol.66, 1776, pp.160-167). See also Dr William White on York (*Phil. Trans.*, Vol.72, 1782, pp.35-43); the Rev. J. Aikin on Warrington (*Phil. Trans.*, Vol.64, 1774, pp.438-444); and Dr Richard Pulteney on Blandford Forum (*Phil. Trans.*, Vol.68, 1778, pp.615-621, including an estimate of births to Dissenters).

40 There is no complete set of the Carlisle Bills in this country. The complete set reprinted in the companion volume, *The Development of Population Statistics*, was made up of those in the possession of the City Library, Carlisle, together with those in the possession of the National Library of Medicine, Washington, DC. I am indebted to the City Librarian, Carlisle, and to Dr J. H. Cassedy of the National Library of Medicine for enabling me to complete the set. The correspondence between John Heysham and Joshua Milne (who constructed the Carlisle life table) is given in J. Milne, *A Treatise on the Valuation of Annuities and Assurances on Lives and Survivorships*, 2 vols, London 1815; and H. Lonsdale, *The Life of John Heysham, M.D.*, London 1870. The Carlisle Library possesses the correspondence between William Wales and John Heysham, reprinted in an appendix to this chapter with the permission of the City Librarian.

41 *Phil. Trans.*, Vol.50, 1757-58, I, pp.356-363.

42 A comparable example of time-lag is that relating to the inclusion of questions on fertility in British Censuses. First suggested (in detail) by Gregory King in the 1690s (King's journal in the Public Record Office, T.64/302), the 1911 census was the first to include them. But it is true that King's suggestions were not published, as far as I know, until 1956. (See my paper 'Some aspects of the development of demography', *Journal of the Royal Society of Arts*, Vol.104, 1956.)

43 [Arthur Young], *Proposals to the Legislature for Numbering the People*, London 1771, esp. pp.7-14 & 33-38.

44 W. Wales, *op. cit.*, pp.77-78. Wales seems to have been far more in favour of improved vital statistics than of a census. In a letter to Heysham, dated 28 August 1781 (Heysham MSS collection), he wrote: 'It is greatly to be lamented that we have no law, or that it is not better enforced, to Oblige all births and deaths to be carefully Registered. It is impossible to say how many salutary and valuable ends might be answered by it, both of a public and a private nature. The latter might, one would think, tempt every parent to see his Child registered.'

45 For November and December 1753 and in the *Supplement* for the year 1753.

46 British Museum, *A Bill, with the Amendments, for Taking... etc.*, K. Great Britain – George III 357.d.10(40), State Paper Room.

47 The 1836 Act, which introduced civil vital registration, was less satisfactory in that it placed responsibility upon the registrar. It was found necessary to amend this in 1874.

48 As regards age at death, an appended schedule showed the detail in which this was to be recorded – 1 month and less; 1-3 months; 3 months to 1 year; single years thereafter to 5 years; 5-year groups thereafter to 20 years; and 10-year groups to 100 years, except 5-year groups for 40-45 and 45-50 years. A list of causes of death was also given as a model.

49 For marriages, provision seems to have been made only for those celebrated according to the rites of the Church of England.

50 Various amendments to the Bill were made during its passage through the House of Commons. But it is by no means clear what those amendments were. See *Journals of the House of Commons*, Vol.XXVI, pp.731, 736, 771, 800, 810.

51 The Archbishop of Canterbury so protested in the debate on the 1836 Registration Act and argued that, while there was need for improvement of the system of parochial registration, why should the existing arrangements with the clergy be disturbed? (see *Hansard*, Vol.XXXV, cols.82-83).

52 R. E. C. Waters, *Parish Registers in England*, London 1883, p.22. Potter had obviously given considerable thought to the proposal and had had discussions with Corbyn Morris (see Corbyn Morris, *op. cit.*).

53 All citations from the debate are, unless otherwise specified, from Hansard's *Parliamentary History of England*, Vol.XIV (1747-53), cols.1317-1365.

54 The Bill was also attacked in an anonymous pamphlet, *A letter to a member of parliament on the registering and numbering the people of Great Britain*, London 1753. The author wrote that 'in Theory I join with you that it may be useful, but from Practice, I from long Experience judge it must be disadvantageous to attempt the Knowledge'. He did not believe the proposed census would give accurate results, and argued that any inferences drawn from them would be incorrect. In support of his view he referred to the poor results of the 1694 Act, suggesting that the main purpose of that Act was really to number the people and not to levy taxes.

55 Hansard's *Parliamentary History*, Vol.14, 1747-53, col.1319, claims that the Bill was thrown out by the House of Lords at the second reading, but I have not been able to find confirmation of this.

56 See the amended Bill in *Bills Public*, Vol.III, 1757-59, No.98, House of Lords collection. The references in the *Journals of the House of Commons* are in Vol.XXVII,

pp.123, 241, 265, 272, 309. Potter was associated with the Bill.

57 *Considerations on the Bill for Obliging all Parishes in this Kingdom to Keep proper Registers of Births, Deaths and Marriages...*, London [1759], esp. pp.10 & 24. According to Henry Higgs, the author was Maseres.

58 He excluded marriages from this because he regarded the Hardwicke Act (1753) as having done all that was necessary for them.

59 In some degree, the feeling of malaise was not unlike that in the early sixteenth century – a feeling that the world was running down.

60 P. Mombert, 'Die Anschauungen des 17. and 18. Jahrhunderts über die Abnahme der Bevölkerung', *Jahrbücher für Nationalökonomie und Statistik*, October 1931, pp.481-503.

61 I. Vossii, *Variarum Observationum Liber*, London 1685, p.34, stated the population of Rome at 14 millions.

62 *Lettres Persanes*, letter CXII; *Œuvres de Monsieur de Montesquieu*, Amsterdam & Leipzig 1764, Vol.V, pp.286-289.

63 *De l'Esprit des Lois*, Bk.23, ch.24, *Œuvres...*, Vol.III, pp.43ff.

64 See especially M. Messance, *Recherches sur la population...*, Paris 1766, pp.270-271; and *Nouvelles recherches sur la population de la France...*, Lyon 1788, pp.1-2 & 4-5. In the latter Messance claimed that, as a result of the publication of his earlier book, one no longer heard the anti-patriotic cry, 'La France est dépeuplée, elle est en friche, elle est sur le penchant de sa ruine', though this cry had resounded for ten years, and unfortunately throughout the 1756 war.

65 On the level of mortality in the seventeenth and eighteenth centuries, acceptable statistics are still rare, though much valuable work has been done since the 1950s. But there is ample evidence of high mortality associated with epidemics and harvest failures in Europe, and especially of mortality from plague.

66 It is not surprising that there is a wide range of variation in the estimates of the number of Jews and Moors leaving Spain after 1492 and 1609-14 respectively. M. Colmeiro, *Historia de la Economica Politica en España*, Vol.II, Madrid 1863, pp.57ff., thought the nearest figures would be about 160,000 Jews and for Moors about 200,000-300,000 leaving by land or sea in 1609-10. But he believed the total exodus of Moors would be much larger, allowing for those who left of their own accord before the decree for expulsion was promulgated, deaths in local uprisings and from other causes, departures not registered by the officials &c. This view is not shared by K. Häbler, *Die wirtschaftliche Blüte Spaniens im 16. Jahrhundert und ihr Verfall*, Berlin 1888, Exkurs I, pp.144-159. He regarded as too low Gonzalez's estimate of about 100,000 but as too high the figure of 400,000 given by Moncada. E. J. Hamilton, in supporting Häbler's general interpretation of the unsatisfactory Spanish population statistics of the period, and arguing for a growth of population in the sixteenth century and no decline until the seventeenth century, goes even further. He suggests ('The decline of Spain', *Economic History Review*, May 1938, pp.168-179) that few Moors were actually expelled, many remaining behind under the 'protection' of the landowners, and thinks that the 'figure of 101,694, exclusive of nursing infants, compiled by the royal commissioners in charge of deportation, was apparently much more complete than economic historians have believed'. Hamilton also doubts if the expulsion of the Moors significantly affected the Spanish economy, arguing first, that since the Moors had a semi-servile status in Spain.

they could scarcely have made a potent contribution to the country; and secondly, that if they were also able and industrious, it is surprising that they did not develop the geographically similar Barbary States when they returned. But a semi-servile legal status is no guarantee of a similar *de facto* status, and it would need to be demonstrated that the Moors had really been unable to act in Spain. As regards the Barbary States, it does not appear, according to H. C. Lea, *The Moriscos of Spain*, London 1901, pp.360ff., that the exiles had much opportunity there. In fact Lea claims that most of those who were deported probably died. For Hamilton's comments on population growth in Spain in the sixteenth and seventeenth centuries, see also his *American Treasure and the Price Revolution in Spain, 1501-1650*, Cambridge, Mass., 1934, pp.298ff., and *War and Prices in Spain, 1651-1800*, Cambridge, Mass., 1947, p.35. It should be noted, on all the above, that the state of knowledge of the demography of Spain in the sixteenth and seventeenth centuries is far from satisfactory. Apart from T. Gonzalez, who published the original data relating to the sixteenth century (*Censo de Población de les Provincias y Partidos de la Corona de Castilla en el Siglo XVI*, Madrid 1829), the major attempts to analyse the data are by Häbler, *op. cit.*; A. Girard, 'Le chiffre de la population de l'Espagne dans les temps modernes', *Revue d'Histoire Moderne*, 1928, pp.420-436, 1929, pp.3-17; and J. R. Almansa, 'La población de España en el siglo XVI', *Revista Internacional de Sociologia*, October-December 1943, pp.115-136. Since World War II new studies have been undertaken. Thus H. Lapeyre (*Géographie de l'Espagne morisque*, Paris 1959) estimates that the number of Moors expelled was around 272,000; in proportion to the total population, the numbers were highest from Valencia and Aragon. A very good general survey of Spanish population history is given by J. Nadal, *La Población Española (Siglos XVI a XX)*, Barcelona 1966, who cites total population estimates for Spain at around 8·5 millions in 1591-94, 7·5 millions in 1717 and 9·3 millions in 1768-69 (p.20). Like other European countries, Spain suffered heavily from mortality from epidemics, especially plague.

67 See J. Nadal & E. Giralt, *La Population catalane de 1553 à 1717*, [Paris] 1960. The stream dried up in the 1640s at about the same time as the occurrence of harvest failures and epidemics (1629-31 and 1649-54).

68 Hamilton, *Econ. Hist. Rev.*, May 1938, suggests that the numbers of priests, monks and nuns perhaps doubled during the seventeenth century, reaching about 180,000 (out of a total population of under 6 millions) by the end of the period. Mathorez, *op. cit.* Vol.I, pp.45ff., cites contemporary estimates suggesting that there were about 270,000 in France in the middle of the seventeenth century, this figure reaching some 500,000 by 1789. The literature of the period is full of complaints of the excessive numbers of these religious celibates. Colbert was certainly anxious to reduce the numbers in France. Bourgeois-Pichat argues (*Population*, October-December 1951, p.647) that the estimates of the numbers of monks, nuns &c. were greatly exaggerated and points out that both Moheau's data and the vital statistics of 1770-84 indicate only about 1 per cent of persons aged twenty years taking religious vows. Bourgeois-Pichat also regards as greatly exaggerated the accounts of lay celibacy. Yet in spite of exaggeration there is a core of truth as regards the nobility and upper *bourgeoisie*. The role of the court and the pressure for conspicuous consumption would have tended far more in that direction in France than in England or perhaps even – after the 1623 legislation – in Spain, and the reports

in J. Mathorez, *Les Étrangers en France sous l'Ancien Régime*, Paris 1919, should be taken into account.

69 Häbler, *op. cit.*, pp.115ff., points out that although there were earlier efforts to stimulate population growth and discourage excessive luxury, the first systematic attempt came in 1623. See *Novisima Recopilación de las Leyes de España*, 1805, Vol.V, Lib.X-XII, pp.10-11. It should be noted, however, that the encouragement of population growth was, at least in principle, a traditional objective in Spain. Thus the *Forum Judicum* declared that 'the law of nature is framed in the direct hope of progeny when the nuptial contract is entered into with all due solemnity', and was thus against excessive inequalities in the ages of partners to a marriage. 'Therefore, that an end may be put to practices whose results are unfavourable to future generations, we now decree, that, hereafter, women shall always marry men who are older than themselves, and a marriage under other circumstances shall not be valid, if either of the parties should object.' Such a decree suggests, of course, the derivation from Augustan legislation (*The Visigothic Code*, trans. S. P. Scott, Boston 1910, pp.77-78). The local *fueros* or customs also favoured marriage and families (E. Gans, *Das Erbrecht in Weltgeschichtlicher Entwicklung*, Vol.III, Stuttgart & Tübingen 1829, pp.401-404), and so did *Las siete partidas*, the general compilation of laws prepared during the reign of Alfonso X and issued around the middle of the thirteenth century. (See *Las Siete Partidas*, trans. S. P. Scott, Chicago, New York & Washington 1931, pp.410-412, Part II, Title XX, Law I: 'The people should endeavour to beget offspring, in order to provide inhabitants for the country'; and Law II: 'What things persons should avoid in order not to be prevented from having offspring.' The objectives were qualitative (i.e. 'eugenic') as well as quantitative.)

70 The Act of 1666 is given in detail in Isambert, Decrusy, Taillandier, *Recueil général des anciennes lois françaises*, Vol.XVIII, Paris 1829, pp.90-93, but the Acts of 1667 (extending legislation to all families) and 1683 (repealing the Acts) are scarcely more than noted. See also E. Esmonin, *La Taille en Normandie au temps de Colbert*, Paris 1913, pp.260-262, and S. T. McCloy, 'Government aid to large families in Normandy, 1764-1786', *Social Forces*, March 1940, pp.418-424. It would seem that the existence of the Acts was not well known at the time. But in any case, given the probable level of mortality, the families which the Acts wished to promote were unrealistically large.

71 See, for example, C. Weiss, *Histoire des réfugiés protestants de France depuis la revocation de l'édit de Nantes...*, Vol.I, Paris 1853, pp.104ff. Weiss is perhaps the most widely cited of historians on this question. But see also R. L. Poole, *A History of the Huguenots of the Dispersion*, London 1880, pp.165ff.; and H. M. Baird, *The Huguenots and the Revocation of the Edict of Nantes*, London 1895, Vol.II, pp.99-101. A recent study surveying the various estimates suggests that a conservative figure for the number of emigrants in the period 1681-1720, as a result of the Revocation, would be about 200,000 (W. C. Scoville, *The Persecution of Huguenots and French Economic Development*, Berkeley & Los Angeles 1960, pp.118-130.) The author doubts, however, whether the emigration accounts for the economic stagnation in France.

72 Estimates of the demographic effects of the Thirty Years' War are also subject to very wide variations and must be regarded with some scepticism, particularly as our knowledge of the populations of the various German states of the time is very unsatisfactory. As was pointed out by C. V. Wedgwood, *The Thirty Years' War*,

London 1938, pp.510ff., contemporary estimates are most unreliable, especially as 'Princes seeking to evade financial responsibilities, States claiming damages, citizens asking exemption from taxes – all these naturally painted the condition of their country in the dreariest colours. In the list of damages drawn up for the Swedish government, the number of villages destroyed was represented in some districts as more than the total number of those known to have existed.' But whatever the margin of error, most historians accept the view that there was a major devastation – not primarily from direct war deaths, but from mortality associated with epidemics and starvation. This is accepted even by R. Ergang (*The Myth of the All-Destructive Fury of the Thirty Years' War*, Pocono Pines, Pa., 1956, pp.24-27), who was concerned to demolish the myth of total ruin; he considered that Hoeniger (who also attacked the myth) went too far in estimating the loss of population by the end of the war as not above one or two millions.

Ergang's major weakness is the absence of any detailed studies of local population data, such as have been brought together by Günther Franz, whose compilation (based especially on various local studies) is probably the most comprehensive (see G. Franz, *Der Dreissigjährige Krieg und das deutsche Volk*, 2nd edn, Jena 1943, 3rd enlarged edn, Stuttgart 1961). Franz disagrees with the views of Hoeniger. He believes that in many areas – such as Mecklenburg, Pomerania, Hesse, the Palatinate, Thuringia and Bavaria – the losses were very great, while in others the population was maintained or even increased. Taking the country as a whole, he concludes that about 40 per cent of the rural population were victims of the war and epidemics, and about 33 per cent of the urban population (3rd edn, p.47), though it is by no means clear how these overall figures were computed.

At the same time, there seems little doubt that many contemporary writers were convinced of the loss of population and of capital equipment, and this second loss may help to account for the opinion of some seventeenth-century writers that there was overpopulation – e.g. the writings of Seckendorff and J. J. Becher. The real 'population fanaticism' occurred in eighteenth-century writings. See O. Jolles, 'Die Ansichten der deutschen nationalökonomischen Schrifsteller des sechzehnten und siebzehnten Jahrunderts über Bevölkerungswesen', *Jahrbücher für National-ökonomie und Statistik*, 1886, pp.193-224, and C. E. Stangeland, *Pre-Malthusian Doctrines of Population*, New York 1904, ch.6.

73 The literature on colonization and pro-natalism in eighteenth-century Germany is extensive but badly needs pulling together. Population considerations were influential, affecting economic policy, religious toleration and moral standards. See M. Beheim-Schwarzbach, *Hohenzollernsche Kolonisationen*, Leipzig 1874; M. L. Hansen, *German Schemes of Colonisation before 1860*, Smith College Studies in History, Vol.IX, Nos.1 & 2, October 1923-January 1924, Northampton, Mass.; E. Frohneberg, *Bevölkerungslehre und Bevölkerungspolitik des Merkantilismus*, Gelnhausen 1930, esp. pp.85-120; O. Jungels, *Deutsche Bevölkerungspolitik seit dem Zeitalter des Merkantilismus*, Frankfurt am Main 1939, pp.10-43.

74 This was the advice given to the government in 1720. Similar advice had been given in 1689, namely, increasingly to 'Germanize' the Kingdom, to 'temper with German blood the Hungarian blood, given to revolution and unrest, and thus to establish a steadfast loyalty to, and love for their natural and hereditary King and lord'. See R. F. Kaindl, *Geschichte der Deutschen in Ungarn*, Gotha 1912, pp.39-42.

For many European states the drive for immigrants and the prohibition of emigration must have created a peculiar situation. Migrants from the German States went not only to Prussia and Hungary but also to Spain and Russia and agents used a wide range of propaganda and other methods to stir up emigration in the desired direction. Probably the most remarkable case was that of Kaspar Thürriegel, who in 1767 was appointed commissioner to implement the Spanish immigration policy and who sent his emissaries wherever likely human material might be found. It is said that in Bavaria he even tried to provoke a revolutionary mass migration to further his ends (see Schünemann, *op. cit.*, Vol.I, pp.237 & 308). Looking at these eighteenth-century movements as a whole, it is clear that migration was a much more important factor in Europe than is sometimes realized, and that the migration of Germans was especially marked (see I. Ferenczi, *Kontinentale Wanderungen und die Annäherung der Völker*, Jena 1930, pp.9-12). Clandestine emigration from France was also important – in addition to the flight of the Huguenots. Among the prisoners in the Bastille, 1659-1789, were thirty imprisoned for enticing Frenchmen to emigrate or to join foreign armies. Russia, Spain, Prussia and the British colonies were the main destinations for the emigrants concerned (see F. Funck-Brentano, *Les lettres de cachet à Paris*, Paris 1903).

75 Perhaps the most important of these provisions was the series of Acts and orders, issued from 1747 onwards, which removed the existing restrictions on marriage, i.e. the abolition of the *politische Eheconsens*. This did not last very long, however. Early in the nineteenth century, as in many of the German States, the restrictions were resurrected, largely under the influence of Malthusianism. For the abrogation of the restrictions in Austria in the eighteenth century, see F. Herzog, *Systematische Darstellung der Gesetze uber den politischen Ehe-Consens im Kaiserthume Oesterreich*, Vienna 1829, pp.7-13. The impact of Malthusianism on marriage policy is discussed in my contribution to D. V. Glass (ed.), *Introduction to Malthus*, London 1953, and by J. Knodel, 'Law, marriage and illegitimacy in nineteenth-century Germany', *Population Studies*, March 1967.

76 The reported deaths from plague in the London Bills of Mortality for the year ending 19 December 1665 amounted to nearly 69,000. Allowing for under-reporting, Bell estimates plague deaths to have been at least 100,000 (W. G. Bell, *The Great Plague in London in 1665*, London 1924, p.312). Earlier 'Great Plagues' occurred in London in 1563, 1593, 1603 and 1625, and it is possible that at least one of these was more devastating than the 1665 outbreak (see I. Sutherland, 'When was the Great Plague?', in D. V. Glass & R. Revelle (eds.), *Population and Social Change*, London 1972). There were outbreaks of plague in many other English cities in 1665 and 1666. According to Shrewsbury the last seventeenth-century plague deaths which he found recorded were two in Redruth, Cornwall, in 1671 (J. F. D. Shrewsbury, *A History of the Bubonic Plague in the British Isles*, Cambridge 1970, p.537, and more generally ch.9). But two plague deaths were reported in the London Bills of Mortality for 1679 (the deaths were in the parish of Rotherhithe – see [W. Heberden], *A Collection of the Yearly Bills of Mortality*, London 1759, Bill for 1679). These were the last plague deaths reported for London in the seventeenth century. Plague, as a major cause of death, disappeared later in continental Europe – the more easterly the area, the later the date.

77 See, for example, one of the gin recipes in J. C. Drummond & A. Wilbraham,

The Englishman's Food, London 1939, p.236,

78 W. Whiston, *A New Theory of the Earth... wherein the Creation... Deluge and... Conflagration, as Laid Down in the Holy Scriptures, are Shown to be Perfectly Agreeable to Reason and Philosophy*, London 1696, pp.174-181. The appendix was reprinted separately and had reached its sixth edition by 1755.

79 R. Cumberland, Bishop of Peterborough, *Origines Gentium Antiquissimae: or, Attempts for Discovering the Times of the First Planting of Nations*, London 1724, esp. pp.142-156.

80 [R. Wallace], *A Dissertation on the Numbers of Mankind in Ancient and Modern Times: in which superior Populousness of Antiquity is maintained*, Edinburgh 1753. A French translation was published in London the following year and a Paris edition appeared in 1769.

81 Such rates – primarily, periods of doubling – were discussed by Sir Matthew Hale, *Primitive Origination of Mankind*, London 1677; John Graunt, *Natural and Political Observations*, 1662, p.63, and in the various works of Sir William Petty, while many of the pages of Gregory King's journal (in the Greater London Council library) are given over to these calculations. (King's journal, which contains drafts of his *Observations*, will be reprinted by Gregg International Publishers Ltd.) On the Continent, Süssmilch persuaded Euler, the mathematician, to prepare a table showing the periods required for doubling with various rates of natural increase.

82 Pp.11-12. It was this belief in the 'prolific virtue' of mankind which led him eventually, in his subsequent book, *Various Prospects of Mankind, Nature, and Providence*, London 1761 – a book from which Malthus derived the immediate inspiration for his *Essay* – to maintain that Utopias were impossible, for the better the form of government, the sooner would mankind increase beyond the means of support, and the more quickly mankind become miserable again (Prospect IV).

83 Pp.109ff.

84 *Political Discourses*, 2nd edn, Edinburgh 1752, Discourse X, 'Of the populousness of ancient nations'. F. H. Heinemann, *David Hume: The Man and his Science of Man*, Paris 1940, pp.7-15, gives an account of the relations between Hume and Wallace concerning the publication of both Hume's and Wallace's books, copies of which were sent to Montesquieu by the Earl of Morton. Hume read Wallace's *Dissertation* early in 1750 and produced his own essay because of the doubts which Wallace's study had raised in his mind. On finding that his work was to be published before Wallace's, Hume wrote to Wallace, stating his intention to refer to the *Dissertation*, and Wallace replied (see the copy of his letter, dated 26 September 1751, in the Wallace MSS, University of Edinburgh): 'As for your intended note relating to my Discourse on the numbers of mankind I have very great reason to be much pleased with it. If ever my little work shall be published such an encomium cannot fail to be an useful introduction to it and create a mighty prepossession in its favour.' Hume later helped in correcting the proofs of Wallace's *Dissertation*, and this appears to have become fairly widely known and misinterpreted. Hence a note dated 19 November 1764 (Wallace MSS) states: 'And because some were pleased to say that Mr. David Hume... had made Mr. Wallace's bad language good by his corrections of the press, Mr. Wallace has kept many of the proof sheets which he corrected (and they are in this bundle). These corrections were both few and

of little consequence as may be seen here by inspecting the corrections themselves
and by letters inclosed here in which he acknowledges that they were but very few;
Mr. Wallace hearing this calumny kept all he could find but some were lost before
he heard that such a thing had been said.' The relationship between Wallace and
Hume was both 'correct' and cordial, and Montesquieu, to whom both had written
in modest terms, commented on this in a letter to Hume in 1753 – 'Le public qui
admirera les deux ouvrages n'admirera pas moins deux amis qui font ceder d'une
manière si noble les petits intérêts de l'esprit aux intérêts de l'amitié. . .' (J. Y. T.
Greig, *The Letters of David Hume*, Oxford 1932, Vol.I, p.178). Wallace subsequently defended Hume against an attempt to excommunicate him.

85 *Op. cit.*, p.163.

86 Edinburgh 1809. The edition was described as 'revised and corrected'. It did
at least contain one change – 'pompous arguments' was replaced by 'showy
reasonings'.

87 *Various Prospects of Mankind*, pp.6-7.

88 William Bell, *Dissertation on the following subject: What Causes principally contribute
to render a Nation Populous? And what Effect has the Populousness of a Nation on its
Trade?*, Cambridge 1756. An MS note on the flyleaf of the Goldsmiths' Collection
copy says: 'Far above the level of the ordinary academic essay: a really important
tract', and a printed catalogue entry adds that the *Dissertation* was translated into
German in 1762 under the title of *Quellen und Folgen einer starken Bevölkerung*. McCulloch, on the other hand, refers to Bell's essay as 'confused and contradictory; and
consists of little more than worn out homilies in praise of virtue, simplicity, agriculture, and so forth, with tirades against luxury and the "elegances of life";
and attempts to show the mischievous and dangerous nature of commerce'.

89 *Op. cit.*, pp.2-3.

90 *Op. cit.*, pp.4-10.

91 I— B— MD, *A Vindication of Commerce and the Arts*, London 1758, reprinted in
J. R. McCulloch (ed.), *A Select Collection of Scarce and Valuable Tracts on Commerce*, London 1859, pp.489-561. This collection, used in the present study, forms one of
the series of Overstone volumes of tracts.

92 *Op. cit.*, p.504.

93 Temple's rules for increasing populousness stressed commerce, religious toleration and a general naturalization Act, but also provided for conquest and for
fighting wars by hiring mercenaries from other nations. But his most outstanding
thesis was the need to increase the range of wants of man. 'To want nothing is the
existence of a post, or a God' (p.506), and the former category applied to mankind.
His policy was that of the industrial revolution, and his reference to African natives
has a strangely familiar sound: 'But should two or three great geniuses arise among
their princes [among the Africans, that is], succeed each other, and incline to
refine the people, and bring them under a good police, it would be absolutely
necessary to introduce a great number of imaginary wants among them, in order
to establish the arts, and bring them under a regular government' (p.505).

Similar views are expressed in [Anon.], *Political Observations on the Population of
Countries*, London 1782, namely (p.17): 'As men in the rude state of nature can have
few ideas, they can have few wants, and of course few motives to exert their industry
or ingenuity. . . Introduce new objects of gratification, and you give them ideas

of happiness, and create new wants, to remove which all the latent faculties of the mind and body will be called into use.' The author referred explicitly to the population controversy (which was then in its second stage) and rejected the idea that declining numbers – if there had been such – were necessarily a disadvantage, or that power was inevitably associated with population size. As for the situation in England, 'instead, therefore of complaining of a diminution of inhabitants, supposing such a diminution has happened, we ought rather to rejoice that we have been relieved from a burdensome superfluity, and to wish the diminution more rapid since a change of circumstances has rendered us unable to find employment for those we have' (p.45). The decline in population would stop as soon as it was no longer beneficial.

94 [John Brown], *An Estimate of the Manners and Principles of the Times*, London 1757. A third edition was reached in the year of publication. On the reception of Brown's *Estimate*, see James Bonar, *op. cit.*, p.183. A second volume was published in 1758.

95 *Op. cit.*, Vol.I, p.153.

96 *Op. cit.*, Vol.I, pp.186-188. He made the following general remarks on England: 'The Metropolis seems to augment in its Dimensions: But it appears, by the best Calculations, that its Numbers are diminished; And as to the Villages thro' *England*, there is great Reason to believe, they are in general at a Stand, and many of them thinner of Inhabitants than in the Beginning of this Century.' These conclusions probably derive from Brakenridge's papers.

APPENDIX 1

Letters from William Wales to John Heysham

From the Heysham Collection, reprinted by permission of the Carlisle City Library

Christ's Hospital August 28th, 1781

Sir,

I beg leave to return you my warmest thanks for your valuable present of "Observations on the Bills of Mortality in Carlisle for 1780", as also for the same thing for 1779, by Mr. Archdeacon Law, which I believe he was so obliging as to call with himself, when, unfortunately, there were no person at home but a maidservant who could only tell me "it was left by a Mr. Law". And there being no name to it left me totally at a loss how to find out the person whom I was obliged to for it.

I am very happy to find that my Scheme, for some call it so, meets with your approbation: and I have the further happiness to find it meets with the approbation of all, who like you, think the general interests of mankind deserving of their care and attention; and through the assistance of such I have now reason to flatter myself with collecting the registers from a very considerable part of the Kingdom. As you propose making the same collection for the County of Cumberland I have taken the liberty of enclosing to you a few blank forms which I have dispersed in every part of England which I could come at, and if it meets with your Approbation, will send you as many as there are parishes in the County of Cumberland; which, I think, are but between 50 and 60 in all: but it would make no difference if they were three times the number, as I have plenty.

Your Table of the enumeration of Carlisle tends to overturn (as every one else which I have seen does) Dr. Price's notion that there is no material difference between the number of houses and the number of families. In Carlisle the difference is very great indeed. But it is so in every great Town, Nottingham alone excepted, which the Dr. has produced as an example, and that town happening to prove so, has, I suppose, led him into the mistake.

It is greatly to be lamented that we have no law, or that it is not better inforced, to Oblige all births and deaths to be carefully Registered. It is impossible to say how many salutary and valuable ends might be answered by it, both of a public and a private nature. The latter might, one would think, tempt every parent to see his Child registered.

But notwithstanding this defect, which I observe you particularly complain of at Carlisle, you would particularly oblige me by filling up, or procuring to be filled up for me two of the enclosed papers for the two parishes of Carlisle, and to add the 10 Years from 1758 to 68, on Acct. of Mr. Alderman Hodgson's Enumeration. My reason for this request is that I intend to attempt an estimation of the Absolute number of Inhabitants in the whole kingdom, by observing the proportion of births and deaths to the whole number living in as many places as I can procure them from. If you have many Dissenters, I shall be obliged to you for the best hints you can give me, of the effect their births and deaths have on the register.

And after all these requests, let me beg pardon for the liberty I have taken in making them. I the rather hope you will grant it, as you must have suspected what sort of a Person I was before you wrote to me, from my undertaking. Inquisitive persons must be troublesome ones; but knowledge cannot otherwise be had. Make such use of me in return as I may be able to be of, & you'll oblige

your obedient & very humble Servant

Wm. WALES

Sir,

I take the first opportunity of thanking you for your last valuable letter, which contains every thing, I think, that I could wish or expect from Carlisle. I have also sent you by the Carlisle Coach a parcel of papers, which I believe will be sufficient for the County of Cumberland which I hope you will find is greatly increased. I don't think of doing any thing on the subject until March next, so that you need not be anxious about the sending them back before that time. If I find reason to alter my mind I will take the liberty of letting you know it. I need not request you to procure the Baptisms & burials of desenters where you can, as well as such other circumstances as may tend to explain or illustrate the facts themselves. I hope you will give me leave to acknowledge my obligations to you in the publication: I would not do it without asking your Consent.

I am, Sir, very respectfully,

Your greatly Obliged and Obedient Servt.

Wm. WALES

Christ's Hospital
Novr. 17th 1781

Should these Papers be too few pray let me know.

Sir,

I received your kind letter of the 27th of November, but have been too ill to answer it before; I however sent to the Bull & Mouth, where the Coach goes from, to inquire after the parcel and they promised to write down to the several Inns, where the Coach stops, concerning it, so that I hope you have, long before this time, received it. If you have not you will greatly add to the many obligations your kindness has conferred on me by giving me another line, & I will immediately send more papers. I am exceedingly sorry you should have had so much trouble concerning it, and am, with great respect & thanks,

Your obliged & Obedient Servant,

Wm. WALES

Christ's Hospital
Dec. 10th, 1781

Sir,

I am favoured with yours of the 2nd along with the parish registers for the ward of Eskdale in Cumberland, which I return you many thanks for, and am exceedingly happy to hear you are in a likely way to procure the Registers for the other two wards.

I was aware, from experience, how difficult you would find it to procure returns from so great a number of parishes; but *self*, dear *self* made me loath to drop any hints that might discourage you. I am sure you must have had a great deal of trouble, and I am only sorry that I know not how I can, in any measure, return the obligations I am under to you. – I however flatter myself that if it should ever happen that I can be of service to you in any respect that you will command me; I do assure you it will give me as much pleasure as the service you have done *me* has, and I know not how to say more on the subject.

I shall be greatly obliged to you for the absolute number of the inhabitants when you have them. I have procured all the actuall enumerations that I can where I have procured the Registers, and for this reason. By taking the medium proportion between the number of births in a great number of Cities, Towns of different sizes, and Villages, and the number of persons actually liveing in them; if I can come at extracts from near the half of the parishes in England, I think we may come nearer the absolute number of the inhabitants from thence than by any other means that has yet been proposed; unless that an actuall enumeration of the whole Kingdom was undertaken; which there is, at present, no hopes of. The same may be done by comparing the burials.

I was in hopes to have seen Dr. Price's last thoughts on this subject some time ago. His bookseller told me it would be out very soon, last March; but I hear no tydings of it yet. If it comes out at all it must be soon now, as the town will presently be empty. We talk strongly of a Dissolution of Parliament in a few weeks; as the present Ministry think they will be able to get a parliament chosen that will carry the motion for an alteration in the representation. For my part I think it the most unwise Scheme that ever was formed; as the Boroughs will undoubtedly take care to chuse men who will be staunch to their interest when they know that such a thing as their disfrancisement is intended.

I am fully convinced with you that if a general inoculation could be brought about, it would be one of the greatest things that ever was done for the preservation of human life; but I much doubt whether, as it is now carried on, it does much good. – I think it does much hurt in London, on account of its keeping infection continually present. Before inoculation was practised there did not die of the small pox above one in 14 of all that were born, and now there dies about one out of [?]8, which is an amazing difference. I am, Sir, with the most sincere wishes for your health and happiness

Your obliged and obedient Servant,

Wm. W A L E S

Christ's Hospital
June 10th, 1782

Sir,

I return you thanks for two packets of Registers which I received from you this afternoon, as well as for your current count of the Bills of Mortality and diseases in Carlisle for the last year. I am of opinion great benefit might be derived from the publication of such accounts annually in every place where it could be done by a judicious person. Beside your three for 1779, 80 & 81 I have seen none of the kind except one by Dr. Haygarth of Chester for 1774 and one by Dr. White for York, which the Archbishop was so obliging as to send me last year amongst a Vast Number of extracts from Registers in his Diocese.

I have begun to arrange the materials for those Counties which I have no farther expectations from, but shall not think of publishing any thing before next Spring; by which time I hope to obtain such materials as will enable us to guess with tolerable certainty at the state of population in most parts of England. I am, Sir, with great respect,

Your greatly obliged & obedient Servant,
Wm. WALES

[marked Recd. Sept. 1st, 1782]

Christ's Hospital,
January 30th, 1784

Dear Sir,

I have been for some days in pain because I fear you must have thought me long in replying to your two valuable packets of the 10th & 11th Inst., but I can assure you, extraordinary as it may seem to you, that I have not been able to procure the paper you wanted till this moment. It is indeed a very difficult matter to get a paper after the day it is published on, unless you have some acquaintance with the publisher, or have a friend who takes it, and happens not to have lost or destroyed the paper you want; neither of which was my case. The publishers of papers here are extremely carefull not to sell a paper which is enquired for after the day it was published on, as they very seldom are enquired for, but for purpose of proving the publication of them, in order to found a prosecution on it; and to tell you the truth I employed a friend, who is happy in a *modest assurance*, to steal it off the file in a Coffee house. – The letter is, I think, rather exceptionable, & it is not to be wondered at that the publisher would not sell it me.

I am desired by Dr. Maskelyne to return you his sincere thanks for the Account you have sent him of the meteor from Mr. Greatorex, which is a very precise and valuable one; he also desires me to request you will be so kind as return his thanks also to that Gentleman for his obliging kindness, & to tell him that he could not have made it more perfect than it is, unless he had mentioned whether it was to the eastward or westward of him when it was at its greatest altitude, and that scarcely, he supposes, admits of any dispute, from other observations.

I am greatly obliged to you for the Register & particularly for that of Mary Port, which is indeed a prodigy.

You will not wonder that objections were made to your paper at the Royal Society when you learn how things are carried on there. It is, in a great measure become lately a *genteel* Society, rather than a *learned* one. No man of learning has lately had any chance of admission, unless he was at the same time a man of fortune; and these two Qualifications come but too seldom together. Would you believe that in the present *committee of papers* there are but three, out of 21, who have ever given a paper to the Society; & of those, two have given but one each – one an Anatomical, the other an account of the Romansh Language. – The third is Sir W. Hamilton, Bart. – I believe there are not three others who are capable of giving a paper worth printing. You may therefore readily conclude that their approbation and rejection of papers depends more on little puralitties such as their having been printed before, though in a private manner, rather than on their merit or demerit, of which they can scarcely be judges. The Disposition of the present president cannot bear near him a man who is disposed to judge for himself, & will not take his word for every thing: and hence it is that no man of real Science is admitted into the Council. – He has at last, however, drove them to open rebellion, & what the consequence will be, twelve months may discover.

I am, Sir,
Your greatly obliged & Obedt. Servant,
Wm. WALES

Dear Sir,

I sincerely return you thanks for your valuable favour of the 28th July enclosing me accounts of the state of population in Cumberland and Allerdale Wards, as also your excellent and very useful Observations on the Bills of Mortality in the City of Carlisle for 1782. It is greatly to be regretted that Gentlemen who have opportunities of information, and abillities to do it, do not follow the example set them by yourself, Dr. Haygarth of Chester Dr. Percival of Manchester, and Dr. White of York, in publishing similar Accounts of other Cities & Great Towns. It is impossible to say how many useful purposes such Accounts may be put to. Indeed Government ought to encourage the compiling & publishing such Accounts, as they would in time lay foundations of immense use in the science of finance. Instead of which I am sorry to say, they have passed a bill which will render the only tolerably pure fountain of information that we had totally useless. I mean Bills of Mortality.

The Case you mention of Ann Liddle appears to me a very extraordinary one indeed. I never before heard of any thing that bears the least resemblance to it – but it is true I have not read much on these subjects. I think you say that in the Cases recorded by Dr. Fothergill, it never came to his knowledge that the pain was occasioned by insects lodged in the bone? How came they there? or the seeds or eggs which produced them? I remember, many years ago, as they were digging a Coal-Pit in the neighbourhood of the place where I then lived, that in the midst of a perfectly solid rock, of the nature which I think they call Toadstone in Derbyshire, a small, spherical cavity, of about an inch diameter, was broke into, and in this cavity were found about 20 small, red insects, so nearly resembling those which run in the grass & are called by the farmers *Tings*, that they could not be distinguished from them by any person that saw them; they all died almost as soon as they were exposed to the air. I have heard also of Toads being found in large blocks of Marble. – How are we to account for the generation of these animals, &c. on the principles generally received?

You may depend on my using my interest, if needful, with such of the Council of the Royal Society as I am acquainted with, to have your paper printed in the Transactions. The Society at Large have no power in this matter.

I am sorry you have occasion to charge the clergy of your county with indolence. I have found but too much of it in many other places. I am exceedingly thankful however for what you have been able to procure me, and shall be happy at all times, to express my gratitude for it, as opportunities come in my way. I have not any county so compleat as that of Cumberland, unless I except Yorkshire, Nottingham, and Warwick. You have not sent me the numbers of the houses in the several parishes of Leeth and Eskdale Wards which were assessed to the Window Tax in

1781, and therefore, when you find your self at leasure, I shall be greatly obliged to you for them.

I am sorry I cannot apply to Mr. Howlett, as you wish me to do. Mr. H., with less liberality than I could have expected from him, has, in many places, and I suppose in all where he had influence, endeavoured to prevent my receiving extracts from Registers, &c., by telling the Clergy that if they did not give them to my friends it would be conferring the greater obligation on him. I have ever followed the direct contrary practice with respect to him; because I thought it rather advantageous that Authorities should be multiplied. I am, Sir, with the utmost respect & esteem

Your obliged & obedient Servant,

Wm. W A L E S

P.S., I hope you will come to no disgrace on acct. of the unworthy Member who wrote the frank I send this by.

Sir,

I return you many thanks for 13 Registers received by Mr. Barton, who appears indeed to merit all you have said of him. I find he has some thoughts of settling in London; and if so, shall be exceedingly happy in the acquaintance of so sensible a person.

I believe I shall be able to find out where the registers belonging to the Quakers are kept, and perhaps to procure the necessary extracts from them.

I have enclosed you a few more papers, if you should either want them in Cumberland or have an opportunity of dispersing them in any other part; but I cannot desire you to take any trouble about them, unless the opportunity fall directly in your way.

If you see the Gentleman's Magazine, you will observe that some person has made an Attack on Mr. Howlett, who is engaged in the same pursuit with my self, partly justly & partly unjustly but he has not objected to my mode of applying the evidence of parish Registers. I am, Sir, very respectfully,

Your obliged & obedt. Servt.

Wm. W A L E S

CHAPTER 2

The controversy and the participants

It was soon after the appearance of the first edition of Wallace's *Dissertation* that the initial paper in the controversy was published – Brakenridge's paper in the *Philosophical Transactions* of the Royal Society.[1] Brakenridge had been struck by the decrease, as shown by the London Bills of Mortality, in the numbers of burials and baptisms since 1743, in contrast with the increase between 1704 and 1728. This, he believed, 'plainly shews that the inhabitants were increasing till about the year 1728; and that from thence to 1743, they remained in the same state nearly; but that afterwards, during the last ten years, till 1753, they were constantly diminishing. For it is evident, that the number of inhabitants must always be in proportion to the number of births, and burials considered together.' Brakenridge made various computations of the actual size of the population of London, one based upon an assumed death rate – using Petty's estimate of one person in thirty dying each year – and another, which he regarded as less satisfactory, based upon estimates of the number of houses and of persons per house.[2] By his first method, allowing for omissions from the Bills, he found that the population of London had fallen from 875,760 in 1734-43 to 748,350 in 1744-53, a decline of over 120,000. He attributed the fall in population to the use of spirituous liquors, the increasing fashion of remaining unmarried, and the increased trade in Northern England, which prevented people from migrating to London. Although he agreed that there had been a great increase in building in London, he thought that this was due to the enlargement or rebuilding of houses and to the fact that people were simply moving across London from the east to the west parts of the town. That Brakenridge used an assumed death rate, and applied it to the earlier and later periods, is not surprising. The major contributions to demography since the seventeenth century – and these were few, in spite of the stimulus of John Graunt and Edmund Halley – had tended to emphasize the similarities or universalities of vital rates and ratios, rather than their differences. What is perhaps somewhat surprising is that Brakenridge should accept a decline of 120,000 population coupled with a large-scale move from east to west, the combination surely meaning, had it been true, a visible depopulation of east London.

A second paper by Brakenridge extended the thesis to the population of England and Wales as a whole.[3] In the absence of poll taxes, there were, Brakenridge said, only two ways of estimating the population of England, namely from the number of houses or from the amount of bread consumed. As to the first method, he assumed that six persons to a house would be an acceptable average for the whole country, and he applied this ratio to the number of houses obtained from the Window Tax Office.[4] Taking the number of houses assessed 'before the year 1710, and near about that time', namely 729,048, he allowed a further 25 per cent for cottages omitted. He did not believe a larger allowance was indicated, for 'surely the Surveyors, if they had any care of the Public Revenue, would never omit above one in Five. He thus arrived at 911,310 houses and, using his multiplier, a total population of not more than 5,467,860. Since that time the population had grown; but not greatly. He did not think that, at this latter period, it could be more than 6,257,418 'or six millions, all ages included; for it must be remembered, that in our wars since 1710, there could not be fewer lost than 200,000, which is to be deducted from that number'. The method used in arriving at this increase was scarcely beyond reproach. He took 1 in 40 to be the average annual death rate in the Kingdom – being the mean of 1 in 30 in the Bills of Mortality and 1 in 50 in the very healthy areas – and then, basing himself on Derham's observations that the ratio of births to burials in the Kingdom at large was about 1·12 to 1,[5] and taking the population as around 6 millions, arrived at an annual natural increase (excess of births over deaths) of 18,000. Making no allowances for emigration or war losses, he arrived at about 6,250,000 in 1755. Even less acceptable was his attempt to check his first calculation by an estimate of the amount of bread consumed. That he thereby arrived at a similar figure is purely fortuitous since he did not know either the total quantity of bread produced or the average quantity consumed per person.[6] It is clear that there had already been some questioning of Brakenridge's earlier conclusions, for he noted the argument that the decrease in the number of burials might have been occasioned by a greater healthiness. To this he replied that births had also fallen and that, in any case, as regards the presumption of greater healthiness, 'the decrease of the people diminishes the practice of physic, which makes some of that profession imagine, that the times are more healthy'.

Brakenridge carried the argument still further in a third paper.[7] He now believed he could prove not only that there had been no population increase in the British Isles, after deducting losses at sea and through war and emigration, but that the population of England and Wales would actually be declining if it were not for immigrants from Scotland and Ireland. To arrive at these conclusions he used three approaches. First, he calculated – by using Halley's life table for Breslau, his own previous estimate of the population of England and Wales, Webster's estimate for Scotland and an estimate of the population of Ireland – the numbers of 'fencible' men, that is, men aged 18-56 years, capable of bearing arms. Taking these men, according to Halley, to be a quarter of the total population, he argued that a quarter of the annual natural increase would thus also represent the annual increase in the numbers of fencible men, and he found this to amount to 8250 for Great Britain. If he could then prove that annual losses at sea and from war and migration amounted to the same, obviously – he thought – there could be no population growth. He had little difficulty in proving to his own satisfaction that during the previous sixty-six years, since 1690, the annual losses through these causes were at least 8250 men. The population of Great Britain could not, therefore, have increased. It is scarcely worth drawing attention to the fact that Brakenridge employed double-counting in estimating losses, for such errors are slight in comparison with the fundamental lack of reliability of the computation as a whole.[8]

Brakenridge thought he could find confirmation of his argument in the statistics of corn exports – again without reliable data – and then, in a postscript, he returned to the use of the Window Tax statistics. According to the most recent returns, made 'after the year 1750', there were 690,000 houses charged to the tax. Allowing 200,000 cottages omitted at this and the earlier surveys,[9] there would be 890,000 houses around 1750 as compared with 929,048 around 1710. Hence the population had probably declined, perhaps from about 5,570,000 to about 5,340,000 persons.[10]

Apart from the critics to whom Brakenridge referred in his second and third papers, two other objectors went into print to attack him, namely George Burrington and Richard Forster. Burrington, a former Governor of North Carolina, was concerned exclusively with the state of the population of London.[11] His own arguments were, however, of the same order as those of Brakenridge. He attempted to show that, because of inaccuracies and the exclusion of Dissenters &c., the true numbers of births and deaths were considerably in excess of what Brakenridge had allowed, and that the disparity had increased with the number of Dissenters; that a multiplier of seven persons per house should be used, instead of six; that there were more houses in London than formerly; that enlarging buildings, to which Brakenridge had drawn attention, increases the number of persons they contain; and that though there might have been a slight fall in the population living within the walls, the total population of London had grown. Burrington thought that the population of London, including Marylebone and St Pancras, was around 900,000, and he anticipated further growth during the next forty years to bring the numbers to about a million.

Forster's criticism was more pertinent and, in parts, more soundly based. In his first note on Brakenridge's papers, in which he communicated the results of his own inquiries in the parish of Great Shefford, in Berkshire, he emphasized the importance of having basic population data to which to relate statistics of births and deaths.[12] He wrote: 'All reasoning without this preliminary is really not much better than groping in the dark'. His own estimates of the population of the Kingdom were scarcely of a higher order than those of Brakenridge, being in part based upon the hypothetical numbers of people needed to cultivate the 'good acres' of England, together with an allowance for townfolk, and in part upon no more realistic assumptions regarding the consumption of wheat. But he drew attention to the fact that, in his village, the number of persons per house was, by actual inquiry, under five, and suggested that if the statistics of houses given by Brakenridge omitted cottages, an allowance of more than 25 per cent would have to be made for omissions. In Shefford more than two thirds of the houses were cottages and he believed that, for the kingdom as a whole, the proportion would be at least a half. He thus arrived at 1,458,096 houses around 1710 (including cottages) and a total population of 7,290,480. His estimate for 1755 was, however, arrived at simply by adding to the 1710 estimate the increase of 789,558 (excluding war and other losses) given by Brakenridge in his second paper.

Dissatisfied, perhaps, with the empirical basis of his own estimates, and certainly prompted by the calculations in Brakenridge's third paper, Forster carried out a wider survey and published a second paper summarizing the results and their implications.[13] For Great Shefford and eight other contiguous parishes his inquiry, which he claimed to have conducted with the 'utmost care', showed a total of 588 houses, of which only 177 paid the window tax, while in Lamborn parish (which contained a market town) there were 445 houses, of which tax was paid by only 229. He then allocated Brakenridge's 690,000 houses charged to the tax around 1750 into 200,000 in the country; 200,000 in country towns; and 290,000 in 'cities and flourishing towns'; and to these figures he applied the correcting factors he had obtained, namely 588 to 177, 445 to 299, and 690 to 200. The latter was Brakenridge's factor and was accepted by Forster on the assumption that 'without all doubt he [Brakenridge] had some reason for pitching upon such numbers; and as they could not be taken from country towns or villages, must be assumed from the present state of some flourishing place'. The calculation yielded a total of 1,427,110 houses, comprising 374,058 in the larger towns and 1,053,052 in the rest of the kingdom. For the former Forster used a multiplier of six persons per house (to allow for servants), and he applied his own multiplier of five to the latter, arriving at a population of 7,509,608, a figure which he did not claim to be exact but nevertheless was 'in hopes, that, upon trial, it will be found nearer the truth, than any thing hitherto advanced'. He attempted to obtain some confirmation of his result from the operation of the Militia Act but even he agreed that the check was dubious. He also analysed the baptisms and burials for three parishes (Lamborn, Welford and Shefford) in which they were apparently well recorded, and found that over the period 1614-1756 (with a gap for the Cromwellian period) there was a ratio of 83 burials to 149·4 baptisms.[14] He emphasized the importance of direct empirical inquiry and insisted that 'where certainty may be had, it is trifling to talk of appearances and conjectures'.[15]

Since, at the end of his paper, Forster had said that Brakenridge's views were 'from beginning to end, to say the best of it, ill timed' – he was referring to their publication after the outbreak of the war with France – it is understandable that Brakenridge should have replied with some indignation.[16] But the reply, though making a few points against Forster, scarcely disposed of his objections. Brakenridge began by saying that his statistics of the numbers of houses had been obtained from a public office (presumably the Window Tax Office), that only the number of cottages was unknown and that, nevertheless, they were known in some degree in that they did not appear to amount to as many as 300,000. He believed, in fact, that they were nearer to 200,000, for 'in some places, that I was perfectly acquainted with, I found many of the day labourers rated to the two-shillings duty, and there did not appear to be one house in ten omitted'. So he did not imagine there could be a million houses in total. But even if there were, the returns showed about one in seventeen as being empty. Taking the inhabited houses at 941,200 and multiplying by six would still not yield more than 5,647,200 population, or 'near about five millions and an half; which at the utmost, is what I insist on to be the real number'. Next he attacked the arbitrariness of Forster's allocation of houses between large towns and other types of areas, though without realizing that his own assumptions had in large part been equally arbitrary. He also regarded Forster's inquiries as inconclusive since they related to only nine parishes as compared with perhaps 7000 in the kingdom as a whole, and to one market town as compared with a total of perhaps over 300 in the nation. He did not appreciate that Forster had at least tried to collect reliable data for a number of parishes and appeared to forget that he himself had derived his multiplier from a single unspecified parish in London. He added that a 'late survey' of Middlesex, London, Westminster and Southwark – an area in which 'the poor are as numerous as in most places in the Kingdom, because of the numbers of labouring people that flock hither for imployment' – had shown 87,614 houses, of which 19,324 were cottages and 4810 uninhabited, giving about the same proportion as he had used. Forster's computations from the militia were next attacked and, finally, referring to the data on baptisms and burials in the three parishes, Brakenridge asked: 'But does he imagine that this proportion (the ratio of burials to baptisms) is general all over England? If so, we should increase in a rapid manner indeed! for then we should double our people in 35 years, if it were not for our losses; which no reasonable man will venture to say.' But in fact, though Forster had interpreted his table to indicate that there was very substantial natural increase, he had also said: 'and if other gentlemen would take the like pains (and it is next to nothing) in four or five parishes in each county and in every great town, we might perceive, by one cast of the eye, whether our people are in an ebbing or flowing state.'[17]

Public disputation between Brakenridge and Forster ended at that point because, as has been indicated before, the Royal Society closed down on the correspondence. Forster did reply, however, and his reply is available in manuscript.[18] He surveyed the arguments put forward by Brakenridge and made a number of comments which may be summarized as follows. First, he doubted the estimates of not more than 200,000 cottages excluded from the window tax returns and noted that there had been no satisfactory explanation as to what these statistics were and whence they had come. Instead, Brakenridge had changed his basis and taken a new ratio of 2 to 1 for houses to cottages. As regards this new basis, 'The Learned World will be so good as to observe, that for this there is not still the least Authority'. Forster agreed that his own survey of houses was based on too few data. He now gave results for ten parishes, widely scattered through Southern England, and showing a total of 1045 houses, of which only 347 paid tax, yielding the same ratio as given in his previous paper, and leading him to believe that this ratio would apply to southern England as a whole. There were two other reasons which dissuaded him from accepting Brakenridge's estimate of less than a million houses in the kingdom. First, the poor always constituted the larger part of any population – the implication being that the bulk of the houses would not pay tax – and secondly, the hearth tax returns of 1685 had shown 1,300,000 houses, and 'whoever is tolerably acquainted with England must be sensible, that there have been a great deal more than 100,000 new houses erected since that time'. For the rest, he doubted if the window tax surveyors, with small salaries and large areas to cover, could make accurate surveys, claimed that Brakenridge had misinterpreted the parish register statistics which Forster had cited,[19] and had wrongly used the data relating to the militia,[20] though he agreed that these data were very unsatisfactory. In general, he believed that commerce and employment stimulate population growth and that the population had probably doubled during the past seventy years.[21]

The first part of the population controversy attracted relatively little attention and did not appear to spread much beyond the readers of the *Philosophical Transactions*. It has been considered in some detail here mainly because the types of argument put forward by Brakenridge and Forster are closely similar to those which dominated the later dispute. At the same time, the outside world was not entirely unaffected. In an economic survey, *The Present State of Great Britain and North America*, the author, reputed to be John Mitchell, drew attention to Brakenridge's work, while throwing some doubt on the validity of the statistics of houses in 1710.[22] Many foreigners had come to England since the Glorious Revolution, and Mitchell doubted the fall in population implied by the apparent reduction in the number of houses between 1692 – which, coming from the hearth tax returns, he was willing to accept[23] – and 1710. However, there was little doubt of a fall in

IN Parifhes of about an Hundred Families, and wherein the Regiftry of the Births, Burials, and Marriages hath been well kept, Enquire,

1. The Number of the Inhabitants, Male and Female.
2. Married and Unmarried, and their Trades.
3. Widdows and Widdowers.
4. The Age of each Perfon, Man, Woman, and Child.
5. The Number of Families and Hearths.

As in the following Scheme, *Viz.*

Hearths.	Males.	Females.
3.	*John Smith*, Taylor, 45. 17. 15. 1.	His Wife 40. 16. 14. 4.
2.	*Richard Sims*, Carpenter, 52. 30. 22. 11.	His Wife 46. 24. 12. 2.
4.	*Robert Hughs*, Shoemaker, Widdower, 50. 16. 14. 2.	18. 6. 1.

And put the Births, Burials, and Marriages into the following Scheme, for the 7 laft Years.

	Born.		Buryed.		Married.
Anno 1676.	Males	Females.	Males	Females.	
77.					
78.					
79.					
80.					
81.					
82.					

Defcribe the Soyl and Scituation of the Parifh, and the Reputed Number of Acres which it containeth.

Schedule for a seventeenth-century demographic inquiry

population between 1692 and 1758, for which year the window tax returns gave only 961,578 inhabited houses. Taking six persons per house as the appropriate multiplier, Mitchell inferred that the population in 1758 was not more than 5·7 millions,[24] and that it had probably been about 7 millions in 1692. He concluded: 'Such a decrease of people indeed seems to be unavoidable from their great concourse to the towns, in which they decrease very fast; and as the country is thereby deserted, we cannot have lost less in that, than a million and a half within a century, and perhaps two millions; especially if we consider, how many go abroad, and are taken off by the army and navy, at the same time that they flock to the towns.' The author of the *Considerations on the Trade and Finances of this Kingdom* also drew attention to the decline in population implied by the reduction in the number of houses since 1759.[25]

But the real sound and fury began when the Rev. Richard Price took over Brakenridge's arguments and developed them. Price, who was the dominant figure in the controversy, was a Nonconformist minister, brought up in an atmosphere of nonconformism – an Arian who became preacher to a Presbyterian congregation in London and was later involved in the Unitarian movement. He was well-known as a preacher, but still more widely known as a writer, and his published work, including books and pamphlets on the American war, on religion, on national finances and on insurance, was very extensive. He was, in fact, one of the most noted men of his day. As the *Edinburgh Review* put it: 'His life was more connected with the greatest events of his age, than usually happens to men in so private a station, and of habits so retired and peaceable. His connexion with the American and French revolutions, his long friendship with Franklin, his correspondence with Turgot, and at last the hostility of Burke, rendered him conspicuous during life, and entitle him to some place in the history of his times.'[26] He was a friend of the North American colonists and was invited to become a citizen of the United States and to assist Congress in the regulation of their finances, an invitation which he refused, writing that he felt the 'warmest gratitude for the notice taken of him, and that he looks to the United States as now the hope, and likely soon to become the refuge, of mankind.'[27] He was generally considered the most authoritative writer of his time on life assurance and annuities,[28] though the Government lost money by selling annuities for premiums based on his life table, the Northampton table, which over-estimated current mortality.[29] Greenwood wrote of him: 'My guess is that Price was an able, self-confident, original-minded man, who knew a good deal about many things, and had no exact knowledge of anything.'[30] That is perhaps not entirely fair: but it would not be unjust as an assessment of his contribution to the population debate.

Price's association with the controversy arose partly out of his interest in annuity problems. He was concerned that many societies were being set up, professing to provide annuities for widows, and that the principles on which these societies were run were, in his view, actuarially unsound. He thus undertook a large correspondence with groups wishing to establish annuity schemes, and wrote at length on the general subject, with the object of providing accurate information on correct assurance practice – information which, as he said in the introduction to his nephew's book on the same problem, 'is rendered the more necessary by the multitude of *bubble*-societies which were some time ago established and some of which are

53

still existing in this Kingdom'.[31] At the same time it may have been his radicalism and his discontent with the contemporary political scene which persuaded him to believe, as his nephew wrote, that 'the increasing burthens which oppressed the poor, together with the growing luxury and extravagance which pervaded the higher ranks of society, were, in his opinion, making dreadful inroads into the population of the Kingdom...'[32] In holding this belief he was, of course, sharing the sensations of *malaise* which oppressed many of the moralists and anti-trade writers of the period.

Price's first note on the controversy sprang directly from his work on actuarial matters and appeared in a paper addressed to Benjamin Franklin, and read before the Royal Society in 1769.[33] In this paper he commented on the meaning of life tables and calculations of the expectation of life derived therefrom and suggested that, by using the expectation of life at birth, it was possible to estimate the population of a given town from the Bills of Mortality, assuming that yearly births and deaths were equal. 'Find by the Table, in the way just described, the *expectation* of an infant just born, and this, multiplied by the number of yearly births, will be the number of inhabitants.'[34] This is, of course, quite true provided that the population concerned is stationary and has the stationary age and sex composition appropriate to its fertility and mortality. At the same time, to construct a life table, as Price did, from the births and deaths alone, is also only valid if the above-mentioned conditions apply. Thus, little value can be attributed to Price's estimate of the population of London at the time he was writing – especially as he tried to make allowances for the fact that births and deaths were not equal for London – or to the comparison between that estimate and Brakenridge's earlier computation. The point is, however, that Price, too, came to the conclusion that the population of London had been larger in 1737 than in 1769 and argued that, taking the earlier period as based on the births and burials of 1716-36, and using the life table methods referred to, 'it will be found that the number [of inhabitants] then was 735,840, or 84,260 greater than the number at present. *London*, therefore, for the last 30 years, has been decreasing; and though now it is increasing again, yet there is reason to think that the additions lately made to the number of buildings round it, are owing, in a great measure, to the increase of luxury, and the inhabitants requiring more room to live upon'.[35]

This statement is not exactly unambiguous, and clarity was not improved by Price's further comment that this calculation assumed the same 'proportion of the omissions in the *births* to those in the *burials*' at the two dates[36] and that, as this appeared not to be the case, there having been instead a greater omission of births in relation to burials at the earlier date, 'this must render the difference between the number of inhabitants now and formerly less considerable than it may seem to be from the face of the Bills'.[37] Price added: 'I have observed that *London* is now increasing. But it appears that, in truth, this is an event more to be dreaded than desired. The more London increases, the more the rest of the Kingdom must be deserted; the fewer hands must be left for agriculture; and, consequently, the less must be the plenty and the higher the price of all the means of subsistence. *Moderate* towns, being seats of refinement, emulation and arts, may be public advantages. But *great* towns, long before they grow to half the bulk of London, become checks on population of too hurtful a nature, nurseries of debauchery and voluptuousness; and in many respects, greater evils than can be compensated by any advantages.'[38]

This paper by Price was reprinted in 1769 as a pamphlet and included, with some additions, in the first edition of the *Observations on Reversionary Payments*, which appeared in 1771 (London). In the second edition of the latter treatise, published in 1772 (London), additional emphasis was laid on the demographic situation. The 'Advertisement' to that edition informed the reader: 'in this kingdom, it appears that, amidst all our splendour, we are decreasing so fast, as to have lost, in about 70 years, near a quarter of our people'. Price thought that his evidence left little room for doubt on that score, though he hoped that, if he were wrong, 'some better-informed person' would demonstrate it to the public. The evidence, given in a 'Supplement', was an argument based upon the principles of Braken-ridge. It consisted of statistics of the numbers of houses at various points of time – 1,319,215 in 1690, cited from Davenant; 986,482 in 1759; and 980,692 in 1766, the two latter figures cited from *Considerations of the Trade and Finances of this Kingdom*. From that series Price inferred that 'our people have, since the year 1690, decreased near *a million and a half*'.[39] He urged, among other action, that the country should 'enter immediately into a decisive enquiry into the state of population in the king-dom', but it is clear that he did not anticipate his conclusions being refuted by the results of such an inquiry.[40]

During the same year, 1772, Price again drew attention to the population question in a pamphlet on the national debt, on this occasion linking depopulation with the burden of the national debt as one of the main causes.[41] He once more claimed that the population of the kingdom had fallen by about a quarter – defining the period as eighty years – from about 6 millions to about $4\frac{1}{2}$ millions. The evidence was that given in the second edition of the *Observations on Reversionary Payments*,[42] plus an account, by an unnamed correspondent, of the depopulation of Norfolk, offering no statistics but deducing a fall in numbers from the decline of most of the smaller towns, the excess capacity of the churches (even allowing for the fact that 'churches were in a degree, in popish times, the works of ostentation rather than necessity', and that 'a church was often built, though some neighbouring church might have held the parishioners of both'), the decay and disappearance of many houses, and the presence of a system of roads, paths &c. apparently indicative of 'the former great population, as in the present condition of the place they are altogether needless'.[43]

In the preface to the third edition of *Observations on Reversionary Payments* (London 1773) there was a reference to Arthur Young and other (unnamed) 'ingenious persons' who differed from Price as to the state of the population. Price presumably had in mind not Young's pamphlet proposing a census,[44] but his letter in 1772 to the *St James's Chronicle*,[45] in which he claimed that 'the positive assertions he has ventured on the number of the people, engrossing farms, etc. are by no means attended with any but conjectural proofs; no positive ones; that is, he offers us such and such *opinions*, supported by *arguments*; which, if you approve, you may accept; and if not, reject'. This was different from Price's work on annuities, for there 'he commands your assent by facts; not solicits it by arguments founded on supposi-tions'. As for the detail, Young cast doubts on the validity of Price's historical statistics of the numbers of houses in the kingdom. The fact that Houghton and

Davenant gave widely different totals for the position around 1690 suggested that the authority for either figure was extremely 'fallible'.[46] As to the comparison with the statistics for more recent years, 'the list of 1691 gives 56,826 more houses in *Yorkshire, Middlesex, London, Kent, Essex, Surry* and *Sussex*, for that year, than for 1758, which is simply impossible'.[47] Moreover, as regards the current figures, a gentleman 'equally eminent for his abilities, his eloquence, and his accurate investigation of these affairs' had told him that a study of the returns for specific parishes showed the returns for 1759 and other years to be false and throughout to understate the number of houses. This destroyed the whole basis of the argument that the population was declining. Nor was Young satisfied by the ratio of persons per house. Institutions were omitted and London entirely excluded from the calculation.[48] Thus he remained unconvinced that the population of the kingdom was less than 5, and perhaps less than $4\frac{1}{2}$ millions, as Price had declared. He once again urged that a census be taken and mentioned that he was collecting 'lists' relating to the course of the population and did not doubt that he would be able to convince the public – 'as far as any authority, except directly numbering the people, will allow' – that our numbers were increasing considerably. This was shown by the large increase in the numbers of births in various places since the Restoration, but 'Dr. *Price*, though he has been so conversant in such registers, takes not the least notice of this; from which I conjecture, that he also might find it thus'.[49]

Price defended himself, but did not reply at any great length. He claimed, in the preface to the third edition of his *Observations* that 'hitherto all my enquiries have served only to confirm me in my first conviction'. The growth of a number of large manufacturing towns did not mean that the population of the kingdom as a whole had increased. 'In truth, it would have been strange if our numbers had not been declining; for I can scarcely think of any great cause of depopulation, which has not for the last 80 years been operating among us.' But although Price purported to answer the objections raised by Young and the other critics, he did not in fact offer any substantial additions to the evidence he had already given. The statistics cited to show that five persons per house would be too large a multiplier for the kingdom as a whole were not amplified to any extent. There was a note asserting that the number of houses given in the house and window tax returns 'must probably be the full number of such houses in the Kingdom'.[50] For the rest, Price added only a postscript containing a general discussion of the 'influence of the different states of civil society on population', in which he again argued that the enclosure movement had depopulated the countryside and that, so far as England was concerned, 'the circumstances of the lower ranks of men are altered in almost every respect for the worse'.[51]

Arthur Young returned to the attack, on both general and specific grounds, in *Political Arithmetic* (London 1774).[52] On general grounds he put forward the view that employment creates population, that employment was acting more powerfully than ever and that, consequently, there could not be depopulation.[53] On specific grounds he repeated the arguments of his 1771 pamphlet, attacked the estimates of the numbers of houses cited by various writers and gave some examples of the inaccuracy of the window tax returns. According to his information, 'the last public lists of 1759 and 1766, are known by experiments to be false'. 'Catalogues' were taken in a variety of places in Yorkshire and elsewhere, and the numbers were always larger than those reported by the surveyors, who generally paid little notice to houses exempt from the tax. And if the numbers of houses were known, there was still the question of the correct multiplier; Price and others had usually collected information only on the number of persons per family and not per house. Moreover, he had little doubt that the number per house had also increased as compared with the figure eighty years earlier. And he criticized Price's correspondent from Norfolk, whose arguments were not convincing and could largely be explained by other causes than depopulation.[54]

A few years after the appearance of *Political Arithmetic*, Price produced a collected version of his various arguments. He had persuaded his nephew, William Morgan, who had become the actuary to the Equitable Assurances Society, to write a treatise on assurance,[55] and Price took the opportunity of including as an appendix an 'Essay on the Present State of Population in England and Wales'. The basis of the argument was once more the statistics of houses as reported in the window tax returns, followed by a discussion of the fall in the yield of the duty on beer, wines and spirits. Almost immediately, William Eden queried Price's use of these materials. He questioned the meaning of Davenant's hearth tax returns for 1690, the reliability of the window tax returns, the inferences in respect of the London Bills of Mortality and the interpretation of the Excise duty on liquor. He himself did not put forward any alternative hypothesis; he had wished only to show that 'with equal plausibility, and by similar modes of proof, it is easy, from such dark materials, to produce opposite inferences; and it is surely neither unfair nor unreasonable to presume that each inference is inconclusive and fallible'.[56] Price replied with a speed which compares very favourably with modern publishing: his 'Essay', with some corrections and an appendix commenting on Eden's analysis, was published as a separate pamphlet in 1780.[57] Much of his rejoinder consisted of a discussion of the scope and reliability of the statistics used – a discussion which was unlikely to convince either writer of the validity of the other's use of the data. But the 'Essay' also persuaded three other political arithmeticians to participate in the debate, namely William Wales, the Rev. John Howlett and Sir Frederick Morton Eden; and with them, new empirical inquiries assumed much more importance.

Price's arguments were very heavily based upon the window tax statistics and he thus tried to justify his use of those statistics. William Wales, though accepting Price's approach, was extremely doubtful of the data used.[58] Wales was a mathematician – mathematics master at Christ's Hospital School – and also an astronomer. He had been appointed by the Board of Longitude to accompany Captain Cook on the second round-the-world voyage of the *Resolution*, and also sailed with Cook in the *Resolution* on his last voyage.[59] He had read Price's contribution when it first appeared as an appendix to Morgan's book and had been struck by the unsatisfactory statistics from which the conclusions had been drawn. Reliable data, Wales believed, could be obtained only if actual surveys were carried out by people who had no connection with the taxation system. Since even those who believed in the decline of the population acknowledged that it had actually increased in the main manufacturing and commercial towns, the survey should be conducted in country towns and villages. Accordingly, Wales drew up a list of questions to which answers were needed and sent them 'to every acquaintance which I had in the

REV. SIR,

A QUESTION having arisen, whether the Number of the Inhabitants in this Kingdom has increased or decreased since the Revolution, it is conceived that great Light would be thrown on it, if the Number of Baptisms and Burials for each Year in the Three following Periods were procured from as many Parishes as possible in different Parts of the Kingdom: Your kind Assistance in this Inquiry will greatly oblige, Sir,

Your very humble Servant,

London, Christ's Hospital,   W. WALES.
May 17th, 1781.

Parish of
County of

Years.	Baptized.	Buried.	Years.	Baptized.	Buried.	Years.	Baptized.	Buried.
1688			1741			1771		
1689			1742			1772		
1690			1743			1773		
1691			1744			1774		
1692			1745			1775		
1693			1746			1776		
1694			1747			1777		
1695			1748			1778		
1696			1749			1779		
1697			1750			1780		

If the Register be defective in any of these Years, a Period of Ten Years, as near to the Period here given as possible, may answer the same Purpose.

William Wales's questionnaire

country, as well as to every other person that I could get recommended to' (p.7). But the list included questions on the number of houses in 1750 and subsequently, and also on the omissions from the window tax returns. And though he had a number of answers, there were also great difficulties. His friends met much local opposition, including threats and blows and he himself encountered similar hostility. This being so, he decided not to press the survey, but instead to collect statistics on baptisms and burials from the parish registers, and in this enterprise he was given substantial co-operation.

In his study Wales began by accepting in principle the possibility that the population of London might have fallen, though he did not accept Price's figures on the magnitude of the fall. He disagreed with the argument of decadence and considered that 'providence has cast my lot in an age which is as desirable as any that have preceeded it for many generations' (p.21). He believed that London had become a healthier city, especially since 1740, and concluded that in reality the population had increased. But his main concern was with the rest of the country, and he drew upon three sets of data.

First, there were the data from his incomplete initial survey. This had provided him with figures of the numbers of houses around 1750 and around 1780, for various districts (parishes, villages and some townships) in the North and West Ridings of Yorkshire, Derbyshire, Northamptonshire, Suffolk, Sussex and Somerset. Somerset had shown a fall; so, too, had Northamptonshire, but the surveyor of that area had assured him that, nevertheless, the population had increased. Taken as a whole, the group showed a considerable growth, though the number of houses covered was only some 28,500 in 1700. Secondly, the parish register inquiry collected baptisms and burials for pre- and post-1750 periods. A wider range of counties was involved, and returns had been collected for thirty-eight parishes. Here both baptisms and burials had increased, the former more than the latter. A third collection consisted of baptisms and burials for 142 parishes, comparing the situation around 1740-50 with that in the 1760s and 1770s. Again both baptisms and burials had grown in numbers, the former more than the latter. There were, finally, enumerations reported for ten communities – mostly fairly large or large towns – at two points of time, and in every case save one there had been a growth in population. Wales concluded: 'In every instance the places have been taken indiscriminately; that is, just as I could procure them; and I have omitted no place which I could procure: it may, therefore, be fairly concluded that they represent, justly, the state of the Kingdom in general; and this argument cannot be overturned but by producing a greater number of parishes which tend to prove the contrary; or an equal number of facts of a more certain nature' (p.69).

That Wales could not have been entirely happy with his range of statistics is evident from the fact that he continued to collect information, though he did not publish a revised edition of his book. He issued a printed questionnaire, dated 17 May 1781 – it is reproduced opposite – and sent copies to a number of people who might be able to help. The Heysham manuscript collection contains several copies of the blank questionnaire – judging from the letter of 28 August 1781, fifty or sixty copies may have been sent to Carlisle originally – as well as a good deal of additional information on numbers of houses and people, sent to Heysham from various parishes in Cumberland. Heysham may perhaps have collated the material and sent a fair transcript to London. Wales obviously envisaged using the new material in several ways. First, he hoped to have a fairly wide range of comparisons between the actual numbers of houses and the numbers assessed to the window tax in 1782, as well as comparisons between numbers of houses and numbers of families. In addition, it is likely that he intended to estimate the absolute increase in the populations of the areas covered by applying a constant ratio of baptisms to total population assumed to be at the 1781 level. But he also suggested (letter of 10 June 1782) that by doing this for a large number of different types of community – for 'near half the parishes in England' – he would be able to 'come nearer the absolute number of the inhabitants. . . than by any other means that has yet been proposed; unless that an actuall enumeration of the whole Kingdom was undertaken. . .' He was clearly not aiming at a random sample of parishes, though he tried to stratify his material. He must have greatly extended his collection of statistics in respect both of areas and of time coverage. By autumn 1782 he was beginning to order his new material and was hoping to have obtained, by the following spring sufficient to 'enable us to guess with tolerable certainty at the state of population in most parts of England'. But nothing appeared, and there is no reference to impending publication in the last dated letter (30 January 1784) in the collection.

In the correspondence, William Wales referred twice to John Howlett, another of the main contributors of new work – first to the unfavourable review of Howlett's book and, secondly, to his apparent attempt to 'monopolize' the subject by asking local clergy not to take part in Wales's survey (probably the first survey, rather than the new one, was in question). John Howlett, who was vicar both in Dunmow and Great Badow, wrote several books associated in one way or another with population questions and with economic progress in England.[60] He also contributed to Arthur Young's *Annals of Agriculture* and to one of the county agricultural surveys. Unlike Wales, he did not explain how or when he became interested in scrutinizing Price's arguments. In the preface to his main publication – *An Examination of Dr. Price's Essay*, Maidstone, n.d. [1781] – he notes only that he was engaged on his book when Wales's volume appeared and was glad that 'as far as we have adopted the same mode of investigation, our researches have been directed to different questions' – a somewhat disingenuous remark if Wales's comments were true. At any rate the two sets of data were complementary and gave almost identical results, thus affording 'additional weight to the general argument, and mutual confirmation to each other's conclusions' (Preface).

Howlett began by an attack on some of Price's prejudices, most particularly on his statement that 'great towns do more towards obstructing the increase of mankind, than all plagues, famines and wars. . .' (p.9). He argued that although great towns might be great evils, they are also sometimes 'indications or causes of greater advantages; . . . the natural concomitants of overflowing wealth, of extensive manufactures, of a wide and flourishing commerce'. In any case the crude death ratios were not always in favour of the villages as against the towns. A substantial part of the book is taken up with similar criticism of Price's arguments about the effects of migration, of the continental wars, of the engrossing of farms and enclosure of commons and waste grounds and of luxury. And like Wales, there is a fairly elaborate reply to Price's use of the London Bills of Mortality, the returns of the window tax, and produce of the hereditary and temporary excise.

The positive section consists of parish register data, collected through the local clergy, on baptisms and burials for two periods, the first 'beginning about the Revolution' and the second covering the period 1758-60 or 61. Taking these data together with those presented by Wales, and thus covering several hundred parishes in total, he concluded that, altogether there was an over-representation of the northern part of the country, 'there cannot a doubt remain that our people are almost *doubled*' since the Revolution (p.129). Further, in sharp contrast to Price's claim that the rate of decline in numbers had become steeper in recent years, Howlett presented an analysis of the baptisms and burials for 162 parishes, fairly widely dispersed over the country, for two five-year periods, the first beginning with the year 1758, 60 or 61 and the second with the year 1773, 75 or 76. His analysis convinced him that, taking the joint evidence of baptisms and burials, the population had grown by more than one eighth in a period of ten years – 'much faster than before' (p.131). Towns, too, had increased in population, as shown by local enumerations.

Finally, Howlett made two attempts to estimate the total population of England and Wales around 1780. First, he tried to 'correct' the window tax surveyors' returns by comparing them with enumerations in a number of communities. On that basis he argued that in 1780 there must have been over 1·6 million houses. This figure was then multiplied by an average number of persons per house, based on local surveys (or estimates) of $5\frac{2}{5}$, a figure which he considered on the low side since it did not allow for higher ratios in London. The total population would thus amount to 8·69 millions (p.146). The second estimate was arrived at by comparing the local returns for the numbers of men ballotted for the militia with the ratios of such men to the total numbers of inhabitants in the places for which enumerations or surveys were available. By using a variety of places, averages could be struck and these then used as multipliers in the same way as for the houses. A figure – again regarded as low – of about 7·9 millions was reached. The general conclusion was that 'the inhabitants of this Kingdom must have increased one third since the revolution, about one sixth during the last twenty years, and that their present amount cannot be less than between eight and nine millions' (p.152).

Howlett's work was criticized in two publications. The anonymous author of *Uncertainty of the Present Population of this Kingdom* (London 1781), took a sceptical view of the writings of all the contributors to the controversy, though on balance tending to agree with Price. Eden was dismissed as being 'so general and superficial, that nothing very determinate or satisfactory can be expected' (p.8). Wales and Howlett are chided for their comments on the window tax returns. It was not clear that the surveyors did exclude the untaxed houses; in one example which could be tested – the parish of Tenterden in Kent – a correspondent had assured him that the full total number of houses was to be found in the parish duplicate. What would be required was evidence to show, from enumerations, that the number of houses had actually increased while the numbers reported by the surveyors had fallen. This to some extent had been done by Howlett for several parishes for recent years and Price's claim that depopulation had continued during the last twenty years was 'directly and fully refuted'. But as for the comparison between 1690 and the mid-eighteenth century, Howlett's probable misinterpretation of the tax returns threw great doubt on the reliability of his arguments. Nor was it sufficient to show that there had been increases in some districts – in Yorkshire, for example, admitted by everyone to have grown in population; that was not incompatible with a decline at the national level.

As for the evidence from parish registers, there was the question of the representativeness of the sample and also of the differing degree of completeness of registration over time. Wales's sample was not representative. Moreover, registration was less complete in the earlier period (1740-50). And the evidence of increased population from Howlett's use of the register data was 'not greater than what may fairly be accounted for, from the probable imperfection of registers in the first period, the great diminution of dissenters since that time, and the different degrees of mortality' (p.28). What was really required was 'correct and well-authenticated information from two or three principal towns, and thirty or forty villages and country-parishes in every province throughout the nation...', covering numbers of houses and proportions of men allotted to the militia, as well as parish register data. If the first two sets of data 'mutually agree with each other, and with the register testimony of advanced Population, we may be as fully convinced of our increased numbers, and may be nearly as sure of what is their present actual amount, as from the most correct and accurate survey' (pp.31-32). But if they differed, and especially if the omissions in the surveyors' returns were found to be small, then depopulation would have to be accepted as a fact.

Wales did not reply to the criticism of his work; as was pointed out earlier, he did not continue to publish on the subject. Howlett, by contrast, published several books, most of which had some bearing upon population. But he did not appear to reply explicitly to the comments in the pamphlet on the *Uncertainty of the Present Population*, though he was not unwilling to defend himself in print and he did so in response to a critical review by 'G.W.' in *The Gentleman's Magazine* (Vol.52, 1782, pp.369-375, 473-475, 525-526). Part of the review dealt with factors influencing population growth. But the first half of the review was a technical critique, explaining, in contrast to Howlett's argument, that an excess of burials over baptisms in a given place was not evidence of out-migration, nor an excess of baptisms evidence of an inward flow. Nor could it be claimed that a decrease in the number of burials was necessarily an indication that mortality had fallen. Indeed, 'unless an exact register of all migrations in every parish, whether *to* it, or *from* it, were carefully kept', every conclusion that can be drawn from a comparison between the births and burials would be 'extremely fallacious...' (p.372). Changes in completeness of registration would also have to be taken into account. On the other hand, since the ratio of baptisms to the population (i.e. the crude birth rate) was generally constant over the country, the number of baptisms could be used as an indicator of population growth. And, on that basis, the population of England must in fact have increased at least as much as Howlett had concluded. Howlett did not accept G.W.'s strictures on the factors associated with population growth, but he accepted the first half of the technical criticism. He could not agree that the number of baptisms could be taken as an index of population size. It would be necessary to know whether the number of Dissenters had increased, and in any case the baptismal registers were the most 'deficient' of all the registers (pp.473-474).

Howlett was not entirely consistent. Thus in a pamphlet on the influence of enclosure on population he used ratios of baptisms in two periods to argue that population growth had been greater in recently enclosed parishes than in those not enclosed.[61] And in writing on the population of Ireland, he used the tax returns and a multiplier of five persons per house to estimate that the population had increased from about 1 million in 1672 to over 2 millions in 1772, without justifying in any detail the reliability of his data.[62] In a later pamphlet, discussing the numbers of people in receipt of parochial assistance, Howlett threw overboard another of his methods of estimating the population of England on the basis of the window tax returns. He wrote: 'I take the present opportunity, indeed I think it absolutely incumbent upon me in order to prevent future errors, to acknowledge that that calculation of mine deserves no credit; it being founded on an entire misconception of the manner in which the district and county surveyors make their collective returns of cottages. This mistake seems not only to have escaped the notice of the public in general, but even the acute penetration of Dr. Price himself. What he intimates to be my mistake on this head is merely his own misapprehension; and I must also take the liberty to observe, that the other mistakes he imputes to me have no existence but in his own imagination. This I will satisfactorily evince, should I ever again publish on the general subject of the population of this Kingdom, for which I have by me very ample materials.'[63] He did not again publish on that general subject, though he lived to see the first of our periodic censuses, that of 1801. But he did return to the question in a letter written in 1797 to John Middleton and published in the latter's *View of the Agriculture of Middlesex* (London 1798). There he referred once more to the (undisclosed) erroneous principle in his earlier calculations and to his later unpublished 'more minute and accurate investigation of the subject', from which he had been led to conclude that the population (of England and Wales) 'did not amount to seven millions and a half, and that at present it does not exceed eight millions'.[64]

In the fifth edition of his *Observations on Reversionary Payments*, Price included what were to be his final comments on the debate on population.[65] He again referred to the contrast between Davenant's figure of 1·3 million houses in 1690 and the much smaller – and, indeed, consistently declining – numbers returned under the window tax for the eighteenth century. He had little to say in favour of Howlett, drawing attention particularly to the fact that Howlett's tax return statistics did not agree with those furnished centrally by the Tax Office and that he had in any case misinterpreted the statistics. No allowance for defects in the tax returns would be so large as to convert a decline into an increase. In addition, Howlett had overestimated the number of persons per house for his multiplier. As for local enumerations, many were for those industrial areas which everyone knew were growing in population.

For William Wales, Price had more respect, though he did not accept his data as valid. Where Wales showed an increase in the number of houses between 1750 and 1780, Price claimed that in part that was only apparent; many single houses occupied by two families had been converted into two houses, thereby reducing the tax burden. The argument from baptisms and burials was not conclusive. In part the data had been misinterpreted and there was also the question of the reliability – and especially comparative reliability in different periods – of the parish register material. Price believed that the registers had been more deficient at the time of the Revolution than in his period and generally doubted whether they could be used to provide evidence of population growth. Further, Price remained convinced that the population of London had fallen – still basing himself on the diminished numbers of burials and births. Adding to all this the fact of the decrease in the yield of the hereditary and temporary excise on beer, and taking into account the 'growing distress among the lower orders of people', he saw no reason to alter his conclusions, though his opinion was 'by no means a clear and decided conviction'.[66]

Richard Price died in 1791, and with his death much of the earlier controversial vigour was lost. But the general interest in population provoked by Price's contributions was maintained, and showed itself in publications on the economic circumstances of the country and in the various county reports on agriculture. One such report has already been refered to – that of John Middleton on Essex. Other reports containing discussions and estimates of population include that on Berkshire by William Pearce;[67] and on Cambridge by Charles Vancouver.[68] And in one of the special reports Sir John Call attempted to see whether population was increasing, by comparing the baptisms and burials in the period 1788-97, extracted from 'the registers of four dispersed and distant parishes in every county'. He did not try to arrive at a total figure for the population of the country, but was in no doubt that there had been an increase. 'All I shall beg leave to have granted is, that the increase has not been less than one-third part, in the course of ten years, to the end of 1797, on the total, whatever it might have been at the beginning of the period; and the increase of the population has been regular and progressive for thirty years past, if not for more. . .'[69] There were also less detailed – and more grandiose – estimates in the publications of Henry Beeke, a well-known writer on taxation. In a work published in 1798, he argued that the population of England and Wales must be at least 11 millions, that of Scotland $2\frac{1}{2}$ millions and that of Ireland about 4 millions. And in a subsequent study, published in 1800, he put the figure for England and Wales at between $10\frac{1}{2}$ and 11 millions, with the increase probably continuing 'at the rate of considerably more than 100,000 annually, after deducting all commercial and military waste'.[70]

There was still time, before the 1801 census, for one last direct contribution to the controversy, and this was produced by Sir Frederick Morton Eden in 1800.[71] Eden, who is remembered primarily for his writing on the state of the poor[72] knew that the Census Bill was being debated in Parliament, but nevertheless considered it useful to construct his own estimate, based partly on the information presented in his earlier book and partly on additional data collected mainly for agricultural areas. In essence, he followed two approaches in his work. First, he had data on the numbers of baptisms, burials and marriages and assessed houses for a range of parishes and also data on total population for a more limited series of places. From this material he derived a series of ratios and applied them to the figures for assessed houses for England and Wales – he had obtained these latter from the Tax Office the previous year (1799 or 1798 – the date is not specified). The manipulation gave him three estimates of the total population, ranging between 8,935,500 and 10,710,000 and he concluded that, allowing for seamen and soldiers, the population of England and Wales was almost 11 millions.

Secondly, he used Sir John Call's collection of parish registry data as a model for a survey of his own in which he attempted to collect similar information for 200 parishes (four for each county) for four periods from 1688-97 to 1793-99. In fact, only just over half the parishes supplied returns. But the data showed an excess of baptisms over burials for each of the periods and, assuming the same ratio of baptisms to population as in his earlier estimate, he estimated the total population at the time of the Revolution was about 6·6 millions. This was substantially higher than Gregory King's estimate, but, of course, was still in keeping with the conclusion that the population of England and Wales had increased very substantially during the eighteenth century.

Like all other contributions to the controversy, Eden's estimates suffered from many defects. The novel aspect of his particular study, however, was his effort to eliminate errors resulting from the under-enumeration of houses by the tax assessors. Eden had no doubt that the assessments were incorrect and that the size of the error was greater at the time he was writing than in the earlier periods. The error would not matter if he could obtain a valid ratio between assessed houses and total population for the point of time for which the calculation was being done. But it is most unlikely that the ratio was valid either in respect of the representativeness of the sample of places covered or of the accuracy of the population totals for those places. And the estimate of the increase over time was itself subject to a variety of errors, including one which continued to obtain in many nineteenth – and some twentieth – century calculations, namely the implicit assumption of a constant birth rate.

The final results of the 1801 census, when they appeared in 1802, put an end to controversy in the form initiated by Brakenridge and later resuscitated by Richard Price. Whatever might have been the actual course of population during the eighteenth century, the figure of some 9·168 millions for England and Wales in 1801 gave no support to the decline which the 'pessimists' claimed was taking place.[73] For all the errors in their methods of estimation and in the basic data on which they drew, the 'optimists' were more nearly correct in their assessment than was Richard Price, who had dominated the actuarial and demographic establishment of the period. Indeed, taking into account the probability that there was under-enumeration in the 1801 census, even some of the higher estimates of the 'optimists' were not far from reality.

Price's nephew, William Morgan, attempted to defend his uncle's reputation by arguing that the 1801 census had shown the average number of persons per house to be lower than had been claimed by most of the 'optimists', and that the essential fault lay with the surveyors of windows, who had not given correct returns of the house exempted on grounds of poverty. Had those returns been accurate, he claimed, Price would in fact have over-estimated the population of England and Wales. But, as has been shown, the under-reporting of houses by the surveyors was stressed by most of the 'optimists', a circumstance of which Morgan must have been fully aware. He also conveyed the impression of serious doubts about the reliability of the census returns. 'These accounts,' wrote Morgan, 'if they be correct, contradict both observation and experience, not only in giving the proportion of inhabitants to a house much greater than they have been found in former enumerations, but more particularly in making the number of males to exceed that of females; – a circumstance I believe seldom or ever known to have taken place in any other part of the world.' But this latter conclusion was arrived at by attributing all the armed forces, seamen and convicts to England and Wales alone, instead of to Great

Britain or to the British Isles. If only a modest number were attributed to Ireland – say 25,000 out of a total of over 470,000 men in these categories – and the remainder rateably distributed between England and Wales and Scotland, an excess of females would have emerged.[74] Morgan further criticized the census in that, given the way it had been devised and carried out, it was 'hardly possible to imagine a measure so ill-fitted for obtaining any useful information. It appears to have been instituted for the mere purpose of determining a controversy; and even in this it has totally failed of its object.' The question of whether the population was growing or declining was a matter which would still remain the subject of future discussion.[75]

At least that final judgement by Morgan was a sound one. The question of whether the population was actually growing *was* answered by the successive enumerations, the results of which tended to give support to Malthusian fears rather than to the fears exhibited by Price. The question of whether – or, rather, how and why – the population had been growing during the eighteenth century has continued to be a subject for discussion until the present day. Rickman, Finlaison and Farr tried to answer it during the nineteenth century: the 1801 and 1841 censuses tried explicitly to provide the statistical basis for a more realistic answer. In the twentieth century Brownlee and Griffith added their estimates of the course of population during the eighteenth century, while social and medical historians and sociologists have debated a variety of explanations for the substantial increase in numbers implied by all computations subsequent to those of Price. But we still lack definitive answers to the detailed questions on the course and magnitude of the increase, on the relative contributions of mortality, fertility and marriage, or on the specific factors associated with the probable decline in mortality.[76]

If there are still no definitive answers today, the participants in the eighteenth-century controversy can hardly be criticized for their inability to provide such answers. The basic data at their disposal were poor and limited – much more limited than is now the case for historians studying the period, for many parish registers have been transcribed and the results of many local enumerations have been collected and examined with a technical expertise not possible two hundred years ago. A comparable expertise has been applied to the examination of some of the early tax returns which, in any case, were rarely open to close scrutiny by contemporary writers.[77] Further, almost two centuries of census taking and a century and a half of civil vital registration have provided materials which have not only been of immediate relevance, but have also facilitated the more fruitful use of earlier and poorer demographic statistics. Not least important, historical demographers today write with the great advantage of hindsight. They can begin their studies of the eighteenth century with the statistics of population and houses reported by the 1801 census. Though no doubt subject to errors, these statistics are far more reliable than the data available during the eighteenth century and they reveal a situation very different from that which Price believed was implied by the window tax returns.

Greenwood, whose comment on Richard Price has already been cited, had little to say in favour of the other participants in the population debate. His view was that '...the eighteenth century political arithmeticians of England made no advance whatsoever upon the position reached by Graunt, Petty and King. They were second-rate imitators of men of genius.'[78] This assessment is justified technically, but it is nevertheless unreasonable. It would have been surprising to find a continuing crop of 'men of genius' in a field which received so little public support and in which the basic data were so unsatisfactory. Graunt, with his great intellectual and imaginative leap forward, had practically exhausted the possibilities of analysis offered by the London Bills of Mortality. Gregory King, who admired Graunt's work (but not Petty's), was able to draw upon some of the unpublished enumeration data collected under the 1694 Marriage Act and to persuade competent friends and acquaintances to undertake detailed local censuses of direct value to him when he estimated the age structure of the population and the numbers of persons per house. But King's work was inaccessible, save in the extracts published – and not always correctly interpreted – by Davenant.[79]

The eighteenth-century political arithmeticians began with a handicap: none of the materials available to them was as useful as the Marriage Act statistics had been to Gregory King. They tried to overcome this handicap by collecting their own data and by persuading acquaintances to co-operate in that activity. The period from the first controversy onwards saw many 'sample surveys' of parish register entries and a wide range of local enumerations.[80] By modern standards, the samples were certainly not well-designed Nevertheless, 'representativeness' was the aim of much of the work, even if the actual practice fell short of it. 'Field surveys' were carried out, in spite of some local hostility and in spite of the superstition regarding 'numbering the people'. Many of the local enumerations were undoubtedly inaccurate, and so no doubt were the transcriptions of local register and tax materials.[81] But the intellectual climate encouraged initiative, and some of the local studies were admirable – Heysham's enumeration of Carlisle, for example, and the particularly valuable census of Corfe Castle parish, Dorset, at the end of the century.[82] The initiative spread to Ireland, too, and Whitelaw's report on his enumeration of Dublin in 1798 is still worth studying, not simply for historical reasons, but as a discussion of the problems involved in organizing a local census – including those of training and supervising enumerators – and as a pioneer attempt to classify the population by social status.[83] Medical statistiticians, too, were stimulated to reanalyse existing information, especially the available Bills of Mortality, and to collect new materials – for example, from the records of dispensaries.[84] It is true that the census and vital statistics of the nineteenth century had to be built on new foundations; that was unavoidable. But it was to a large extent the controversy which stimulated interest in population questions and publicized the deficiences of the existing statistical systems.[85] By the end of the century there was a much wider awareness of the need for reliable census and vital registration data. The circumstances which finally led to the provision of such data will be discussed in the next chapters.

NOTES

1 'A letter from the Reverend William Brakenridge, D.D. and F.R.S. to George Lewis Scot, Esq., F.R.S., concerning the Number of Inhabitants within the London Bills of Mortality', *Phil. Trans.*, Vol.48, II (1755), No.XCV, pp.788-800. William Brakenridge (spelled Braikenridge in the register of Oxford alumni) came from Glasgow and first studied at Aberdeen. He was incorporated from Queen's College, Oxford, successively MA, BD and DD, and subsequently became Rector of St

Michael Bassishaw, London. In 1745 he became librarian to Sion College and was later elected President. (Information from the Guildhall Library, London.)

2 He decided upon six persons per house – found by 'experiment', in 'a certain parish in London'.

3 'A letter to George Lewis Scot, Esq., F.R.S., concerning the Number of People in England; from the Reverend William Brakenridge, D.D. Rector of St. Michael Bassishaw, London, and F.R.S.', *Phil. Trans.*, Vol.49, I, No.XLV, 1756, pp.268-285.

4 A brief survey of the development of the house and window taxes is given in F. M. Eden, *An Estimate of the Number of Inhabitants in Great Britain and Ireland*, London 1800, pp.20-25. The effect of the window tax was naturally heaviest on the poor as is indicated by John Heysham's description of the outbreak of typhus in Carlisle in 1781: 'It broke out in a house in Rickergate which contains about a half a dozen very poor families; the rooms are exceeding small, and in order to diminish the window-tax, every window, that even poverty could dispense with, was shut up: hence stagnation of air, which was rendered still more noxious by the filth and uncleanliness of the people'. See J. Milne, *A Treatise on the Valuation of Annuities and Assurances . . .*, London 1815, Vol.2, pp.737-738.

5 He was referring to the statement given in Derham, *op. cit.*, 1st edn, 1713, p.177n, that 'in England in general, fewer die than are born, there being but 1 death to 1^{12}_{100} births'. The observations are extremely slender, to say nothing about their accuracy.

6 If it should be thought that this calculation is ludicrous, as indeed it is, it should also be noted that modern writers arc capable of comparable estimates. Mr Rew, in the discussion of Gonner's paper, *J.R.S.S.*, February 1913, p.297, mentioned that Dr Thorold Rogers, who on one occasion was 'very contemptous of the estimates made by certain statisticians of the English population in the Middle Ages', in turn 'claimed that he could give the population with practical certainty by calculating the amount of bread which people consumed'.

7 'A Letter to George Lewis Scot, Esquire, concerning the present Increase of the People in Britain and Ireland: From William Brakenridge, D.D. Rector of St. Michael Bassishaw, London, and F.R.S.', *Phil. Trans.*, Vol.49, II., 1756 No.CXIII, pp.877-890.

8 Brakenridge, as a corollary, makes a statement very reminiscent of Wallace: 'We may in general likewise observe, that in all Europe the annual increase of people must be much less than it was in some former ages. For the advancement of trade in the maritime countries, must greatly augment the loss of their fencible men' (p.885, *loc. cit.*).

9 That is, instead of the 25 per cent given in his earlier paper.

10 He referred to criticisms of his use of the Bills of Mortality for London, including objections that they were inaccurate and incomplete. He did not believe, however, that this amounted to very much or that the inaccuracies had increased – he did not, for example, think there were more Dissenters than previously. He agreed that his estimate of the decline of London was not reflected in a corresponding increase in the number of empty houses, but thought that this was because there were now fewer houses – when a new house was built, it replaced two or three or more earlier ones, or existing houses were turned into warehouses – and also that thc decrease in population might have borne most heavily on lodgers and children,

the falling numbers of whom would not result in many more houses being empty (pp.887-890, *loc. cit.*).

11 George Burrington, *An Answer to Dr. William Brakenridge's Letter Concerning the Number of Inhabitants, within the London Bills of Mortality,* . . ., London 1757. Burrington was twice Governor of North Carolina. He was dismissed during his first term of office for attempting to assault Chief Justice Christopher Gale and threatening to burn or blow up his house. He was again appointed in 1731 and was apparently an effective Governor, spending much of his own fortune on the province. He retired in 1734 and was murdered in London in 1759. (*Dictionary of American Biography*, Vol.3.)

12 'An Extract of the Register of the Parish of Great Shefford, near Lambourne, in Berkshire, for Ten Years: With Observations on the same: In a Letter to Tho. Birch, D.D. Secret R.S. from the Rev. Mr. Richard Forster, Rector of Great Shefford', *Phil. Trans.* Vol.50, I, No.XLIII, 1757, pp.356-363. Forster came from Lancashire. He was originally at All Souls College, Oxford, where he took his BA in 1729 and became a Fellow of Brasenose, receiving his MA in 1732. He was Vice-Principal of the College and then Senior Bursar, being subsequently (1747) appointed Rector of West Shefford, Berkshire. He died in 1766. (Information received from Brasenose College.)

13 'A Letter to the Rev. Thomas Birch, D.D. Secr. R.S. concerning the Number of the People of England; by the Rev. Mr. Richard Forster, Rector of Great Shefford in Berkshire', *Phil. Trans.*, Vol.50, I, 1757, No.LVII, pp.457-465.

14 But this does not deal with the question of the supposed recent fall in population.

15 'For a century now past', he wrote, 'the English way of philosophising (and all the rest of the world is come into it) is not to sit down in one's study, and form an hypothesis, and then strive to wrest all nature to it; but to look abroad into the world, and see how nature works; and then to build upon certain matter of fact.'

16 'A Letter to the Right Honourable the Earl of Macclesfield, President of the Royal Society, from the Rev. William Brakenridge, D.D. F.R.S. containing an Answer to the Account of the Numbers and Increase of the People of England, by the Rev. Mr. Forster', *Phil. Trans.*, Vol.50, I, 1757, No.LVIII, pp.465-479.

17 *Op. cit.*, p.462.

18 Birch MSS 4440, No.176, letter from Forster dated 2 December 1760. It is not clear from this and from Forster's letter of 4 December 1760 (Birch MSS 4440, No.189) whether there was also another, earlier reply.

19 He wrote: . . . 'it is very certain, that were ye Births ten times ye Burials; yet were ye Consumption proportionable some way or other, ye real Increase wou'd be nothing. Whereas my Table (which is nothing but ye Registers methodized) has not one word of ye Burials. It shows, that ye Christenings are doubled in a certain Term, & therefore ye People are doubled; which is so plain, that I am in hopes, no Body will call for a proof of it.' Thus he assumed a constant birth rate, as did other writers of the period.

20 Brakenridge had used a multiplier of 4 to 1, based on the proportion given by Halley for men aged eighteen to fifty-six years. But the Act of Parliament specified an age range of 18 to 50 years and allowing for exempted men (lame &c.), Forster felt that his own ratio of 5 to 1 was justified.

21 Forster also attacked Brakenridge's use of the ratio of 100 burials to 112 births,

taken from Derham. He believed that Derham had really taken this from Gregory King and that though King was to be respected, he was also liable to some criticism – for example, for his thesis that there were more women than men alive. Forster had surveyed various parish registers and had found a ratio of 100 burials to 173 births.

22 [John Mitchell], *The Present State of Great Britain and North America, with Regard to Agriculture, Population, Trade, and Manufactures, impartially Considered*, London 1767, pp.108-118.

23 In fact the 1692 data were given by John Houghton, though some writers took them to have come from Halley, because of a reference made by Houghton to Halley's assistance in computing the acreage of each county of England and Wales. Houghton gave 1,175,951 houses (the date for this return is not given) as compared with 1,319,215 given for the year 1690 by C. Davenant. See R. Bradley (ed.), *A Collection for the Improvement of Husbandry and Trade... communicated... to the Collector, John Houghton F.R.S.*, Vol.I, London 1727, pp.67 & 73-75; Lord Somers & others, *A Second Collection of Scarce and Valuable Tracts*, Vol.4, London 1750, table facing p.80; [C. Davenant], *An Essay upon Ways and Means of Supplying the War*, London 1695, table facing p.76. Gonner, *op. cit.*, p.262, says that both Houghton and King (the latter in Chalmers's reprint) gave the population in each county, but I can find no trace of this.

24 Mitchell gave no authority for his multiplier except to say there is 'an observation that every marriage produces four children' – presumably adding the parents to the children and getting a total of six persons. Even if he were correct on his fertility data – which he could not know – his estimate would make no allowance for mortality (the fertility ratio itself obviously comes from Graunt).

25 [T. Whately], *Considerations on the Trade and Finances of this Kingdom*, 2nd edn, London 1766, pp.97-98. He claimed that the tax burden was responsible for a fall in the number of houses in England and Wales from 986,482 in 1759 to 980,692 'now', without saying to which date the 'now' referred.

26 *Edinburgh Review*, Vol.XXV, June-October 1815, p.171.

27 W. Morgan, *Memoirs of the Life of Richard Price, D.D., F.R.S.*, London 1815, p.80; R. Thomas, *Richard Price: Philosopher and Apostle of Liberty*, London 1934, *passim*.

28 See W. Morgan, *A Review of Dr. Price's Writings on the Subject of the Finances of this Kingdom*, London 1792.

29 See the discussion in Chapter 4.

30 M. Greenwood, *Medical Statistics from Graunt to Farr*, Cambridge 1948, p.48.

31 W. Morgan, *The Doctrine of Annuities and Assurances*, London 1779, Introduction, p.ix. The theory described by Morgan had been applied by the Equitable Assurance Society – the first to do so. In the introduction Price urged the Society to adopt new tables based upon a lighter mortality than that originally applied – the mortality of London in 1728-50, which period included two years of especially heavy mortality, 1740 and 1741. He also advised the Society to take care not to accept 'bad lives'. 'It must be ruined, should it ever become, not a resource for the living and healthy, but a refuge for the sick and dying' (p.xix).

32 W. Morgan, *Memoirs*, pp.85-86.

33 'Observations on the Expectations of Lives, the Increase of Mankind, the

Influence of Great Towns on Population, and Particularly the State of London, with Respect to Healthfulness and Number of Inhabitants', *Philosophical Transactions*, Vol.59, 1769, pp.89-125. It was also issued as a separate pamphlet (London 1769) and reprinted, with additions, in the various editions of the *Observations on Reversionary Payments*.

34 'Observations on Expectations. . .', p.97.

35 *Op. cit.*, pp.107-108.

36 That is, the omissions of births and deaths from the London Bills of Mortality.

37 *Op. cit.*, p.108. Price believed this was perhaps due primarily to a decrease in the number of Dissenters, but gave no reasons for so believing. But, indeed, he gave no real reasons for believing that the omissions of births relative to burials had changed over time.

38 *Op. cit.*, pp.118-119.

39 *Observations*, 2nd edn, pp.362-365. He claimed, in this connection, that 'a flourishing commerce, tho' favourable to population in some respects, is, I think, on the whole, extremely unfavourable; and, while it flatters, may be destroying; particularly, by increasing luxury, the worst enemy of population as well as of public virtue; and by calling off too many persons from agriculture to unhealthy trades and the sea-service'.

40 He did not, in the Supplement, give any information as to the ratio of persons per house used in his estimates, though it is clear that this ratio must have been about $4\frac{1}{2}$ persons per house. But in the enlargements and corrections at the end of the volume (pp.401-404) he commented on Brakenridge's estimates and there asserted, on the basis of surveys of Leeds (1770), Shrewsbury (1750) Holy-Cross (a suburb of Shrewsbury) and Northampton, that $4\frac{1}{2}$ persons per house was probably, and 5 per house certainly, an excessive allowance. He placed the population of England and Wales at probably not over $4\frac{1}{2}$ millions and certainly less than 5 millions.

41 R. Price, *An Appeal to the Public on the Subject of the National Debt*, 2nd edn, London 1772, pp.45-46, 85-97.

42 The possibility of inaccuracy in the window tax returns was not entirely excluded – at least Price said that 'if there is any room for doubt, it may be removed, with little expence or trouble, by an order to the collectors of the house and window duties to make more careful returns' (*Appeal*, p.87).

43 The correspondent expressed views which anticipated later theorists. Thus he said: 'Mankind seldom grow thin in any country, through the defect of the natural powers of procreation; these powers, almost all over the world, far out-run the business of keeping up the stock, and are even capable, when not obstructed, of making a very rapid increase of the species.' He claimed that even famine, pestilence and war would be counterbalanced by propagation, which was encouraged, rather, than diminished by them. On the other hand, propagation was affected by the 'manners and political circumstances of a people', that in 'the most refined state of civilisation, few children are produced and brought up by the highest and lowest classes of mankind', and that 'in proportion, therefore, as luxury increases, and civilisation grows greater, the *vis propagandi* (if I may so call it) decreases; and if with this increase of civilisation, the individuals of these classes increase in number, the mischief is so much greater' (pp.92-93). In essence, this was also the view of

Price, but Price (and other writers lamenting depopulation) were rather more crude in their account of luxury as a cause, and did not generalize their attitude in the form of a negative correlation between the degree of civilization and the level of overt fertility.

44 [A. Young], *Proposals to the Legislature for Numbering the People*, London 1771, esp. pp.4-6, was apparently attacking John Mitchell in referring to those who claimed 'that population declines; that we have lost a million and a half since the Revolution'. Young was generally sceptical of the validity of any of the calculations made, and it was part of his case for a census that 'the calculations drawn up from the number of houses are, in all probability, fallacious: that they are mere *guesses* we well know; for by what rule is the number of souls *per* house to be determined? How is the medium to be found out between the palace, and the cot?... Besides, how are we to know that the number *per* house is always the same?' Nor did he think highly of attempts to determine the ratio of persons per house by surveying a few areas, for 'an accidental agreement between the common supposition *per* house, and the real numbers in any small district, cannot, with accuracy, be extended to the kingdom at large'. In urging that a census be taken, he said that if, 'contrary to expectation', the population were found to be falling, repetition of the census every five years would show where the fall was most important and thus help to explain the causes (p.27). Young's proposal included 'the publication of the tables of population, as an essential part of the plan'.

45 Letter dated 28 March 1772, published in *St James's Chronicle* and reprinted in *Political Arithmetic*, London 1774, pp.322-331.

46 Young referred to Houghton's total as having been calculated by Halley. In this he seems to have been wrong, for Houghton made no statement to that effect.

47 Young asked why Price had taken no notice of Brakenridge's figure of 911,310 houses in 1710, less than the figures for the later years. It was true that Brakenridge did 'not mention the office whence he got the list; but his character is too well established to suppose him utterly mistaken'.

48 He also argued that it was useless to give the number of persons per family (as was done in some instances) when the number per house was wanted.

49 Young also, of course, denied Price's assertions that enclosures had evil consequences for population growth.

50 *Observations*, 3rd edn, p.375n(b). What Price had mainly in mind here was that the returns did distinguish between the separate dwellings in a given tenement, for it was to the advantage of the landlord, as regard his tax liabilities, to insist upon that distinction. But this did not dispose of the question of their general accuracy.

51 *Ibid.*, pp.379-394.

52 See esp. pp.61-96.

53 It was presumably because of his theory of the relation between employment and population that he did not agree with Wallace (or Price) about the ill-effects of increasing manufacturers. He did not believe that simplicity of living encouraged population growth, for simplicity would really mean less employment. For Young the characteristic of a populous country was – many people, but labour expensive. Labour was more expensive in Holland than elsewhere and he believed Holland to be the most populous (i.e. most densely peopled) country in Europe.

In an earlier publication, Young had written more generally on the subject of population and suggested six means of promoting agriculture and population. These means included the framing of new poor laws – the existing laws, he believed, encouraged 'idleness, drunkenness, and tea-drinking' among the poor and were thus 'highly pernicious to the welfare of the Kingdom'. Young also advocated the abolition of tithes; the conversion of waste land into arable farms; the reduction of the population of London; and a great reduction in the 'prices of the necessaries of life, and those of labour in proportion' ([A. Young], *The Farmer's Letters to the People of England*, 2nd edn, London 1768 (the first edition appeared in 1767)).

54 Part 2 of *Political Arithmetic*, London 1779, contains only one specific reference to the controversy, namely: 'All guesses at the number of people are fallacious. – There are no data sufficient for the calculation. – Besides, *depopulation* is the fashion with a set of men who wish to decry the state of the nation; and they have found writers visionary enough, from very fallible materials, to pronounce, with an authoritative air, that we are not four millions and an half' (p.25n).

At one time Young had envisaged producing a book on the population of England and had collected materials for that purpose. But in 1780 or 1781 he was asked to give some of his data to John Howlett and apparently did so – including tables of baptisms before and after the Revolution and for two more recent thirty-year periods. Presumably, the knowledge of Howlett's inquiry persuaded Young to give up his own project. (M. Betham-Edwards (ed.), *The Autobiography of Arthur Young*, London 1898, pp.97-98.)

55 W. Morgan, *The Doctrine of Annuities and Assurances on Lives and Survivorships, Stated and Explained*, London 1779.

56 W. Eden, *Four Letters to the Earl of Carlisle... to which is added a Third Letter*, 3rd edn, London 1780, p.xxxiv. William Eden, first Lord Auckland, was a political figure of some eminence. Trained as a barrister, he entered Parliament and was chosen as one of the first Lords of the Board of Trade and Plantations when that was set up.

57 R. Price, *An Essay on the Population of England*, 2nd edn, London 1780.

58 *An Inquiry into the Present State of Population in England and Wales*, London 1781.

59 *Dictionary of National Biography*

60 *Dictionary of National Biography*. Howlett was at St John's, Oxford, and obtained the BA in 1755, the MA in 1795 and the BD in 1796.

61 John Howlett, *An Enquiry into the Influence which Enclosures have had upon the Population of England*, London 1786, pp.23-30.

62 John Howlett, *An Essay on the Population of Ireland*, London 1786, pp.3 & 22. In this criticism of Price, Howlett had written: 'All public accounts, in consequence of the imposition of any public tax, will always be extremely uncertain. There are never wanting a number of persons who are interested to attempt connivance and concealment... Nor let it be said that this will equally take place, at every period, and that consequently, the deception must be as great at one time as at another' (*An Examination of Dr. Price's Essay...*, pp.41-42.

63 John Howlett, *The Insufficiency of the Causes to which the Increase of our Poor, and the Poor's Rates have been commonly ascribed*, London 1788, p.61n. In this pamphlet Howlett attempted to estimate the mortality of children in the Houses of Industry in various parts of the country (chiefly Norfolk and Suffolk) as compared with children in general in various parishes. His conclusion was that mortality in the

Houses of Industry was much higher than that in the parishes in general, and that this was not because the Houses of Industry contained poor children (he appeared to find that in his own parish of Dunmow mortality was lower among the children of the poor than among the children of the richer families).

64 P.563. A second edition of Middleton's survey of Essex was published in 1807. By that time, the returns of the 1801 census were available and are given in detail for Middlesex. Howlett's letter was omitted. But Middleton noted (p.591), with reference to Howlett's earlier estimate of the population within the Bills of Mortality as being between 800,000 and 900,000, 'It now appears that Mr. Howlett's calculations relative to London, were surprisingly near giving the true number of inhabitants'.

65 London 1792, 'Postscript', pp.297-347. This edition was edited by William Morgan. Since Price died in 1791, this was the last edition to which he could have contributed revisions and additions.

66 *Op. cit.*, p.346.

67 William Pearce, *General View of the Agriculture in Berkshire*, London 1794, pp.13-14.

68 Charles Vancouver, *General View of the Agriculture in the County of Cambridge*, London 1794, pp.193 & 211-212. Some reports discussed population increase without giving estimates of numbers – e.g. William James & Jacob Malcolm, *General View of the Agriculture of the County of Buckingham*, London 1794, p.27.

69 *Communications to the Board of Agriculture*, Vol.2, London 1800, pp.479-493; Sir John Call, 'An Abstract of Baptisms and Burials in Four Parishes of Fifty Counties in England...'

70 [Henry Beeke], *Letter to a County Member on the Means of Securing a Safe and Honourable Peace*, London 1798, pp.69-73; *idem.*, *Observations on the Produce of Income Tax, and on its Proportion to the Whole Income of Great Britain*, 2nd edn, London 1800, pp.117-118. In the second work, Beeke noted that he hoped soon to produce a book on a 'View of the Progress and Present State of the Population of England and Wales, containing authentic documents that confirm all I have said on this subject in its fullest extent' (p.117). Presumably this project collapsed with the taking of the 1801 census.

71 F. M. Eden, *An Estimate of the Number of Inhabitants in Great Britain and Ireland*, London 1800.

72 F. M. Eden, *The State of the Poor*, 3 vols, London 1797. He was a nephew of William Eden and was one of the founders – and subsequently Chairman – of the Globe Insurance Company.

73 The figure represents the corrected enumeration returns for England and Wales plus a proportionate share of the armed forces and mariners – it being assumed that these latter categories were attributable to the various divisions of the British Isles in proportion to the civilian population of those areas. Rickman's calculation is a somewhat mixed one in that it includes the population of Ireland, as estimated from the hearth tax, as well as estimates for the islands. See [John Rickman], *Observations on the Results of the Population Act, 41 Geo. III*, London 1802, p.9.

74 The sex ratio of a population depends upon (1) the sex ratio of live births; (2) relative male and female mortality; (3) the age-structure of the population (itself heavily dependent upon the level and trend of fertility); (4) the extent of sex-selective immigration and emigration.

75 R. Price, *Observations on Reversionary Payments*, 7th edn, London 1812, Vol.2, pp.210-212 & Vol.1, pp.x-xi. Morgan was also clearly sceptical of the statistics of houses – especially because the inhabited houses contained more than one 'family' per house, while at the same time there were some 57,000 uninhabited houses in England and Wales. He appears to have overlooked Rickman's note that the 'uninhabited houses' included new houses in process of completion but not yet able to be occupied, and did not allow for the possibility of geographical maldistribution of houses in relation to population. Incidentally, he also referred to the Census Act as having been passed in 1802 – though perhaps that incorrect reference was really a printing error. In addition, though one of his suggestions for the kinds of questions which should have been included in a satisfactory census schedule was sound – the ages of the population, by single years under five and thereafter in five-year groups – the other is one which was actually included, namely the births and burials in each district for the past three or four years. Indeed, as will be seen in the next chapter, the coverage of parish register data on baptisms and burials collected at the 1801 census was far more extensive than Morgan requested. In sum, it does not seem that Morgan had closely examined the provisions and results of the 1801 census.

76 Some of these matters are discussed subsequently.

77 The hearth tax returns have been the subject of particularly close scrutiny by modern archivists and historians, the window tax returns much less so. The only detailed comment on the window tax I have come across – I was referred to it by Mr W. Kellaway of the Institute of Historical Research, University of London – is W. R. Ward, *The Administration of the Window and Assessed Taxes 1696-1798*, London 1963 (this is a reprint of a paper which was published in *The English Historical Review*, October 1952). Although the author gives a very useful account of the administrative problems involved – including a discussion of the quality and qualifications of the officials – he does not deal with the tax statistics as such.

78 M. Greenwood, *Medical Statistics from Graunt to Farr*, Cambridge 1948, p.49.

79 In a manuscript written after he had completed his *Natural and Politicall Observations*, King stated that his previous figure for the total number of households in England and Wales in 1690 was too high – the consequence of the way in which the figures had been extracted from the hearth books. His revised estimate was 1·24 or 1·25 millions instead of his earlier figure of over 1·3 millions. The participants in the controversy could not have known of this revision, for the King manuscript was not accessible for study until 1949, when it was loaned to me by the Museum Book Store, which had acquired it. See the discussion in D. V. Glass & D. E. C. Eversley (eds.), *Population in History*, London 1965, pp.184-185.

80 Many of the contributors to the discussion of population – including the medical statisticians – tried to assess the extent of omissions from parochial registration (there were frequent estimates of the numbers of births and deaths to Dissenters in the areas examined) and from the London Bills of Mortality. Howlett made an elaborate estimate of these latter omissions, analogous to the earlier work of Maitland (see J. Howlett, *An Examination of Dr. Price's Essay*, ch.2, esp. pp.68-71 & 83-93). Whereas Maitland had estimated that 2114 burials were omitted from the London Bills in 1729, Howlett's estimate was 9173 for 1780 (excluding the figure of 2100 deaths which he estimated was the reduction in child mortality resulting

from the 1767 Hanway Act, by which poor infants were sent out of London to be nursed in the country).

81 Apart from inaccuracy as such, one of the difficulties lies in knowing what definitions were used in enumerating local populations – who was included in, or excluded from, a 'house', for example. A few enumerations were reported in considerable detail, and show quite clearly the coverage. But many simply reported the totals of 'houses' and 'population'. On this, see the very useful study by R. Wall, 'Mean household size in England from printed sources' (in P. Laslett (ed.), *Household and Family in Time Past*, Cambridge 1972). Wall lists the results of a large number of local returns, including many published in the various issues of Arthur Young's *Annals of Agriculture*.

82 Heysham's work, including his Bills of Mortality, is discussed subsequently. The 1795 enumeration of Corfe Castle parish, an industrial district at the time, is given in detail in J. Hutchins, *History and Antiquities of the County of Dorset*, 2nd edn, 3 vols, London 1796, Vol.1. The enumeration recorded age, sex, marital status, household composition, occupation and 'probable weekly earnings'.

83 The Rev. James Whitelaw, *An Essay on the Population of Dublin*, Dublin 1805. Unfortunately – though understandably, because of the expense involved – the book contains only a digest of the much more comprehensive material actually collected, which included a particularly detailed list of the inhabitants of one of the largest and poorest parishes, St Cathrine, giving age, sex and occupation, as well as the educational status of the children. A table facing p.14 allocates the population of each parish (males and females separately) to one of three 'social classes', namely: upper and middle classes, servants of the upper and middle classes, and lower class. The text indicates that, in the unpublished enumeration materials, this allocation must have been done separately for each household. The enumeration yielded a total population of 170,794 (excluding the suburb of Spring-garden): 21·8 per cent upper and middle class, 10·7 per cent servants of the upper and middle classes, and 67·5 per cent 'lower class' (i.e. with children having been allocated to the class of their families). The average number of persons per house was 11·5. Incidentally, Whitelaw specifically refers to the population controversy.

84 William Black's work is an example of the serious and sensible use of available data and of the collection of new data. See my introduction to the reprint of his book (the 2nd edn of 1789), *An Arithmetical and Medical Analysis of the Diseases and Mortality of the Human Species*, forthcoming.

85 It should be remembered that interest in the controversy extended well beyond the group of political arithmeticians. This is evident from the success of John Brown's *Estimate*, and from Oliver Goldsmith's well-known poem on depopulation ('The deserted village', first published in 1769. In the preface to the poem, Goldsmith wrote: 'In regretting the depopulation of the country, I inveigh against the increase of our luxuries...' See J. Aikin, *The Poetical Works of Oliver Goldsmith, M.B.*, London 1796, p.37.). Equally, George Chalmers's *Estimate*, which went through many editions, devoted a large section to the population question. And a foreign resident, writing on England at the end of the century, considered the question sufficiently important to spend a chapter on it, advocating a complete enumeration as the only means of settling the dispute. See F. A. Wendeborn, *A View of England towards the Close of the Eighteenth Century*, 2 vols, London 1791, Vol.1, p.126.

Wendeborn lived in England for many years, for most of the time as preacher to a German community in London. His book was originally published in Germany, the English translation was also published in Dublin, and there was a Dutch translation. Wendeborn apparently knew many prominent people in England and abroad and he was elected to membership of two of the best known European Academies. (See *Allgemeine Deutsche Biographie*, Vol.21, Leipzig 1896, pp.712-714.)

Forster's letters to Birch

Published by permission of the Trustees of the British Museum

Revd. Sir,

I never read Sr. Willm. Petty without admiring his great Candour & Moderation, who tells us, that He had drawn up an Answer to every Paragraph of Monsr. Azout's long Letter: But that he suppressed it, because it looked like War against a worthy Person, with whom he intended none. What we admire, we are apt to imitate. I have drawn up a long Reply to Dr. Brakenridge's Answer; but am resolved to throw it aside, as I design not ye least Quarrel, & content myself with stating ye bare matter of Fact.

In his first Letter to Mr. Scott[1]* Dr. Brakenridge informs us, that in Q. Anne's time there was a Survey made of all ye taxable Houses in *England* & *Wales*, & ye Number of them amounted to 729,048. To this He adds, by way of Supposition, that in this Survey one fourth part more must be allow'd for Cottages. So that ye whole number of Houses in ye Nation, at that time, did not exceed 911,310.

In a Second Letter to ye same Gentleman,[2] He acquaints us, that "there are at present 690,000 Houses charged to ye Window Tax, besides Cottages, that pay Nothing: And tho' ye No. of Cottages is not accurately known, *it appears from Account given in*, that they cannot amount to above 200,000." By this it appears, that, at present, there are not above 890,000 Houses in England & Wales.

You will please to observe, that ye former of these Computations is merely hypothetical. To this I have no Objection to make. Every one is a proper Judge of ye force of it.

But the latter is a more Serious Concern; It being of a positive Nature, founded upon ye Authority of *Accounts given in.*

What these Accounts were; & whence Dr. Brakenridge had them, I expressed a very strong desire of knowing, in a Letter addressed to yourself.[3] And was in hopes, if ye Dr. shou'd ever take ye Trouble of answering me, that He woul'd have satisfied this one Quere, as it was evidently the only Motive of my Writing.

But this He has not thought proper to do: So far from it, that he seems to have dropt both his former Numbers, & to have adopted a New one, being now of ye mind, that ye rated Houses are to ye Cottages, as about two to one. The Learned World will be so good to observe, that for this there is not still ye least Authority.[4]

Dr. Brakenridge objects to my Survey, that it is too scanty. The objection is undoubtedly very just. But if we extend our prospect, we shall not mend ye matter at all. In my former Survey, I took in ten contiguous Parishes, containing about 100 Square Miles, in order that it might not be said, I picked out such, as best suited my purpose. I have now taken ye contrary Method, & got an Account of several detached Parishes, scatter'd here & there, as I cou'd prevail upon my Friends to send in their Accounts

---

* The numbers in Foster's letter of 2 December 1760 would appear to suggest footnote references. But there are no such references or any other equivalent materials among the manuscripts.

		No. Houses	No. pay
Peasemore	Berks Hills	42	10
Letcomb Regis	Do. Vale	79	22
Chilton	Wilts	117	27
Shalborne	Berks & Wilts	172	74
Compton Abbas	Dorset	50	12
Stanton Harcourt	Oxon.	99	23
Southleigh	Do.	65	21
Catworth Magna	Huntingdon	69	43
Cottingham	Northamp.	300	84
Clayton	Sussex	52	31
		1045	347

Here out of 1045 Houses only 347 pay, which approaches so near to what I produced in my former paper, that it is highly probable, the proportion of Cottages to Taxable Houses, in Country Villages, is somewhat more than 2 to 1, throughout ye South of England; which is full four times as much as Dr. Brakenridge is at present willing to allow.

And here it may be proper to take Notice of my Numbers, which ye Dr. has taken so much pains to confute, never considering that they were mere Suppositions, & armed with an express caution, of being liable to very great Objections. Nay, I had before called all such Computations (I confess, I meant Dr. Brakenridge's as well as my own) by ye plain Appellation of Random Guesses. I do assure you, Sir, had ye Dr. kept himself within ye Pale of Hypothesis, he had never met with any Opposition from these Quarters.

I have seriously consider'd what He recommends to me about ye method of reasoning by Induction; & cannot discover, how it can lead to *Paralogism* (by which I understand proceeding upon mistaken Principles.) Every Body knows that Induction is an imperfect way of Argumentation; but then it is an honest one. It lays ye whole force of ye Argument before you; & therefore no body can be deceived by it. It appears to me, that ye present Philosophy (Experimental) is carried on entirely by this method; & above all, were it to be laid aside, ye Political Arithmetician wou'd be stript of ye most valuable part of his Patrimony. Grant, who was, I think, ye Father of this Art, measures ye whole Nation from one Parish in Hampshire. Sr Will. Petty is full of it. King's Tables, upon which Davenant raises such a superstructure, can be built upon nothing else. Halley has measured the whole World from 5 years Bills of a Single Town in Germany: & Brakenridge has determined ye number of all ye Families in England & Wales, by one of ye small City Parishes in London.

I must confess, The Dr. has fairly stated ye Dispute between us, where he says, that I make ye number of Houses more than 1400,000, & that of these more than 700,000 are Cottages: Whereas he himself is very positive, that there are not a Million in all. I do assure you, Sir, had he given me one good reason for this Positiveness, I wou'd have surrender'd myself & come over to his opinion: As it is, I will give him two solid ones, why I cannot.

The first is, all Authors, who have treated of this Subject, seem very positive that ye Poor are greatly ye Majority of any Peoples.[5] And ye Reason of ye Thing seems to declare ye same; *The Employed* being vastly superior in number to *ye Employers.* Thus for Instance, it is but a poor Farmer who does not employ two Labourers, & some of them employ a dozen. Master-Miners employ from 50 to 100 under them, & Manufacturers still greater Numbers. In a word, Dr. Davenant acquaints us from Mr. King's Tables, that ye Rich at that Time were to ye Poor, as 50 : 85. His words are 500,000 Families contribute to ye Support of 850,000. But this is my

Second Reason, & what indeed deserves ye most serious Consideration,[6] viz: "That upon a Survey of ye Hearth Books at Michaelmas 1685: there were found to be in ye Nation 1,300,000 Houses." And whoever is tolerably acquainted with England must be sensible, that there have been a great deal more than 100,000 new houses erected since that time. Take but a view of London & its *Environs*, of Portsmouth, Bath, Bristol, Worcester, Birmingham, Woolverhampton, Manchester, Liverpool, Whitehaven, &c. and you will soon be convinced that I am extremely moderate in my Computations.

Dr. Brakenridge acquaints us, that I gave him Advice; I cannot find, I was guilty of such Presumption. Were I inclined to exercise this trifling Talent, I would caution him against a Topic of Argumentation, which has done more mischief in ye World, than all *Aristotle's* sophisms put together, & that is *Authority*, without sufficient Examination. Dr. Derham tells us from King's Tables, that there in England about five Millions & a half of People: And Dr. Brakenridge argues upon it, as Matter of Fact, without consulting Mr. King about it. No body can have a greater veneration for Dr. Derham, than myself; having been honour'd with a small share of his Acquaintance. However it is very certain, that He did not examine this Business with sufficient Attention:[7] For these are Dr. Davenant's Words[8] speaking of Mr. King, "what he says concerning ye Number of ye People to be 5,500,000 is no positive Assertion, nor shall we pretend any where to determine in that Matter. What He lays down is by way of Hypothesis, that supposing ye Inhabitants of England to have been Anno 1300, Two Millions 860,000: Heads, by ye orderly series of Increase, allowed of by all Writers, they may probably be about Anno 1700 five Millions 500,000 Heads; but if they were Anno 1300 either less or more, ye Case must proportionably alter".

It is very true, as I find upon Enquiry, that Orders have been issued out some time for ye Surveyors of ye Windows to give in an Account of ye number of Houses within their respective Divisions. But the Thing is not done; & upon ye present footing, I believe, cannot be done, chiefly from ye Smalness of their Salaries, & ye Largeness of their Departments. I am of Opinion, that if ever ye Thing is performed in a proper Manner, it must be by persons acquainted with, & resident upon, ye Spot. Viz: Either by ye Minister & Church-Wardens, when collecting a walking Brief (which is now a very common Practice) & returned *ex Officio* at visitation. Or by ye Overseers, when collecting their Rates, & returned to ye Clerc of ye Peace at ye Quarter Sessions, or by ye Assessors of ye Window Tax, when taking their view, & returned to ye Receiver General. And indeed if it were done by all ye 3 methods, it wou'd be best. And if ever any, or all these, are order'd to do this, when their Hands are in, they may as well tell us, how many Heads are in Every House, & then all Disputes of this kind will be obviated indeed.[9]

When I talked of judging by appearance, concerning ye Increase of our People, I gave such a reason for it, as deserved ye most steady Consideration, *Viz.* ye Great Facility, with which ye Government raises Soldiers, compared to ye Cruel & Oppressive Methods, made use of in K. William & Q. Anne's Time: For that ye obtaining any Commodity upon easy terms is a plain Indication of ye Plenty of it. What I produced, in Confirmation of this, from ye Registers of my Neighbourhood, Dr. Brackenridge has miserably perverted, by making me prove ye Increase of our People from ye Proportion of ye Births to ye Burials, when it is very certain, that were ye Births ten times ye Burials, yet were ye Consumption proportionable some way or other, ye real Increase wou'd be nothing. Whereas my Table (which is nothing but ye Registers methodized) has not one Word of ye Burials. It shows, that ye Christenings are doubled in a certain Term, & therefore ye People are doubled; which is so plain, that I am in hopes, no Body will call for a proof of it.

Upon this Occasion, I cannot but express my great concern, that ye Dr. was so precipitate in aswering my Paper. I think, he shou'd have waited ye Publication of it, & then he cou'd not have fal'n into such Errors, which seem to flow merely from ye want of knowing ye contents of it.

Another Mistake of ye like Nature he falls into, with respect to ye numbering of ye People by ye *Militia*. I had Information, that, in ye West-Riding of Yorkshire, one Man in 45 completed their Quota. Now ye *Militia* Act levies 32,000 upon ye whole Nation: So that if we apply ye West Riding Proportion to all England, i.e., $32,000 \times 45$ we shall have 1,400,000 for ye whole Number of Balloters: which multiplied by 5^{10} (& this, considering ye Number of Persons excepted, must be under ye truth) will amount to 7,200,000 for ye sum total of our People.

In opposition to this, Dr. Brackenridge tells us, "Halley has clearly shewn that ye Fencible Men are one Quarter of ye whole People": And therefore multiplies my Number of Balloters by 4, & so very adroitly makes me prove against myself. In short, ye Case is this. The Proportion of Men able to bear Arms is differently fixt by different Authors. Mr. King makes them 34 per Cent. Dr. Halley 25 per Cent. & I, from ye Act of Parliament, but 20. However there is no Contradiction in this. All ye Difference consists in ye Definition or Idea of a Fencible Man. Mr. King takes it in ye Old Notion of between 16 & 60. Halley rejected this, with good reason, & substituted between 18 & 56. Whereas ye present Act of Parliament confines its Notion of a Fencible Man to between 18 & 50 years. This, together with a large Quantity of excepted People,[11] made me multiply ye Balloters by 5. And upon farther Trial, I find it answer to a great Degree of Exactness.

Whether ye Proportion of 1 to 45 will hold throughout ye whole Nation, I greatly doubted in my former Paper. To satisfy myself in this, I laid out for Intelligence both far & wide. But my Endeavours were cut short, almost as soon as begun. In a Neighbouring Parish,[12] which contains 445 Houses, there were only 135 Names stuck up on ye Church Door: Whereas there ought to have been 445 nearly, *Viz.* ye same as ye Number of Houses. This manifest Breach of ye Law discourged me from all Attempts this Way.

About a Century ago, it was ye general Opinion, that ye Planting of Colonies weaken'd ye Mother Country; as it takes away great Numbers of People & returns none, or none worth mentioning. The case of Spain was so striking, that it was thought to be unanswerable. However it happen'd that Three of ye greatest Men in ye World, I mean most Intelligent in these Matters, undertook to demolish this vulgar Notion much about ye same time: And these were Pensioner de Witt, Wm. Penn, & Sr. Josiah Child. The purport of these Gentlemen's Reasoning, taken together, is this:

First that there are in all Countries great Numbers of People uneasy in their Present Circumstances, who will remove & nothing can prevent them: And indeed were it possible to prevent them, they wou'd be but a Burden & Disgrace to their Country.

2. It is therefore ye best Policy to give them an Opportunity, aye & Assistance also, to remove into such Situations, as that they may be still subject, & usefull, & beneficial to their native Country. Whereas without this provision, many of them would emigrate into Rival States, where every Man is a double Loss to ye Country, He deserts. As is ye lamentable Case at present of ye Irish Catholics, who strengthen France in ye same proportion, that they weaken us.

3. That Employment begets People; & that wherever Employment is, there is a certain prospect of a Livelihood, & therefore ye poor marry young, & increase prodigiously. Sr. Jos: Child's Words are, "Such as our Employment for People is, so many will our People be".

4. That it was plain matter of fact, that England is more Populous, rich & powerfull, since it planted Colonies, than it was before, It having been found by Experience, as well as by Calculation, that Every Man Employed as He ought to be in America, finds Employment for 4 pair of Hands in Old England. So that Every one, who is lost to us by Emigrating to our Plantations, is ye Cause of three being gain'd to us upon ye real Balance.

And Lastly, that ye Case of Spain is not parallel to ours; That Country having been at first depopulated by driving out ye Moors, & since perpetually harrassed by forceing an Uniformity in Religion. But what has principally kept Spain quite dissimilar to England has been their not being sensible of ye Third particular above mentioned, viz. that Employment begets People, & therefore have never had any considerable manufactures in their own Country; but have constantly supplied their Plantations with foreign wrought Goods. Thus (as I said of England, in my former Letter, concerning E. India Manufactures) are they at vast Expence, in order to maintain ye poor of other Nations, i.e. England, Holland, France, &c. – I have been ye more Explicit in this Article, with a design to throw some Light upon ye next, which is

Our Commerce at Sea: For this, like emigrating to our Plantations, seems to drain us of our People, & has been really joyned along with it, as doing so. But then ye same Solution serves here again. As Every Man in America finds Employment for (i.e. produces) four in Old England: So Every Seaman employed in foreign Commerce, sets on work at least ten pair of Hands in his native Country. This is an Article, wch. shou'd be well understood in a trading Nation, as ye contrary Doctrine, wch. arises merely from a partial View, may tend to make us despise, & neglect That, which does really support us in our present Grandeur, Riches & Power. And therefore to spend a few Words in ye Explication of it, may be doing ye Public a considerable piece of Service.

In the First Place then, Great Numbers are employ'd in felling, stripping, hewing, & transporting of Timber to ye Shipyards. This setts to work numbers in building, fitting, repairing & refitting of Ships, Such as Sawers, Shipwrights, Boatbuilders, Calkers, Joyners, Carvers, Painters, Blockmakers, Ropemakers, Mastmakers, Flagmakers, Oarmakers, Compassmakers, Coopers, Blacksmiths, Anchorsmiths, Shopsellers, Ship-Chandlers, Brewers, Bakers, & all sorts of Victuallers, Such I mean, as deal in provisions; together with Gun-Founders, Shotmakers, Powder-makers, & those that are employed in ye transporting of these bulky Commodities to ye places of their Destination. We must not forget to mention, upon this Occasion, ye multitudes, that are busied in dressing of Flax & Hemp, and in spining, weaving & Making of Sails. Every one of which Trades depends entirely upon our Commerce at Sea; Insomuch that if our Trade were to fail, all these People must leave us, & go to France or Holland &c. to seek for Employment.

Now if such Numbers are employ'd (i.e. maintain'd) in fitting out ye Hull only, together with ye necessaries for Defence & Provision, what shall we say to ye Ship's Lading? Most of This often consists of our own Products, or, which is all one, of things wch. have been purchased before by our own Products. And when a Cargo consists, in a good measure of manufactured Goods, such as Cloths, Stuffs, Linen, Cotton, Hardware, or ye like, it is impossible to enumerate ye Hands employ'd in furnishing of it. In a word, it is plain to Every one, that takes a serious Survey of ye Matter that ye whole Nation is set at work by our Commerce at Sea: Which like ye Weights, or Spring of a Clock, puts & preserves ye whole Machine in Motion.

Nor must we here forget ye Cargoes brought back, wch. mostly consist of Raw Goods, & which set infinite numbers of our People to work: Such for instance, as Sugar, Cotton, Tobacco, Dying Ingredients, Gum, raw Silk, Herba, Caramenia & Vigonia & Spanish Wool, Camels hair, Goats Hair, Mohair yarn, Hides, Skins, Furrs, Iron, Copper, Timber, Deals &c. which without Commerce, we must want, or at best stand to ye Courtesy of others for.

As manufacturers encrease Civil Trades encrease in proportion. I reckon, that every 50 Families maintain a Taylor, Mantua-Maker, Shoe-Maker, Blacksmith, Carpenter, Cooper, Publican, Chandler's Shop, Butcher, Midwife, & ye like, & that Ten of these Aggregates produce a Physician, Surgeon, Apothecary, Grocer, Mercer, Draper, Hosier, Milliner, & a thousand other Trades, which compose our Market Towns. As ye Number of These encreases, ye Demand for Provision must of necessity encrease likewise. This puts ye Farmer upon improving his Land; & consequently encreases ye number of Labourers. This will account fairly & honestly, for what I advanced, in my Second Letter, as it will likewise receive Strength from that, Viz: that it appears by all ye Registers, I have examined, that our People are nearly doubled in 50 years, & now I can assure you, that it is ye unanimous voice of all ye Farmers, that ye Land brings forth double, what it did 50 years ago.

To this way of arguing, Dr. Brackenridge objects, that we ought not to conclude from a small part concerning ye whole, & that we must have accounts from all parts before we can determine any Thing about our Increase. To this I answer, that ye Objection is extremely just, if we speak of an adequate & demonstrative Knowledge: But as ye Dr. himself has employ'd *mediums* only to approximate ye Truth, I hope I may be allow'd ye same privilege, especially if we consider, that ye Hardiness of some of his own *Postulata*, first drew me in to give you this Trouble.

In order to form some Judgement of our Increase, Sr. Will. Petty has furnished us with 2 or 3 *Data*, which, I think, are full to ye point, & which, I hope, will satisfy Every candid Enquirer. About ye time of ye Revolution, he tells us

1. That ye Royal Navy of England consisted of 70,000 Ton of Shipping, and required 36,000 men to man it.

2. That our Plantation Trade employ'd 400 Sail. and

3. That ye whole Trade of England was carried on by 48,000 Mariners.

Whoever compares these Particulars with ye present state of ye Nation, will have abundant reason to conclude, that our Navy & Trade are more than doubled in ye last 70 years. And, as I have shew'd above, that ye Increase of our whole People must attend ye Increase of our Trade, I am in hopes, it will be thought highly probable, that our People are doubled[13] in ye same Period of Time.

Suppose I shou'd give up this Argument & allow, that Trade diminishes ye Stock of People, I think it will then be impossible to account for a Phenomenon constantly observed in ye World; & that is, that in all places, where Trade has resided, there has always been ye most People; As in Idea, Tyre, Carthage, Egypt, Genova, Venice & Holland, In ye Second Instance, two or three hundred thousand People lived upon a Rock, in ye middle of ye Sea, where, without Trade, one Family cou'd hardly have subsisted. And in ye last Instance, I am perswaded, that there are a great deal more than twice as many People in Holland,[14] as cou'd live upon ye Produce of ye Land, without Commerce.

Indeed Dr. Brakenridge brings ye Dutch, as an Instance full to his purpose, as having brought their Country into a Decay by overmuch Trade. But ye Dutch themselves (& I presume they will be allow'd to be proper Judges) assign a quite different Cause. They tell us, that ye Decline of their State is owing to ye Decline of their Trade, & to nothing Else. And Every body is sensible, that about a Century ago, when their Commerce was at its Height, ye united Provinces were ye most populous flourishing Nation, ye World ever saw.

But it seems ye Present King of Prussia has shewn ye Utility of naturalizing Foreigners, by ye great Figure he makes in Europe.[15] Dr. Brackenridge forgets that his Prussian Majesty has been all along doing every thing possible to promote Commerce in his Dominions. Now if ye Dr's. Notion of Commerce be just, then must his Majesty of Prussia have been forsaken of his usual prudence & sagacity, as having been doing & undoing ye same thing. Importing Strangers is increasing his People. Trading at Sea is throwing them away, & therefore he has been counteracting himself & had better been doing nothing.

The Truth of ye matter is, The K. of Prussia thinks what Every Prince in Europe seems to be sensible of at present, & that is what I have been proving, Viz. That Commerce at Sea brings in Money; that Money finds their People Employment, that Employment begets Numbers, & that This creates Grandeur & Power. And therefore they are every one of them doing all in their Power to come in for a share of it.

I entirely acquiesce in what ye Dr. says, that ye Scurvy, Shipwreck, & ye Inclemency of ye Sea do not beget People. To this He adds ye following words, doing me ye honour to speak of me, "But He will say, without These we cou'd not have Trade, which employs great numbers of our People. & therefore what we lose, we may gain another way. And just so He may say of our Wars, that occasion ye Destruction of so many of our People, that they are no loss to us; for we gain by them in their Consequences, in securing our Liberties & Property, & by which our

Trade is preserved & promoted." Here what ye Gentleman says of Trade is true & certain, as I have demonstrated above, Viz: what we loose by ye Sea, our Commerce at Sea more than restores to us by employing our People. But how to make out his Parallel between Trade & War,[16] I confess myself at a full stop. It plainly evinces, that War is sometimes necessary, but which way, it restores us ye Numbers it destroys, I cannot find out. Every common man has Meat, Drink & Cloaths before he enters into ye service, as much as (I believe more than) he has afterwards, & consequently is of equal value with ye soldier, in respect to ye Employment of our People. The only Article, I can think of, in which War gains us any thing to our Stock of People is in providing Arms. Now as one Mechanic will provide Arms for ten Soldiers; & one Sailor finds Employment for ten Landmen, it follows that one employ'd in our Commerce is of equal value to ye Public with 100 Soldiers. How therefore to make these Parallel is a difficulty much above my abilities.

If it shou'd be asked me, whether our Numbers are capable of still farther Increase; I answer they undoubtedly are, to a very great Degree. It is known to Every body, that we pay 500,000 in Cash to Foreigners, for such necessaries, as might be raised in our own Plantations; Such as Flax, Hemp, Iron, Potash, Silk &c. Now cou'd these Articles be supplied by our Colonies, & they undoubtedly might with proper Encouragement, we shou'd not only save so much Cash, in ye Balance of Trade, but encrease our American Subjects to such a Degree, as must set on work a Million of People in Old England in order to supply them with necessaries. Our Ships never carry Cash to our Plantations, being mostly freighted with our own Products & Manufactures; The very Chairs they sit on, & ye Beds they lie on, being furnished from ye Mother Country, as far as they are able to purchase them. I make not ye least doubt, but that were our Trade confined entirely to our Plantations, it wou'd better for the Nation. Every Province abroad wou'd furnish its peculiar staple, proper to ye Soil or Climate. This wou'd supply ye English Markets with all Kinds of raw Goods, & carry back our Manufactures in Return; which wou'd cause such a Circulation of Business, as Europe is quite a Stranger to, & cannot be parelleld in ye whole World, but in China where ye Trade is entirely domestic, i.e. from Province to Province, & is so prodigious that all ye Commerce of this Globe put together is nothing in Comparison to it.

But there is one particular, which I cannot forbear mentioning, as it comes in here very *a propos*, & deserves ye most serious Consideration. It is this, There are as much manufactured Goods imported every Year from ye East Indies into Europe, as wou'd employ ten Millions of People. And if ye Princes concerned wou'd agree to cut off this part of ye Trade, Europe wou'd gain ten Millions of People in a very few years, of which England wou'd come in for a very considerable Share. But till this Scheme can be brought to bear, which, I am afraid will never be, it wou'd be proper not to suffer ye least Article to be exported to our own Plantations, but what is of our own Production, or purchased of such Nations, as trade with us upon an equitable footing. This wou'd, in a great measure, answer ye End of ye Scheme proposed. It wou'd find our Poor Imployment, as far as possible, *Viz.* as far as our Command extends.

No Man Living has a deeper Sense of ye Merit of Mathematical Argumentation than myself. But then we must not go too far; well knowing, that ye best things, when corrupted, become ye worst. And it appears to all considering People, that this sort of Reasoning has been abused. Sometimes it has been applied to improper Subjects, such for instance, as Credibility, Probability, Merit, Virtue, &c. At other times, it has been applied to proper Subjects indeed, but upon wrong or scanty Principles. Thus in ye year 1754, Dr. Brackenridge demonstrated, that ye No. of Houses in London cou'd not be less than 125,302, & that one in 30 died yearly. Whereas in ye year 1758, he tells us, that ye Number of Houses is but little more than 60,000 & that one in 20 may die yearly. Another Demonstration of ye same kind is That, which determines ye No. of People from ye Quantity of Bread consumed.[17] In order to do this, He assumes ye following Principles

1. That as much Land is sowed with Wheat, as with Barley
2. That all ye Barley is malted, nearly.
3. That all ye Malt pays Duty.
4. That all ye People nearly eat Wheat Bread &
5. That one Quarter of Wheat is sufficient for 3 Persons.

Every one of these Principles is either wrong, or at best precarious & uncertain, as I gave reason to suspect in my first Letter.[18] It must be own'd indeed, that Dr. Brackenridge acquaints us,[19] that He has answered this Letter; with what justice he says this let ye World decide. I caanot find where he has said one Syllable in support of this Argument, & therefore conclude, He has a mind to drop it.

As to ye Demonstration, which depends upon ye Number of Houses, that is undecided: as is That likewise about ye Increase of our People from ye proportion of Births to Burials. And here I cannot forbear doing my Antagonist ye Justice to own, that ye Canon, he has established for this purpose is very ingenious, & that when ye Proportion is once fixt, it will perform ye Business with more Accuracy, than any Method hitherto discover'd. Indeed Dr. Brackenridge tells us, yt. Derham from a general view, found ye Proportion throughout ye Nation to be as 112.100 – I wish, He had referred us to ye Place, where Derham says this; All that, I can find, he has added to former Accounts, is from ye Registers of Upminster, Aynho, Leeds & Harwood;[20] And as Leeds is a Flourishing Town, it must be left out of ye Account, as having great Numbers of Dissenters in it. The other three are so far from making out ye proportion, that they are upon an average as 130 : 100. Besides Derham is so far from telling us, that he had accounts from all places, that he says expressly, He was promised Accounts from diverse other Parts of ye Kingdom, but had received none.

Dr. Derham's Proportion of 100 : 112. (for such a Thing he mentions in his Table[21]) is ye Same, I am perswaded, with Mr. King's 17 : 19. I have ye greatest Respect imaginable for Mr. King. His Singular Modesty demands this: And accordingly we quote his Tables, as Things of Authority, tho' we know not, upon what they were built. It had been vastly more satisfactory, had ye Authorities been annexed. He compiled them, we are told, from ye Tax Books, in which an Account was kept of Births, Marriages, Burials, &c. Now as these Branches of ye Revenue were I think, farmed in those Days, it is probable, ye Farmers might deliver in scanty Accounts, in order to beat down ye Price. Sr. Will: Petty detected a notable Instance of this kind in respect to *Dublin*. Besides it is ye Opinion of some larned Men, that King did not always build upon firm Ground, as seems to appear from ye Proportion, he establishes between ye Sexes; allowing but 27 Males to 28 Females; whereas Every body Else allow ye Males to be superior in No.[22] At first sight,

I thought this difficulty might have been solved, by supposing all other Authors to mean ye Births only, whereas Mr. King plainly means ye whole Number alive at ye same time. And as Men are liable to more Accidents, than Women, so more Females might be living at ye same time, than Males, tho' more of ye latter sort were born. But yet it must be considered, that if there were more Women than Men in ye World, there must be more Females buried, than Males somewhere, (for they all die) which is not ye case any where, that I know of. All that can be done this way, till Authority interposes to purpose, is for Every one to contribute what lies in his power for establishing ye Proportion between ye Births & Burials, in all parts of ye Nation, making proper Allowances for Dissenters, where there are such. The following is my Mite; & if I find others make any advances in ye same Business, I believe, I can produce at least ten times as much

	In my Neighbourhood		180
	Chilton Wilts		150
	Melbury Abbas Dors:		221
	Stanton Harcourt Oxon.		149
The Burials are to ye Births	Southleigh Do.	as 100 to	152
	Cottingham Northon.		121
	Clayton, Sussex		182
	Great Catworth, Hunt.		169
	Stoke Damerel, Devon.		206
	Country Places in ye Isle of Wt.		200

$$\overline{}$$
1730

The Proportion here, upon an Average, is as 100 : 173. I must beg to be understood, that I do not propose this as a Standard for ye whole Nation. However, as these places lie very wide, & are not picked for ye purpose, I am in hopes, that ye Ingenious part of Mankind will think it highly probable, that Mr. King's Proportion of 100 : 117 for Country Villages is a great deal too scanty. They may likewise perhaps from hence conclude, that there is no Occasion for an Act to promote Matrimony, nor for ye Importation of Foreigners. That our Breed of People are in no danger of being diminished; & find, but Imployment, & they will obey ye Original Command *Increase* & *Multiply*. Indeed Dr. Brackenridge assures us, that in "many Country Places from their bad situation, there is very little Increase, & in some Towns none at all, & in others a decrease". It will be time enough to consider ye State of these places, when their Names are produced, & their case fairly stated from authentic Records. There is but one named & That is London. I have hitherto purposely forbore saying anything of this mighty City. Not that I am entirely unacquainted with ye Subject; but only because it is so complex & embarrassed, that I despair of being able to make any thing of it; like some of my Country Men, whom I have heard seriously declare, that when they have come to Highgate & taken a view of it, they have declined going thither, merely out of fear of not finding their way out of it again. In like manner, if I enter upon ye Subject, I am apprehensive I shall never find an End. However something I have attempted in this way: But must deferr it, as it wou'd swell this paper to an unreasonable Length; and especially, as it has but little to do with ye present dispute.

What I said, in ye Conclusion of my Second Letter, written above 3 years ago, about ye populous & flourishing Condition of England, is so far justified by ye Event that ye bare mention of it may look like soothing my own vanity, in paying too great a Compliment to own Sagacity. The Face of Things is strangely altered, since I wrote that Letter. It is with the strictest Propriety, that His Majesty calls us *a great People*. Thanks & Praise to ye Author of all Benefits, we are ye greatest People upon Earth: And may he so direct us, that our Successes may neither make us proud, nor negligent.

But Dr. Brackenridge, in ye Conclusion of his Answer, acquaints us, that my "Zeal hurries me on, so that I did not look to ye Date of his Letters; for ye first three were read before ye Society & order'd to be printed, long before ye War was proclaimed". When I first saw this, I do assure you, Sir, I was sufficiently frighted, as supposing I had committed a Mistake (We are ye best of us, liable to it). But upon taking a nearer view of it, I found all ye Force of ye Argument to lie in ye word *proclaimed*. His Letters were wrote, it seems, before ye War was proclaimed. But it happens very unfortunately, that ye War was begun Several Years before it was proclaimed. Several Battles were fought by Sea & Land, Minorca was lost, &c. And as all these Things (& particularly ye carrying on ye War without Declaration) made a great Noise in ye World, ye most Recluse cou'd not be ignorant of it: Which shews this Argument to be a subterfuge of a very coarse Fabric. All ye Animadversion I dare pass upon it is, that if I cou'd have foreseen, my antagonist cou'd have stooped so low, He wou'd have had no Opponent in

> Revd. Sir,
> Your Affectionate Brother
> &
> very humble Servant
> Rich. Forster

Shefford
Dec: 2 1760
[British Museum MSS No. Add.4440, ff.176-185]

Revd. Sir
I am so great a Friend to ye Liberties of Mankind, that I can never be displeased at People for doing what they will with their own. The Transactions are your own, & you may put what you please into them. Upon this footing, I cannot take ye rejection of my Paper ill. How it came to be kept so long afterwards, I cannot imagine. I wish I cou'd reconcile this with Philosophic Justice & Impartiality. If you were equally carefull in ye publication of all your Papers It wou'd be more for your Honour. Be so good to present my Respects to your Committee, & tell them I desire They wou'd appoint one of their Number (an Englishman) to attend to ye Sense only.

The first Sentence of No.XX. of your last Publication p.179. wanted such Inspection. I have consider'd it over & over. And to me it appears stark nonsense.

Again in ye Note upon West Derby it is said, p.226 The District so called of Liverpool. By which it wou'd seem, that Liverpool stands upon a piece of Ground call'd West Derby. Whereas West Derby is a village about 5 miles ENE from Liverpool & gives name to ye Hundred in which Liverpool stands. Besides I think we never say, on this side ye Tweed, that a Town stands in such a District, but in ye County, Hundred, Parish or ye like. I will not find any more faults, that you may not say I am in a bad Humour. I am, Revd. Sir.

Yours &c.

R. Forster

Shefford

Dec: 4 1760

[British Museum MSS No. Add.4440, f.189]

CHAPTER 3

Numbering the people

It was perhaps unfortunate that the 1753 Bill, which proposed a comprehensive system of censuses and vital registration, was presented to Parliament before the population controversy flourished. Had a similar Bill been put forward in the 1780s, it would at least have had the advantage of some change in the climate of opinion. For almost all of those associated with the debate on the trend of population had drawn attention to the value of reliable enumerations. Moreover, many local enumerations had been carried out – some directly inspired by the controversy – without resulting in pestilence or destroying the last remains of British liberty.[1] Richard Price himself cited the results of many of these enumerations and also strongly urged action to ensure reliable registration of births, deaths and marriages as a means of keeping the trend of population under constant survey. Speaking of the inferences he had drawn from the data he had examined, he said 'I beg it may be remembered, that my opinion in this instance, is by no means a clear and decided conviction. I may probably be influenced too much by a desire to maintain an assertion once delivered.' The case could be tested if there were complete and accurate vital registration. 'This is done in other Kingdoms. It has lately been done in France; and the result has been a discovery that the population of France exceeds all that had been conjectured concerning it. Should a like discovery be the consequence of carrying out such an order into execution here, it will give the Kingdom an encouragement which at present it greatly wants; and I shall rejoice in my own confutation.[2] Though this refers to vital registration, which is discussed later, it is mentioned here because Price was proposing to use vital statistics as a substitute for census statistics, for the purpose of calculating the rate of growth of the population – a technique similar to that used by Wales and Howlett, and subsequently recommended by John Finlaison.[3]

Towards the end of the eighteenth century, the attitude towards population growth as such began to change. Concern with the increasing burden of the poor, and with the need to import food, began to erode the earlier mercantilist belief in the advantages of a large and increasing population, and the new views were crystallized by Malthus. But it is doubtful if Malthus's *Essay* was important in persuading Parliament to accept the idea of censuses; the main change very probably occurred before his work was published.[4] Perhaps one of the more important determinants was the fact that other countries had found it necessary, for practical, administrative purposes, to take censuses. (Holland, Spain and the United States were the countries referred to in the debate which finally resulted in the first of our periodic censuses.) And in 1796 John Rickman, who was later appointed to take charge of the census, wrote a memorandum: 'Thoughts on the utility and facility of a general enumeration of the people of the British Empire'.[5] The memorandum was sent by George Rose, MP for Christchurch (formerly MP for Launceston and then Lymington), to Charles Abbot, MP for Helston (Cornwall), who, when he became Chief Secretary and Privy Seal in Ireland, appointed Rickman as his private secretary; and it was Abbot who introduced the Population Bill in the

House of Commons on 19 November 1800.[6] With minor amendments, the Bill was passed on 3 December 1800 – an 'Act for taking an Account of the Population of Great Britain, and of the Increase or Diminution thereof.'[7]

In his speech in the House of Commons, Abbot stressed two objectives. First, to know accurately the current size of the population. Various estimates had been made, but 'all these inquiries and estimates, proceeding without authority, upon such imperfect data, have terminated (as might be expected) in nothing but unsatisfactory conjecture'. It was necessary to 'substitute certainty for conjecture, and instead of approximation have the fact' – and this for practical reasons of general policy and still more because of the 'urgent pressure of our present circumstances'.[8] Secondly, to know the trend of population: 'by showing the increase or diminution of baptisms, burials, and marriages, from the latter of which, I mean the marriages, of which the registers are much more comprehensive, complete, and important, we shall have a correct knowledge of what concerns our increasing or decreasing demands for subsistence'.[9] Both these aims are visible in the schedules provided by the Act. The first aim was to be met by collecting information (for each parish, township or place) on the numbers of inhabited houses, families and uninhabited houses; the numbers of males and females; and the numbers of persons mainly employed in agriculture, trade, manufactures and handicraft respectively. The second was to be achieved by requiring from the clergy in each parish, township or place, lists of baptisms and burials for each tenth year from 1700 to 1780 and thereafter for every year including 1800; and lists of marriages for each year from 1754 (when the Hardwicke Act was implemented) to 1800 inclusive.[10] The Act was also concerned with speedy publication of the results. And although the specified publication programme could not be met in practice, the whole process was nevertheless completed in a remarkably short time. The enumeration took place on 10 March 1801, and the enumeration abstracts for England and Wales were ordered to be printed on 21 December 1801 and for Scotland on 9 June 1802, while the date of the parish register abstracts was 21 December 1801.[11] The abstracts and reports were prepared by John Rickman, who described himself as 'appointed by His Majesty's Most Honorable Privy Council to digest and reduce into Order the above Abstract'. Rickman continued to play this part at the censuses of 1811 to 1831. He may also have been associated with the initial planning of the 1841 census, but he died before it was carried out.[12]

The 1800 Act contained a number of provisions designed to increase the reliability of the census. The individuals designated to act as enumerators were, in the circumstances of the period, not inappropriate: overseers of the poor or substantial householders in England and Wales, with assistance from various church officials and, if need be, from the 'constables, tithingmen, headboroughs or other peace officers'; and in Scotland the schoolmasters or 'other fit persons'. The returns had to be made in a prescribed form and attested before the Justices of the Peace; and there were penalties for wilful default by the various officials involved in the enumeration. Payment was made to the officials and their expenses met. Nevertheless, it is clear that the enumeration was defective. That this should be so in an initial census is not surprising – similar problems are met when a developing country embarks on census taking nowadays. Today such a country would have the benefit of technical advice from various experts on schedule design, on the cartographic

FILLING UP THE CENSUS PAPER.

Wife of his Bosom. "UPON MY WORD, MR. PEEWITT! IS THIS THE WAY YOU FILL UP YOUR CENSUS? SO YOU CALL YOURSELF THE 'HEAD OF THE FAMILY'—DO YOU—AND ME A 'FEMALE?'"

Cartoon : Filling up the census paper

problems, on the training of enumerators and supervisors, and perhaps also on the use of post-enumeration surveys for assessing the effectiveness of the census. In 1801 such advice was not available and it is unlikely that any serious attempt was made to benefit from the experience of the few countries which had taken periodic censuses.[13] Rickman himself drew attention to various defects. In spite of the penalties, not all the parishes had sent in returns.[14] The question on the numbers of families was poorly answered: 'In many counties it has been variously understood, in others not replied to; in the latter case the number of families has been presumed to be, that of inhabited houses.' In Middlesex 'The number of families returned... is beyond the truth, because some parishes in London returned each lodger as a separate family'.[15] Thus Rickman acknowledged that the population was probably larger than was shown by the returns (in the summary of which was included the number of men in the armed forces, the merchant marine and the convict hulks), though his figure for England and Wales, 9·168 millions, was not adjusted to allow for this.[16] In addition, given the fact that there were no nominal lists (as, for example, were produced by Gregory King and also used in the enumeration carried out in connection with the 1694 Act, levying taxes on marriages, births and deaths[17]), and hence no possibility of checking the details of the work of the enumerators, it is very probable that the local returns were inaccurate. John Heysham certainly considered that, in Carlisle, the enumeration was less careful than the local survey carried out in 1796 (though he believed that the 1811 enumeration was 'tolerably correct').[18]

Though there were variations from census to census, the 1801 model continued generally to be applied up to and including the 1831 census.[19] That is, the local returns were in essence statistical summaries, without the supporting authority of lists of names and addresses.[20] Increasing familiarity with the problems of enumeration probably helped to eliminate some of the defects of the first census. In the 1811 report, for example, Rickman noted that 'the enumeration of the whole population may be considered as complete, no place being known finally to have omitted making return'.[21] For the 1831 census the enumerators were supplied with special 'tally sheets' to enable them to make a more accurate count of the numbers required in answer to the questions. On the other hand, the change in 1811 from occupations of persons to occupations of families is likely to have increased the errors. And the question on ages, introduced in 1821, is unlikely to have produced very reliable results. It was a voluntary question. Enumerators were told: 'If you are of the Opinion that in making the preceding Enquiries (or at any time before returning this Schedule) the Ages of the several individuals can be obtained in a manner satisfactory to yourself, and not inconvenient to the Parties, be pleased to state (or cause to be stated) the Number of those who are under 5 Years of Age, of those between 5 and 10 Years of Age... distinguishing Males from Females.'[22] In fact, ages were returned for most of the population – almost 88 per cent – and the omissions were of whole areas rather than of individuals within areas. Nevertheless, it would be unwise to accept the results without a much closer scrutiny than has so far been given to them.[23] In a population with a substantial amount of illiteracy (in 1839-41 some 33 per cent of bridegrooms and almost 50 per cent of brides signed the marriage register with a mark in England and Wales[24]) and with defective vital registration, the first attempt to ascertain ages was not likely to be very successful, especially as the meaning of 'age' was not specified (it was not until the 1851 census that age was defined as meaning 'age at last birthday'). The 1831 census question on age may have produced even less reliable results than that of 1821. For although there had been some pressure to repeat the 1821 question, Rickman was opposed to it and made this quite clear to the committee set up by Parliament to consider the questions to be included in the 1831 census schedule. The committee had before it a sound memorandum from Joshua Milne, but Milne's case was not well argued. By contrast, Rickman's reply was largely irrelevant but superficially quite devastating.[25] The result was that the 1831 census contented itself with asking enumerators to specify the number of males over twenty years of age, and the enumerators were told that if this number 'should differ materially (or otherwise, as compared to the Returns of 1821) from One Half the Total Number of Males. . ., some Error has probably been committed, and the Answer to this Question should be examined, and corrected, if necessary'.[26]

By 1841, however, the situation had changed substantially. With the creation of the General Register Office, the Registrar General became the permanent census commissioner, with a central staff and with the local registrars and superintendent registrars of marriages, births and deaths as his primary agents.[27] A household schedule was used, with the details of each individual in the household being recorded, and the enumeration was defined as being in respect of the individuals present on a specified night.[28] Age was introduced as a standard characteristic to be recorded (marital status was introduced in 1851). The basic area unit for the census became the enumeration district of not more than some 200 houses.[29] With the provision of details regarding each individual, the question of confidentiality of the returns became important and this has always been guaranteed. Census schedules are confidential documents – they cannot be seen or used by other government departments or by outside individuals for a hundred years. Naturally, there have been many changes in the contents of the census schedule since 1841. The range of questions has been increased, and sampling has been used in connection with (or, in 1966, instead of) complete enumeration. Until 1920, each census required a separate Act of Parliament, but the 1920 Act removed this necessity and also provided for the possibility of quinquennial censuses, a possibility first translated into fact in 1966.[30] But in spite of such changes, the 1841 census may justifiably be considered the first modern British census.[31]

As was specified in the Act, the 1801 census collected on a national scale the information on marriages, baptisms and burials recorded in the parish registers for various periods from 1700 onwards. At subsequent censuses, up to and including 1841, the clergy had to make similar returns for the ten years preceding the census; and after the Rose Act of 1812 the records of burials included ages at death. Further, in 1836 Rickman obtained the permission of the Home Office to request from all parishes with registers going back to 1570, returns of marriages, baptisms and burials for 1570, 1600, 1630, 1670, 1700 and 1750, and these data were presented in the 1841 census reports.[32]

Rickman used the collections of parish register material for two purposes: the historical data to estimate past total populations; and the current data for calculating baptism and burial rates, as well as the 'duration of life' for the country as a whole and for various counties. But these enterprises were far less successful than the enumeration of the existing population. The reasons have been discussed in detail elsewhere.[33] Briefly, however, there were three main defects. First, the parish register data were incomplete: many of the earlier registers were missing; and those in existence – including the current registers – did not fully cover the vital events in their areas – not even in respect of the Anglican population. Moreover, the returns submitted were by no means always accurate summaries of the contents of the registers.[34] Secondly, the estimates of population in the sixteenth, seventeenth and eighteenth centuries assumed a constancy of the birth, death and marriage rates over time and also an unchanging degree of coverage of vital events by the parish registers.[35] Thirdly, in his calculations of the 'duration of life' for the nineteenth-century period, Rickman initially worked solely with deaths by age (instead of relating these deaths to the population in comparable age groups and thus computing age-specific death rates), a procedure valid only if the population were a stationary one. Rickman may have been an effective administrator, but he was not a demographer. He tried to study the subject, translated Deparcieux on the probabilities and duration of human life and 'promoted' the translation of Kersseboom's work on political arithmetic.[36] But his approach to life table construction was incorrect, in spite of the fact that there was available at the time a full discussion of life table construction – as well as the example of the realistic life table for Carlisle – in Joshua Milne's *Treatise*.[37] William Morgan, the well-known actuary and nephew of Richard Price, wrote that the 1801 census 'appears to have been instituted for the mere purpose of determining a controversy; and even in this it has totally failed of its effect'.[38] That statement is rather harsh, especially coming from Morgan, who had not apparently criticized his uncle's far less solidly based estimates of the progress of population since the Glorious Revolution. But as a comment on Rickman's efforts in demographic history, it was not entirely unjustified.

NOTES

1 See, for example, C. M. Law, 'Local Censuses in the 18th Century', *Population Studies*, March 1969. The aftermath of the 'sin and pestilence theory' was still visible in the nineteenth century, after four censuses had been taken. In 1835 a contributor to *The Quarterly Review*, reviewing the new British and Irish census reports, wrote: 'When David numbered the people it was justly imputed to him as a sin, for he had done it in a spirit of pride and vain-glory; but the investigations, of which the results are here before us, were undertaken, in the first place, to enable he legislature to exercise an enlightened justice in their fiscal, political, and moral enactments; and, in the second place, to afford to individuals authentic data for the regulation of some of their most important mutual transactions'(*The Quarterly Review*, Vol.LIII, February 1835, p.56).

2 *Observations on Reversionary Payments*, 5th edn, 2 vols, London 1792, Vol.2, pp.346-347.

3 Price had also expressed himself in favour of enumerations. Referring to De Moivre's recommendation that at least there should be periodic enumerations of the population, with ages and occupations, he said that this 'would in some

degree, answer most of the purposes I have mentioned' (R. Price, *Observations on the Expectation of Lives...*, reprinted London 1769, p.39).

4 Given the general impact of Malthus's work – on the technical level it included in rudimentary form the concept of a replacement rate – it is surprising that it had so little discernible effect on British censuses or vital registration. The schedules used in Birtish censuses contained no direct question on fertility until 1911. Yet Malthus was interested in the direct measurement of fertility and its relationship to economic circumstances and told Adolphe Quetelet, at the Cambridge meeting of the British Association for the Advancement of Science in 1833, that Belgium, with the differences between its provinces, would be especially appropriate for the establishment of a 'Statistique vivante'. Quetelet asked him to supply some notes on this matter, and Malthus did so, indicating the most important points for inquiry, namely: the number of births per marriage; the proportion of children born who survive to marry; the number of living children per marriage; the proportion of barren (childless) marriages; the proportion of marriages with five or more living children; the money wages of labour, manufacturing and agricultural, in the different provinces, particularly the wages of common day labour in agriculture; the quantity of wheat which the wages of such day labour will buy in ordinary times; the ordinary prices of different kinds of grain; the ordinary food of the common day labour (A. Quetelet, *Physique Sociale*, 2nd edn, Brussels, Paris, St Petersburg 1869, Vol.2, pp.450-451).

5 The original memorandum was presumably in manuscript. I have found no trace of it, but excerpts were included in W. C. Rickman's memoir of his father, distributed to his friends (the obituary notice in *The Gentleman's Magazine*, April 1841, pp.431-437, is an abridged version, lacking these excerpts). I am indebted to Mr D. C. E. Holland, Librarian of the House of Commons, who allowed me to make use of the memoir – *Biographical Memoir of John Rickman*, 1841). In addition, what must almost certainly be an annotated version of the memorandum was published by John Rickman in a journal which he edited for a few years, *The Commercial and Agricultural Magazine*, June 1800, pp.391-399 (W. C. Rickman lists this as one of the articles written by his father). The initial footnote to the article states: 'This treatise was written in 1796: additional notes accommodate it to the present day.' The article is reprinted as Appendix 1 to this chapter. It should be noted that the title of the published article refers to England and not to the British Empire. But the excerpts from the original memorandum cited by W. C. Rickman in the *Biographical Memoir* (pp.10-12) are identical with passages in the printed article.

6 Hansard's *Parliamentary History*, Vol.35, cols.598-602, reports Abbot's speech, but no other contributions to the debate. The amendments are reported in the *House of Commons Journal*, 41, Geo. III, 5 & 19 December 1800, pp.893 & 915-916.

7 *Acts*, George III, c.15, pp.560-568.

8 Dr Michael Cullen of the University of Edinburgh, who has completed a study of the development of social statistics in Britain in the period 1830-1850, suggested (in correspondence) that the specific circumstance prompting the introduction and acceptance of the Census Bill was the bad harvest of 1800. He drew attention to phrases in Abbot's speech which might very well be interpreted in that way. The phrase already cited in the text – the 'urgent pressure of our present circum-

stances' – is an example. Another and fuller reference occurs after Abbot's introductory remark that it had 'long been a matter of surprise and astonishment, that a great, powerful, and enlightened nation like this should have remained hitherto unacquainted with the state of its population...' He added, 'But, Sir, in times like these when the subsistence of the people is in question, this knowledge becomes of the highest importance. It is surely important to know the extent of the demand for which we are to provide a supply; and we should set about obtaining it immediately, not only for the uses of the current year (for which it must necessarily come late), but also for the year that is to follow...' And he went on to insist that the information to be obtained by the census was important in ascertaining whether the failure to export during the past thirty years, and the need to depend upon other countries, were to be explained by an increased and growing population. Views on the need to expand agriculture, and on the scale of expansion, would be affected by the results of the census.

It is true that 1800 harvest was very poor. The issues of the *Annual Register* for 1800 and 1801 contain many references to the problems and to the means adopted for meeting food needs, to the high price of provisions, to petitions and to riots. The King's speech at the opening of Parliament on 11 November 1800 referred to these problems and to the desirability of preventing a recurrence of such shortages by 'promoting the permanent extension and improvement of agriculture'. The editor of George Rose's diaries summed up the situation as follows: 'The year 1800, though marked by no great political event, obtained a disastrous celebrity as a year of scarcity. At the commencement of harvest the rain descended in torrents, the lowlands were deluged with water, the crops were spoiled, the price of wheat rose to more than 120 shillings a quarter, and people resorted to all sorts of devices to economise the consumption of bread. Potatoes, potato flour, and rice, were the ordinary substitutes, and an Act of Parliament forbade the bakers to sell any but whole meal bread.' (The Rev. L. Harcourt (ed.), *The Diaries and Correspondence of the Right Hon. George Rose*, Vol.1, London 1886, pp.280-281.)

Nevertheless, it is difficult to be categorical in respect of the reasons for the final decision to introduce the Census Bill. One problem is that the reporting of the debate in parliament is incomplete. *Hansard* and the *Annual Register* report only Abbot's speech. The report in *The Times* (20 November 1800, p.2, & 21 November 1800, p.1) covers other speeches – including those by Hobhouse and Sheridan – but in that report the wording of Abbot's speech is somewhat different and so, to some extent, are the emphases. According to *The Times*, Abbot's view was that 'It was of the highest importance that the House should obtain information of the actual state of the population of the country, that they might know how to provide subsistence for the people, not only for the current year, but for those to come'. Moreover, it was important to know the population in the past, so as to be able to discover whether it was population increase which explained why we had ceased to be an exporting country and whether agriculture should be extended. Hence the inclusion in the schedule of data from the parish registers. Further, they also owed it to posterity to collect the information. It would seem, therefore, that the proposal was looking both at the past and the future, even if the stimulus was the present.

Further, Sheridan criticized the Bill; he obviously considered that it would not throw light directly on food needs. 'He saw no objection in ascertaining how many acres of land were sown with wheat, and this could be known by returns made from every parish, and the proportion as contained between the population and consumption. By these means it could surely be determined whether it was a good or bad year, and whether there was wheat enough to supply the population.' But the Speaker ruled that these observations did not apply to the present Bill, though they 'might be moved hereafter as an instruction to the Committee...' The resultant Act did not provide for such information.

Perhaps the harvest failure was the final circumstance which triggered action – though in that case one might have expected to find more explicit contemporary references to the fact. But the food shortage of 1800 was only one of a number of difficulties arising in a war economy (and, after all, there had been food shortages in earlier times). Other difficulties included the increase in poor relief arising – as my colleague Professor Arthur John has told me – from the support to dependants of men in the militia, and the shortage of agricultural labour resulting from conscription and from the growth of war industries. E. L. Jones ('The agricultural labour market in England, 1793-1872', *Economic History Review*, Vol.17, No.2, December 1964) drew attention to these shortages and suggested that when the war ended, some 400,000 men were released from the army and a considerable number from war industry. Realistic data on current and past population would have been relevant to an appreciation of these various problems. And it may not have been entirely fortuitous that Rickman, whose 1796 memorandum had been sent to Abbot, with whom he had subsequently been working (in 1800, according to W. C. Rickman), published what appears almost certainly to be that memorandum in June 1800 in a journal of which he was the editor. Moreover, Rickman himself claimed to be the instigator of the Census Bill. 'At my suggestion they have passed an Act of Parliament for ascertaining the population of Great Britain', he wrote to Southey in December 1800, 'and as a compliment (of course) have proposed to me to superintend the execution of it' (Orlo Williams, *Life and Letters of John Rickman*, London 1911, p.38).

9 This proposal to estimate past population by using the parish register data might well have been derived from Rickman's memorandum. However, Rickman suggested that the census as a whole could be carried out on this basis by using a multiplier to be obtained by enumerating the population in 'three or four distant parishes in each county' and then calculating the ratio of population to burials in these parishes. He obviously had in mind a separate multiplier for each county. The suggestion was not original to Rickman; similar attempts were made by participants in the eighteenth-century controversy.

10 The Hardwicke Act of 1753 did not apply to Scotland.

11 A most valuable survey of the history of British censuses will be found in [L. M. Feery], *Census Reports of Great Britain 1801-1931* (Guides to Official Sources No.2), London 1951.

12 According to his son, the 1840 Population Bill was prepared by Rickman. But this claim is not supported by the manuscript memorandum in the General Register Office, entitled *History of the Census of 1841*. The memorandum (of 142 pages) gives a detailed account of the steps taken to organize the 1841 census and begins with the following statement: 'The Census of 1841, so far as it relates to England and Wales, having been taken on a plan never before attempted and by means

of machinery which was not in existance at the period of any previous Enumeration of the People, it may be proper at the commencement of this Paper to notice that the Act of 3 and 4 Victoria Cap 99 by which it was authorized was framed upon a scheme propounded to the Government in June 1840 by the late Mr. Lister, the then Registrar General of Births, Deaths and Marriages, the details of which will appear in the following Letters addressed by him to Mr. Drinkwater Bethune, the Counsel employed by Government to prepare the Bill.' (The letters referred to are printed as Appendix 2 to the present chapter.)

The apparent discrepancy between the two claims can be resolved by reference to the account given in the *Journal of the [Royal] Statistical Society* and to the two Census Bills of 1840.

It is very probable that John Rickman did assist in preparing the first Bill for the 1841 census (1 June 1840, *B.P.P.*, 1840, Vol.3). That Bill envisaged the census being taken on more or less the same lines as previous censuses, with a similar range of questions (though the 1821 question on age was reintroduced, apparently on a compulsory basis), and vesting local responsibility in the Poor Law officers in England and Wales and the parish schoolmasters in Scotland.

However, the London (afterwards Royal) Statistical Society had set up a committee to make recommendations for the 1841 census, and the report of that committee suggested a radical change in organization of the census (to take advantage of the new Poor Law and civil vital registration administrations), a household schedule listing each individual by name and characteristics, enumerators' transcripts, a much wider range of more specific questions and a centralized tabulation of the data. The committee's report was published in April 1840 and the initial Bill of 1 June must have been a shock. Copies of the committee's report were sent to the Home Secretary, to Lord J. Russell and to Sir H. Parnell (who was to sponsor the Bill in Parliament for the government), as well as to other members of Parliament. According to the Statistical Society, 'the result was, that a Bill which had been previously brought into the House of Commons, and printed, in which it was proposed to take the census according to the imperfect system adopted on previous occasions, and by means of the same obsolete machinery, was withdrawn, and a new Bill, in which the principal recommendations of the Committee were adopted, was introduced in its stead, and subsequently passed'. The amended Bill was printed on 13 July 1840 (*B.P.P.*, 1840, Vol.3) and vested the primary responsibility for the census in the Registrar General and in such other persons who should be 'associated with him' as Census Commissioners. Not all of the Statistical Society's recommendations for census questions were accepted – notably, marital condition, religion and condition of health – while two others were not specified in the detail suggested, namely birthplace and occupation. (See *J.R.S.S.*, Vol.3, April 1840, pp.72-101, & July 1840, pp.204-205; & Vol.4, April 1841, pp.69-70.)

The Bill for 1841 census of Ireland was also amended in committee. Whereas the initial Bill (7 July 1840) contained the usual specification regarding taking an account of the population of each parish, the amended Bill (27 July 1840) prescribed an enumeration of every house, and an account 'of the number of persons dwelling therein, and of the sex, age and occupation of all such persons' &c. (*B.P.P.*, 1840, Vol.3). Unfortunately, there was no civil vital registration system in Ireland and no Registrar General who could act as a Census Commissioner.

13 Charles Abbot corresponded with Rufus King, US Minister to Britain, in part about the US census. In his letter to King of 4 November 1800 he wrote: 'I wished also to have requested the favour of seeing the Act which was passed on 1st. March 1790 for ascertaining the population of America according to which I apprehend the Census was taken in 1791 as a basis for the Scale of Representation.' In effect, however, King appeared to be more interested to have the census data for Britain than Abbot was to know exactly how the US census was taken. (I am indebted to the New York Historical Society for copies of the correspondence between King and Abbot. Unfortunately it has not been possible to trace any of this correspondence in the Abbot files in the Public Record Office.)

14 [John Rickman], *Observations on the Results of the Population Act, 41 Geo. III*, London 1802, p.4.

15 1801 census, *Enumeration Abstract*, 1802, pp.496 & 216. If a lodger provides his own food, he should in modern censuses be treated as a separate household. Failure to distinguish between lodgers and boarders in British censuses resulted in an understatement of the number of 'single-person households', at least prior to the 1951 census (see Alexander Block, *Estimating Housing Needs*, London 1946, esp. Ch.2). It seems very probable that there has also been underenumeration of one-person households in more recent censuses.

16 *Observations*, p.9.

17 For a discussion of this Act and the enumerations carried out under it, see my introduction to W. Kellaway (ed.), *London Inhabitants within the Walls*, London 1966.

18 Joshua Milne, *A Treatise on the Valuation of Annuities and Assurances*, 2 vols, London 1815, Vol.2, p.753.

19 For comments on the ninteenth century censuses of Great Britain, see M. Drake, 'The Census, 1801-1891', in E. A. Wrigley (ed.), *Nineteenth-century Society*, Cambridge 1972.

20 Unfortunately, the returns sent to Rickman for the censuses from 1801 to 1831 no longer exist. But there are some local copies for a few areas in the county record offices and public libraries and these may help to indicate the kinds and magnitudes of errors involved. This is especially so for the 1821 census, for which age was asked on a voluntary basis. The materials extant for the parish of Braintree (Essex) for 1821 suggest that the census operation was conducted in two stages. First, there was a listing of the individuals in each house, the 'exact' age of each individual being stated, but the names of only the householders (and occasionally the name of a lodger). The individual exact ages were then allocated to age groups (by sex) on a separate set of summary sheets, one line being provided for each house. Apparently no printed schedules were provided; it seems to have been left to the local authorities to decide whether or not to produce sheets with printed headings – e.g. as in the case of Croydon for 1811. (For the 1831 census there was a London-printed schedule entitled 'Formula for taking and preparing the account of the resident population', but here, too, each line covered the contents of a house.) Hence both transcription errors and age-reporting errors may have occurred. Scrutiny of a few pages of the Braintree house listings for 1821 suggests that there may have been an excessive reporting of ages in multiples of two and five, but this would need to be checked against the complete return and against any returns available for other parishes. (The Braintree house lists appear to have been kept

locally and used later as a record, for there are notes on the deaths of a number of people. There is also a note that one woman – a householder – whose age was returned as seventy must have been about eighty-three and that she died at the age of ninety-six in 1834.)

The 1811 returns – as exemplified by the list for Croydon – simply provide a summary for each house, e.g. John Tubbs, bricklayer, 3 males, 2 females, total 5. If there were no initial house listing, of the kind used for Braintree in 1821, the likelihood of error in the population figures would probably have been greater.

21 *Abstract of the Answers and Returns made pursuant to an Act, passed in the Fifty-first Year of His Majesty King George III*, London 1812. Preliminary observations, p.xvi.

22 1821 census, *Abstract of the Answers and Returns*, London 1822, p.vi.

23 Dr J. T. Krause has inferred from the 1821 census age data that the birth rate fell between 1821 and 1841. But I doubt whether, without a much closer analysis, the age data are sufficiently reliable to justify an easy acceptance of that conclusion.

24 *Eleventh Annual Report of the Registrar-General*, London 1852, p.v.

25 *Population Bill. Minutes of Evidence taken before the Committee on the Bill for taking an Account of the Population of Great Britain, and of the Increase and Diminution thereof*, 10 & 18 May 1830 (*Reports from Committees*, 1830, Vol.4). See also my paper in the *Journal of the Royal Society of Arts*, Vol.104 (1956).

26 1831 census, *Enumeration Abstract*, Vol.1, London 1833, p.vi.

27 At the 1841 census, the Registrar General was one of three Commissioners appointed to take the census. From 1851 on, he took charge of the censuses. The office of the Registrar General for Scotland was established under the 1854 Act, providing for civil vital registration in Scotland. The 1836 Act had provided it for England and Wales.

28 There were in fact two schedules. Originally, under the Census Act of August 1840, only the enumerator's schedule was specified. An amending Act of April 1841 then provided for an additional householder's schedule, which was distributed to all householders a few days before the census date. Both schedules specified the same information; the information furnished by the householder was afterwards transcribed by the enumerator on his own schedule (which allowed space for more than one house per page), designed to give the details of every individual enumerated in the district for which he was responsible. See the General Register Office Memorandum and also 1841 census, *Enumeration Abstract, England and Wales*, London 1843, pp.1-4. (The Registrar General stated that 'The Householders' Schedule contributed in no small degree to the accuracy of the Returns, particularly from large establishments, while they greatly lightened the labours of the Enumerators on the day on which the Census was taken'.) Since British censuses have always basically enumerated the *de facto* population (and not the *de jure*), it has been necessary so to select census dates as to reduce to a minimum temporary displacements of the population.

29 The enumeration district – part of a registration district – was defined as one consisting of an area which could be covered by an enumerator in one or two days. Before the 1841 census was launched, the Registrar General organized trial enumerations in eight areas to estimate the time taken by an enumerator. He also wrote to seventy-one Registrars of Births and Deaths, asking them to estimate how many persons per 1000 population in their district 'might be found willing

Cartoon (1851): Overpopulation

to fulfil for fair renumeration the duties of "Enumerator" under the Population Act'. In addition, the Census Commissioners tried to discover, by an inquiry through the Superintendent Registrars, the local costs of the 1831 census, but found it impossible to do so.

30 Rickman was not in favour of censuses at intervals of less than ten years. See 1831 census, *Enumeration Abstract*, Vol.1, London 1833, p.xlvii.

31 Feery (*op. cit.*, p.17), referring to the method of household enumeration introduced in 1841, says that 'The method of conducting the enumeration on that occasion has stood the test of time and has not been substantially altered since'. This may seem a somewhat complacent view. But in a literate society, a self-administered household schedule has advantages as compared with a census conducted by enumerators acting as interviewers. It is very probably a less expensive technique; it is less likely to record information obtained from proxies; and interviewer bias, which may become rather important when factual errors have been reduced, is minimized. However, a self-administered schedule needs to be attractive and to be immediately comprehensible, and this has not always been the case.

32 *Biographical Memoir*, pp.16-18.

33 See my paper on 'Population and population movements in England and Wales, 1700 to 1850', in Glass & Eversley, *op. cit.*

34 See the discussion in the subsequent section.

35 In addition, the transcripts of parish register data sent to Rickman were not always accurate. J. D. Chambers ('Three essays on the population and economy of the Midlands', in Glass & Eversley, *op. cit.*, p.352) noted some 'disturbing discrepancies' between the Nottingham parish registers and the abstracts published by Rickman. 'On nine occasions between 1760 and 1800 the totals of baptisms and burials given in the Abstract differ by 15 per cent to 33 per cent from those provided by the registers...' For 1807-10 the discrepancies are still greater.

Mr R. E. Jones of the London School of Economics, who is undertaking research on the parish registers of Shropshire, has also found differences between the numbers in the registers and those in Rickman's summaries.

36 *Biographical Memoir*, p.18.

37 Milne made the point in his letter to the committee on the 1830 Population Bill. He wrote: 'Although enumerations of the people from time to time, and correct statements of the deaths that take place among them in the intervening periods, each classed according to the ages, and distinguishing sexes, are, *together*, of great value; yet, if either of the two be given, and not the other, I consider that no safe inferences of any material use can be drawn from them, unless the population remains stationary, which neither is nor can be the case here or elsewhere' (Milne's italics). Rickman clearly did not understand this and probably misread it. In his reply he wrote, attempting to paraphrase what Milne had said: 'Unless the actual Population and the Age of the Buried can both be obtained, no satisfactory Result as to the Duration of Life, Mr. Milne says,... can be obtained; nor then, unless the Population remains stationary, which he says never happens.' This is clearly nonsense; Milne had said nothing of the kind (*Population Bill, op. cit.*, 18 May 1830, pp.12 & 14). Rickman's use of deaths without reference to an appropriate base population was sharply criticized by T. R. Edmonds ('On the law of mortality in each county of England' and 'On the mortality of infants in England', *The*

Lancet, 1835-36, Vol.1, pp.364-371 & 690-694, esp. p.693), who also argued that Rickman had underestimated the deficiencies in the deaths returned by the clergy for the period 1813 to 1830. But Rickman later changed his views; he calculated age-specific burial rates and he praised Milne and quoted the Carlisle life table with approval, while criticizing Richard Price's Northampton tables. He wrote: 'I therefore hasten to say, that a mortality table proves nothing at all, unless in combination with the number of the living classed in the corresponding periods or grades of life...' (J. Rickman, 'Effect of the increase of population on the mortality; with remarks on the English Population Acts', *London Medical Gazette*, Vol.16, 1835, pp.268-274). Edmonds acknowledged the change of view but said: 'Mr. Rickman, in divesting himself of the gross errors with which he has disfigured his literary productions displays more caution than candour. He attempts to transfer the blame, justly due to himself, to continental writers'. (*The Lancet*, 1835-36, Vol.1, p.693). On the other hand, Edmonds himself had written (*Life Tables, founded upon the Discovery of a Numerical Law regulating the Existence of Every Human Being*, London 1832, p.xii): 'For any useful practical purpose, there is no reason for believing the Northampton Table [of Richard Price] to be a less valuable record than the Carlisle Table; the slight inaccuracy of adjustment of mortality to each age, in the former Table, would be of no sensible value in practice. It is extremely doubtful whether the principle of construction of the Carlisle Table is at all preferable in practice to that on which the Northampton Table is founded, when it is desired to obtain the rate of mortality prevailing over an extensive district... The former principle is decidedly best for indicating the *relative* mortality of different ages. The *truth* of the Northampton Table is not lightly to be called in question, when it is supported by the name of Dr. Price, although its *applicability* to the British population of the present day may be fairly questioned.' But see the discussion in the subsequent section of the present study. Edmonds, like some other writers of the period, was especially concerned to formulate a general law of mortality, of universal applicability, and thought he had done so in his conclusion that the force of mortality falls by 0·6760830 per year from birth to eight years; and rises by 1·0299117 per year from twelve to fifty-five years and by 1·0796923 per year thereafter, being stationary between eight and twelve years (*op. cit.*, p.vi).

Edmonds's 'law of mortality' was the subject of a dispute in the 1860s. Edmonds had referred somewhat disparagingly to the early work of Gompertz, who had formulated a very similar 'law of mortality' in 1825 – one which, in the modified form produced by Makeham, is a powerful actuarial technique. Apparently Edmonds was proposed for a Fellowship of the Royal Society, his sponsor attributing to him the 'invention' of the 'law'. Professor De Morgan attacked Edmonds for failing to make due acknowledgement to Gompertz (*The Assurance Magazine and Journal of the Institute of Actuaries*, Vol.9, July 1860, pp.86-89), and there followed articles by Edmonds (*loc. cit.*, October 1860, pp.170-184, & July 1861, pp.327-340), a reply by De Morgan (*loc. cit.*, January 1861, pp.214-215), a letter from T. B. Sprague, supporting De Morgan (*loc. cit.*, April 1861, pp.288-295) and a letter from Benjamin Gompertz himself, thanking Sprague for vindicating Gompertz's claim to be the 'sole independent publisher of the theory' (*loc. cit.*, April 1861, pp.296-298). Edmonds also wrote two letters to Farr, reiterating his own claims to have discovered a 'law' substantially different from that of Gompertz (Farr Collection, Vol.1, ff.42-44, letters dated 6 April & 25 May 1869).

38 In R. Price, *Observations on Reversionary Payments*, 7th edn, London 1812, Vol.2, pp.211-212. According to Morgan, the census ought to have ascertained the ages of the population – by single years up to age five and thereafter in five-year age groups.

John Rickman's article on the desirability of taking a census

From 'The Commerical and Agricultural Magazine', Vol.2, London June 1800, pp.391-399

THOUGHTS ON THE UTILITY AND FACILITY OF ASCERTAINING THE POPULATION
OF ENGLAND[a]

As the facility of the above measure is of no possible concern till its utility is previously ascertained, there is sufficient cause for giving the latter consideration the priority, in the following discussion.

The arguments which tend to demonstrate the advantages of an ascertained population, claim a superior attention from the reflection, that the wide diffusion of even a minute advantage may make a large sum total of public utility. It must also be allowed, that it is one of those things which do not contain a possibility of damage, so that the arguments in its favour may all be safely reckoned on the affirmative side, without any subtraction. It seems more convenient, on all accounts, to enumerate these arguments separately and distinctly. Such a method will take off the studied appearance of a laboured essay, and be quite in character in a proposal, whose adoption would infer many arithmetical calculations.

1. It will be intuitively granted, that an intimate knowledge of any country can be the only foundation of the legislation of that country, and also of its political relations to other nations. – Without *some* attention of this sort, we might, perhaps, see our legislature grant a bounty on the exportation of wheat, in the year 1800,[b] or the Isle of Man in unassisted hostility against Great Britain. If *some* knowledge of a country be more than useful, be even absolutely necessary, it cannot be denied, that, with the accuracy of such knowledge, legislation and politics must make proportional steps towards perfection – that, without the increase of it, they must be stationary – without its continuance, possibly even retrograde.

2. In the pursuit of this knowledge of political economy, let us consider what may be said to form the grand basis of the power and resources of a nation. Evidently not its extent – witness the endless plains of Tartary: not its fertility or mines – witness the contemptible, the defenceless state of Spanish America. The example of Holland first taught the astonished world what the present power of Britain still inculcates, – "That an industrious population is the first and most necessary requisite to the prosperity of nations." Is it fit that this all-powerful principle should be permitted to remain any longer in its present obscurity? Immediately subsequent to the conviction of the importance of population, naturally occurs the question,

---

(*a*) This treatise was written in 1796: additional notes accommodate it to the present day.

(*b*) Here might be inserted that famed anecdote of the ignorance of our ancestors; who, in Edw. III. laid on a parochial tax; which, at £1.2s. per parish, they supposed would amount to £50,000 or their stupid laws against what they stigmatized under the name of usury.

What is that population? But it is necessary to scrutinize more particularly the many cases in which an accurate answer to that question would be eminently useful.

3. In every war, especially in a defensive war, it must be of the highest importance to enrol and discipline the greatest possible number of men. In England this is already attempted, by the institution of the Militia, whose present good condition only proves the greater advantage to be derived from the farther extent of so excellent a regulation. As the Militia is not paid by the respective counties, there is no possible reason why its numbers should be determined by the wealth of any district, much less by so inaccurate an index of that wealth as is the land-tax. The effect of this inaccuracy is vulgarly stated to vary the proportion of different counties, from one man in twelve to one in twenty-six. Though this calculation is evidently hasty and inaccurate, in the general proportion (whose average cannot exceed one in fifty) yet the statement of the inequality of the burthen is not demonstrably, nor *probably*, false. Supposing it true, the remedy of this abuse would add about 20,000 men to the national defence; and, at the same time, do an act of justice in equalizing a burden too long partially borne. But nothing can be determined in this affair, till we know the separate total of each county. Here we must wait in darkness, till the population is ascertained.[c]

4. Collateral to the last argument is the great importance of knowing (especially at the beginning of a war) the number of seamen in the kingdom. This would be ascertained by an account of the population, which might be so directed as to include many momentous particulars in its execution.[d]

5. The ever-varying price of corn is an evil which more than ever calls for the interfering hand of the legislature, which can only interfere by causing increased importation, or decreased exportation. The uncertainty of the price of corn is an evil to all men. To the consumer *immediately*; and, as soon as his rent is proportion-

---

(c) The Militia establishment has lately undergone many alterations: it was almost trebled by the Supplementary Militia Act, which tended to the desirable equalization, by augmenting the counties, according to the number of taxed houses. Though towns, and the county, would thus be very unequally reckoned, it was certainly an improvement on the old act; the dictate of indolent inaccuracy. Last year the opinion of our rulers suddenly changed, and they thought they had *too many* men in the Militia. The Supplementary Militia were virtually disembodied, and the men mostly went into the Regulars for a bounty. However, the counties were not reduced to their ancient establishment, but a certain aliquot part of the total old and new Militias retained in each; so that, at present, though the number of men is not very different from the old Militia, they are more equally raised on their respective counties. The discovery that has been made, that the English are not afraid to arm in their own defence, may hereafter annihilate the expence of both Regulars and Militia, by a permanent establishment of more numerous volunteers.

(d) The number of seamen in the merchant-service, in peace, may be pretty well determined from the registry of tonnage; about one to twenty ton. But, after a peace, many must quit the profession: of these, the number should be known to Government.

ally raised, the farmer and his labourers are included in the general sufferings. Happy if only so; but an accidental diminution of price absolutely ruins the farmer, who must then retire among his quondam labourers: they, once too ingenuous to seek relief from the parish, are driven, by hard necessity, to that fatal resolution: from that time their spirit is extinguished with their independence. They cease to have any property, and the genius of slavery consigns them to the habitual sloth which ever benumbs her debased subjects. The landlord, who feels, in every expence, the increased price of his tenants' corn, after the trouble and odium of an increased rental, is no richer than before, and the universal alteration of the price of every article is consummated, with much damage, and no possible advantage to mankind. These considerations must interest the feelings of every man.[e] Already we see a board of agriculture established; but the human understanding cannot reason without proper data. No society can confidently pretend to provide the requisite quantity of food, till they know the number of consumers. Here, then, we obtain another view, in which our proposal would be of the utmost utility. On this foundation only can public granaries (emulating those of *ancient* Rome and *ancient* Constantinople) be erected.[f]

6. Many important conclusions might be founded on the increase or decrease of the number of marriages in years past. The causes of their increase, and of consequent, population, might be successfully scrutinized, and attended to, by an intelligent administration. The sum total of human felicity and increasing population (fated eternally to accompany each other) would form a curious and interesting statement from the marriages of different times and places. The influence of the price of provisions in different years – of the price of labour, in different places – of war and peace – would all be ascertained with tolerable precision. On such a foundation what a glorious plan might be sketched by some happy intellect – what glorious superstructure might be raised, by a Government anxious for the good of its subjects![g]

7. To descend from general topics to those particular considerations which persuade the execution of our proposed measure in England, we may venture to be-

---

(e) The imperious interests of our exported manufacturers (the darling object of every Government) will force attention to this subject. The vend of them abroad cannot be continued, even by the superiority of English ingenuity and industry, in spite of dearness of provisions, and thence of labour, in England.

(f) At the death of Severus, Rome had, within her walls, corn for seven years allowing to six men a Roman *modius* per diem. In modern times Berne and Geneva have felt the benefit of a similar arrangement. A pamphlet of the present year (by Arthur Young) has *asserted* that the expedience of such a measure has been refuted a hundred times. Would he condescend to suggest *where* or *how*, through the medium of your Magazine, Mr. Editor?

(g) Though the public intellect far outstrips the tardy improvement of all Governments, yet even they have *begun* to discover the beneficial truth, that the happier their subjects are, the greater taxes may be raised by the Sovereign, more easily, on their increasing wealth and numbers. Lewis XIV, Frederic of Prussia, and the late Empress Catherine, certainly were now and then influenced by this consideration.

lieve, that the real number of inhabitants, in England, is far beyond the usual estimate. Our exertions, in the last war, when we were (not unequally) opposed to half
of Europe, without an ally, and our encreased manufacturing towns, sufficiently
prove that the vulgar statement (never, I think, reckoned at above twelve millions,
in the three kingdoms) is very much below the truth. Even more than 100 years
since, above nine millions[h] were supposed, by Petty, to exist in the three kingdoms.
From the partial researches of modern observers, it is certain that many districts
augment their inhabitants: from the constant importation of grain, in spite of
potatoes, and other efficient agricultural improvements, we cannot doubt the
general fact. Within the eighteenth century our tonnage of shipping, our commerce,
both internal trade and exported manufacture, has more than doubled. Can we
hesitate to believe, that an accurate knowledge of population would be the most[i]
consoling gratification to every lover of his country?

8. We have seen the Government of England terrified by the attempts of certain
obscure individuals, who could not have attracted its notice, but from a higher fear
of more general disaffection. It would certainly tend much to the repose of any
Government, if a general conviction of its inclination and attempts to promote the
public good should pervade the public mind. Any such novel attempt as that
recommended in this paper; which, from its nature, must be of the utmost publicity,
would certainly promote this sentiment, which is little apt to be excited by the
useful, but dull routine of office. A few *undoubted* improvements in the arrangement
of the national police, might easily diffuse this sentiment beyond control. I would
be understood to hint at a more severe or infamous punishment of false weights
and measures – at an arrangement to prosecute all felons at the *county charge,*
instead of that of the injured individual, doubly injured by the expence and trouble
of the prosecution; and, therefore, usually, an unwilling prosecutor – at a systematic
regeneration of the poor laws, especially that part of them which regards certificate
men and removals.[k] But I wander too long from our subject.

9. Another argument (which to some may appear too refined) I would deduce
from the probability that a specimen of the kind proposed, might tend to make
political œconomy[l] a more general study in England. Certain it is, that, at present,
too small a portion of national intellect is engaged in patriotic speculations.
A little attention of Government would produce great things.

(*h*) Nine millions and a half, beside the plantations.

(*i*) France has certainly encouraged her own subjects, and alarmed Europe, by
her vaunted 27 millions.

(*k*) This has been attempted in Mr. Pitt's Poor bill; but has not been acted on:
the bill was so miscellaneous as to take off attention from any single object. A
specific bill against vexatious removals, has been introduced this session, by Mr.
Baker, but thrown out.

(*l*) Political œconomy may be defined to be the scientific application of statistical
survey; the novelty of these phrases is only a proof of the novelty of any regular
attempts to diffuse general happiness. The world is indebted for somewhat *more*
than the phrase, for an effective illustration of its meaning, to Sir John Sinclair's
Statistical Survey of Scotland. A work, performed with unexpected facility, considering it usefully fills thirty-one volumes.

10. At least we may be well assured, that the execution of the proposed measure would much facilitate many other useful enquiries. The mode of investigating population must somewhat resemble that of ascertaining the quantity of that fixed property assessed to the land-tax, – a tax, for so many reasons, the best of all possible taxes, that, doubtless, the only reason against its modern augmentation is the excessive inequality at present discoverable in its operation.[m] Habits of enquiry might most usefully be turned to the solid investigation of the ascertainable property in the nation.

11. An additional argument may be drawn from the great improvement of the Life-Insurance Offices, from the execution of our proposal. The improvement of so useful an institution, in a nation full of various descriptions of annuitants, is not a contemptible argument.

12. Having gone through all these particular arguments, I shall give a concluding one, which is of a cumulative nature. – I would call the attention to *all* the authors, who have written on the state and politics of any nation. Few of them will be found who have not, on some occasion, assumed a certain population of the nation in question. They have not done this for a uniform purpose: indeed, for very different purposes; but all of them tending to demonstrate, by the use they have made of bare supposition, what superior value they might have given to their calculations, had they possessed a foundation of solid materials.

13. HAVING now attempted (at sufficient length) to convince the reader of the utility of the knowledge of British population, it is time to conduct him to the practical part: in introduction to which it will not be incongruous to notice the most famous attempts of a similar nature. The manner in which the usual Census[n] of Roman Citizens was formed, seems to have been by collecting them in their respective municipia, and simply enumerating all who made their appearance. The careful policy of Augustus seems first to have improved this rude method into much utility, at the well-known period of our Saviour's birth. At that time twenty commissioners were dispatched into the various provinces[o] (Cyrenius to Judaea);

(*m*) Our correspondent seems to have formed too favourable an opinion of the land tax. In a nation, without a national debt, and without trade, it should be the *only* tax. But are the creditors of the public, and the foreign trader, to be defended at the exclusive expence of the land-holder? The old land tax is nearly obliterated; and, if our legislators have the usual abilities of their station, we shall never see another without also taxing the interest of the funded property, *at least equally* with the land. It is not, indeed, necessary to lay a direct tax on the merchant; and, from the complex nature of his affairs, it can never be imposed accurately; and, to let him assess himself, is, indeed, "to lead him into temptation." Witness the returns of commercial income, in 1799. Besides, if not taxed, his profits will be charged so much lower to the consumer. It is the same final charge to the public, whether they pay a higher taxation, or suffer an enhancement of all commodities. E.

(*n*) All the various enumerations of the Census yet extant have been collected, and ably commented on, by that eminent philologist, Mr. Moyle.

(*o*) Florus has probably preserved to us the very words of their official instructions: – Ut omnia patrimonii, dignitatis, aetatis, artium, officiorumque discrimina in tabulas referantur. *Flor. Ep.*

and, from their information, property and occupations were ascertained, and the tributes of this mighty empire were equalized. This measure, of course, included an exact enumeration of the people, subjects as well as citizens. The inconvenience which affected Joseph and his wife, and caused their child to be laid in a manger, seems not to indicate much attention in this mode of procedure, to the comfort of individuals, who were dragged far from home, each "to his own city." However that was, the enumeration was (no doubt) sufficiently accurate. The succeeding emperors seem to have neglected the continuance of this salutary measure, since, in the decline of the empire, the tributes were again become arbitrary and unequal.[p] This caused them to diminish so much, that the army and empire went to ruin together.

14. A man, to whom the Romans would have given the appellation of barbarian, seems next to have perceived the advantages of such an undertaking. With a mixed view to military and civil arrangement, Alfred caused the land and inhabitants of his dominions to be ascertained.[q] The extensive crown-lands, reserved by the Norman Conqueror, put him beyond the necessity of taxing his associates, when become proprietors; but he thought it expedient to enumerate the knights' fees, with a military view only. This resolution of his produced the domesday book. An opinion has been formed, that some of our Kings (Edw. I. and IV. and Hen. VIII.) undertook a similar task; but of their attempts no trace remains.[r] In the 24th year of Elizabeth (in fear of Spanish invasion) a muster was made in England, of all men able to bear arms: the return was 1,172,000.[s] This, multiplied by four, gives, for total population, 4,688,000. But, as actual enumeration must always be under the real number, we may safely conclude that England (without Scotland and Ireland) then contained five millions. From that time to the present day nothing beyond conjecture has been attempted.

15. In modern times, Prussia has been the first to enumerate her inhabitants; then America; and, lastly, France.[t] This has been done by an actual enumeration; but this method (fraught with trouble and expence) attempts an accuracy not necessary, or indeed attainable, in a fluctuating subject. It is, perhaps, possible to point out a mode by which all useful purposes might be obtained with little trouble indeed.

16. Though England has, indeed, neglected to enumerate her inhabitants, she possesses materials of the best kind for such an undertaking. I allude to the parish registers, first instituted by T. Cromwell (Henry VIII's Vicar General) for ecclesiastical purposes, with reference to wills: – though parish registers, in general, do not date higher than the middle of the sixteenth century. – Thus, for 250 years, we

---

(p) See Gibbon's Decline and Fall of the Roman Empire.

(q) Since the Dane-gelt was collected at so much per hide of land, it is probable other assessments were levied in the same manner.

(r) At least none is public. I have somewhere heard, or read, that Henry's attempt lies unheeded among other ancient records in the Tower. Perhaps Mr. Abbot may hereafter recover these valuable remains.

(s) See Sir Walter Raleigh's Essay on the first Invention of Shipping.

(t) Austria, Naples, and Tuscany, have made similar attempts, with tolerable success.

have an accurate account of the births and burials of all England. – The name of every benefice which possesses a register, might be obtained from the bishop's offices, who for their own profit, are not inaccurate in the list of parishes within their respective jurisdictions – This done, I would propose a printed letter to be directed "to the Officiating Minister" of every benefice. – If the bishop's countenance in the affair could not be obtained by the Premier, an Act of Parliament[u] must compel an answer, which should contain the births, burials and marriages for the last ten years; distinguishing male and female, and any thing else which may be thought necessary. – Then let three or four distant parishes in each county, be chosen for their insulated situation, where almost every man is deposited in his own church yard. An exact enumeration must be made of these parishes. From the proportion of their burials[x] to their population, sufficient foundation is established, to ascertain by a simple arithmetical operation, the population of the whole nation.

17. We will now attempt to compute the probable expence of the execution of this scheme. – Say, ten thousand printed letters, at 1d. each, about – £40. travelling expenses for the partial enumeration perhaps £300. Two years might complete the operation, during which time it would be necessary to allow some salary to the person or persons employed, – suppose £400. more. These added expences amount to £740. – A sum which constitutes about one hundredth part of the *daily* expence of any future peace establishment. Trifling indeed, must be the benefits of any information, which will not compensate such an invisible expence!

18. It may be perceived, that an extension of this method might inform us (with sufficient accuracy) of the relative state of population at any period, from the days of Elizabeth. The average burials of five or seven successive years, would create an important fund of information on the various influence of the national affairs, which have diversified so long a period.[y] The civil war, the revolution, the continental wars of William and Anne, the energies of various ministries would be all reviewed by this new scale of rectitude. – He who cannot see the momentous consequences of such a scrutiny, can have little penetration; he who has the power of instituting it, without its adoption, can have no spark of patriotism.

19. It may be expected, that this paper should not conclude without some approximating guess at the present population of these nations. – If we have reason to think, that the industry and value of our countrymen, is double that of our rivals, the French; and if the last war proved our resources *equal* to theirs, aided by the silver of Spain, the languid interference of the Dutch, and our previous losses in

---

(u) Some sort of compulsion is necessary. – A person in the North, who sent to thirty ministers, a civil request of similar statements, received answer from no more than fourteen! An astonishing instance of brutal manners in a class of men of liberal education.

(x) As Dissenters do not baptize in the church, and therefore, are not registered on that occasion, the account of burials only would answer our purpose.

(y) It is not unobserved, that many parish registers are deficient; it is presumed, that enough remain to compare with the modern registers of a great number of parishes, whence general inferences might be safely drawn. It would be proper to ask for a statement of dates, etc. of each register, in the communication of births, etc. to be required of each officiating minister.

America; it seems not doubtful, that we must exceed half the French population. – I would guess, that Scotland and Ireland contain about five millions, England about ten millions, and that our eastern and western colonies (with other absentees) complete another million. In all sixteen millions. It is not want of examination that makes me neglect to produce a firmer basis of my supposition. It is, that examination has afforded nothing valuable. The vague result of what I have seen, is, that our numbers have increased as seven to four in this last century.

20. As this treatise contains arguments and facts, rather than rhetoric, no other conclusion is requisite, than a hint to those, who from its perusal, feel a conviction of the UTILITY and FACILITY of ascertaining British Population, that they should not neglect each to forward its execution by word and deed, with the strenuous emulation of good Patriots.

Two letters from T. H. Lister, the first Registrar General of England & Wales, on his proposals for the 1841 census

Extracted from the MS memorandum in the possession of the General Register Office –
History of the Census of 1841

General Register Office
June 27, 1840

My dear Bethune,

After our conversation about the Census on Thursday, I had not time that afternoon to have committed to writing according to your request otherwise than very
hastily and imperfectly the purport of what I had said to you, but I will now do so
more deliberately after having reconsidered the subject.

Without criticising any other plans that may have been proposed for taking the
Census, I will state as briefly as I can my own notion of the manner in which with
respect to England and Wales I think that object may be most easily and effectually
accomplished.

First; I must state that with a view to lessen the difficulty created by the great
numbers who are constantly *in transitu*, and the consequent chance on the one hand
of omission, on the other of reckoning the same persons twice over, I think it essential that the Census should be taken every where at the same, and in the shortest
possible, time – in one day, when possible, and when not, at the most in two –
If this be granted, the first preliminary measure is so to divide the Country with
reference to population and area that no person employed in the Enumeration
shall have more to do than he can do easily in two days. Now the whole of England
and Wales is already divided into *Registrars' Districts*, of which there are 2193
districts, the limits of which are known and published, and which were formed in
persuance of directions for which I refer you to a Circular at page 29 of the Octavo
Edition of my First Report, and on principles and with reference to objects similar
to those which must be observed in forming districts for Enumeration.

As these Registration districts are much too large to be districts for Enumeration,
but (being formed upon similar principles) will always bear nearly the same proportion to such as would be convenient for the latter purpose, I propose that every
Registrar's District should be divided into some integral number of Enumeration
Districts, or in other words, that although the extent of division may be varied,
the Registrar's District should always be the *unit* of which the Enumeration Districts
should be the *fractional parts*. The Enumeration District is to be formed solely for
practical convenience in taking the Census, and it is not necessary that it should be
recognized afterwards in the published abstract, in which I would propose to
notice (with the separate population &c. of each) every Parish and other Division
hitherto noticed in the published Censuses, with the addition of the Registrar's

District, a distinct notice of which is now important on account of the registration of births and deaths.

Having mentioned the *Divisions*, I come next to the *Local Agency*.

The Registrars of Births and Deaths are the only Public Officers whose functions extend to the whole of England and Wales, whose duties resemble those of an Enumerator, and to each of whom is assigned a district containing on the average between 5 and 6000 inhabitants, within which he is obliged to reside, and with the whole of which his occupation as Registrar must render him acquainted. I do not however propose that the Registrars shall be the Enumerators, first, because their districts are too large; and next, because many of them being Medical Men, cannot be required, even for one day, to devote their *whole* time and attention to taking the Census. I propose that they shall be serviceable in other ways – first, in proposing to the Board of Guardians of the Union in which their District lies (or, if there be no Board, to the Superintendent-Registrar), a Plan for the division of their district into smaller districts convenient for Enumeration; and secondly, to submit to them the names of a certain number of Persons competent and willing to be Enumerators and resident within the district, out of whom the requisite number may be selected. I would also make the Registrars the *Receivers* of Instructions and Schedules from the central authority in London – the *Distributors* of such Papers to the Enumerators in their respective Districts – the *Collectors* of the Enumerators' Returns – the *Examiners* by whom Errors, which only local knowledge can detect, should be pointed out and, under their directions, corrected – and finally, the *Transmitters* of such Returns to the Clerks of the Guardians or Superintendent Registrars.

For these duties they are peculiarly qualified by the local knowledge which they must necessarily possess. The majority are very efficient men, and I believe them, with scarcely an exception, to possess all the intelligence requisite to perform such duties very satisfactorily.

I propose that over the Registrars there shall be other local authorities, namely, the Board of Guardians, or, in those few cases where there are none; the Superintendent Registrar, acting under the direction of the Magistrates of the District. Of such Boards and Superintendent Registrars there are about 620, and the District of each comprises, with few exceptions, many Registrars' Districts. These Boards &c. shall settle the arrangement of Districts for which proposals shall be submitted to them by the Registrars, and shall appoint an Enumerator to each District out of the names submitted to them in the Registrars' Lists. It may be advisable, however, that both these acts should be subject to the revision of a Central Authority. They shall receive the Enumerators' Returns from the Registrars, and having inspected them, and having ascertained that the latter have faithfully performed their duties, shall transmit either the originals or certified copies (as the Act may direct, they retaining the originals) to the Central Office where the Returns are to be abstracted.

I will here mention that I would have no Abstracts made but at the Central Office. The duties of the Local Authorities should be confined to the preparation and transmission of correct records of simple facts. The abstraction, condensation, classification and arrangement of those facts should be done upon one uniform system, and upon the responsibility of one person or Board. To have Abstracts made in the Country to be afterwards sent up and used as the materials for other Abstracts to be made in London, is only to divide and weaken responsibility, to make uniformity of system impossible, to increase the chance of error, and to lessen the means of correction.

I would remunerate, by payment of a stated sum, every Enumerator, Registrar, and Clerk to Guardians or Superintendent Registrar, and such payment should be made only upon Certificate from the next Superior Officer (i.e. for Enumerators Registrars should certify – for Registrars, the Clerk of the Board of Guardians or Superintendent Registrar – for Clerk or Superintendent Registrar, the Head of the Central Office) that the services assigned had been duly performed. Whether the payments should be out of Local Rates or the Consolidated Fund is a question with which I do not propose now to meddle.

The Districts should be formed, the Enumerators appointed and the Instructions and requisite Forms issued from the Central Office at sufficiently long periods before the day of Enumeration, which periods ought perhaps to be fixed by the Act.

To the Central Authority should belong, subject to the approval of the Secretary of State, not only the final abstraction of the Returns but the preliminary arrangements of details and issue of Instructions, with such powers as may be requisite to carry the measure into effect. How that authority should be constituted, whether it should be vested in the hands of one or of more, who should be designated in the Act, or appointed by Government, are questions which do not affect my plan and which I do not propose to discuss.

The best enumeration that can be made by going from house to house, must necessarily omit some of the many who are travelling in Coaches, on Railways, Canals &c. – also the houseless poor – and those vagrant and criminal classes who may have no acknowledged home. The means of ascertaining these, and obtaining at least an approximation to the truth, will require consideration and inquiry. There must be some separate means of ascertaining the number of those who are *afloat*.

I had intended to write to you only upon the *means of obtaining* the Census and not upon the extent and nature of the *information* to be sought. But the latter is not quite a distinct subject, as one must be guided not merely by what is desirable in the abstract but what is practicable with the machinery at command. Now if the Census is to be taken in a short time, the Districts must be small, and the Enumerators many, and therefore, perhaps, in many instances, men of *very* moderate education. It is therefore essential that the questions to which they are to record the answers should be few and plain – they should have no difficulties imposed upon them in classifying or adding – that their duties should be limited to ascertaining and setting down, in the plainest form that can be contrived, a few simple facts, and that they should have no more to do than may be very easily done by any sensible man who can read and write. They should have Schedules or Forms, headed with the Registrar's District – the Enumeration District (which may be numbered) and the Parish or Township, and they should insert every house, and the name, age, and occupation of every Inmate. The names should be written *at length*. An Enumerator may sit at home and make *marks*, and no Examiner could detect his Errors. Other questions *may* be asked, but it is dangerous to encumber such an Enquiry. Failure might be risked by attempting more; and if the names, ages, and occupations of the whole or nearly the whole of the Population can be faithfully and fully recorded, the paramount objects of a Census will be gained and little left to be desired.

(*Signed*) T. H. Lister.

To: J. E. D. Bethune Esq.

COPY

General Register Office
July 10, 1840

My dear Bethune,

I have a few more suggestions to make on the Census Bill. I think it inadvisable that the time of the Enumerator should be wasted in recording any particulars which can be obtained as well by other means. Such is the case with respect to the Inmates of all Bulidings of a public description, such as Prisons, Hospitals, Workhouses, and others which agree with these in the circumstance of being presided over by some responsible Head who can give an account of all persons within. I would therefore propose that the Enumerator should in all such cases insert only the Building, describing its nature, and omit the Inmates, and that the Master &c. of every such Institution should be furnished with Schedules and required to insert the requisite particulars respecting the Inmates, subscribing a declaration in the presence of the Registrar who should be directed to collect every Return of this description within a stated time after the day fixed for taking the Census.

I would not have the Enumerator collect these Returns while taking the Census, for this might cause as much loss of time to him as if he were to insert every particular himself. I am adverse to the plan of leaving Schedules at private houses to be filled up by the Inhabitants, for the majority probably would either not fill them up at all, or would fill them up wrong. But the Head of even the humblest kind of Public Institutions must be presumed quite competent to perform that duty with correctness. I do not propose that they should be paid, but I think there should be a Fine for omission or refusal to make such Return, and there should be some Fine also, I think, for punishment of neglect in Enumerators; for as their payment will be small, the fear of losing it may not be sufficient to keep some of them in order. As for the Registrars and Superintendent Registrars, I have a sufficient hold over them. In addition to the advantage of saving time and labour, it may be useful in many respects to have *separate* Returns for all Public Institutions. It may be a matter of doubt with regard to *some* kinds, whether they should be included or not – e.g. *Public Endowed Schools* – and *Colleges* – also *Barracks* – *Arsenals* – and *Garrisoned Forts*, which lead me to another question on which I am doubtful – whether the Enumerators should include the *Military*. If the Army and Ordnance Departments can supply the requisite information, the Enumerators might omit them.

Another class must be thought of – *persons living on board* of *vessels in harbour*. Might not each Harbour Master (and I believe in every Harbour there is such an Officer) enumerate or superintend the enumeration of these? I throw this out for consideration and enquiry.

(*Signed*) T. H. Lister

To: J. E. D. Bethune, Esq.

CHAPTER 4

Marriages, births and deaths

In the discussion of the background of the population controversy, it was emphasized that many eighteenth-century writers were well aware of the deficiencies of parish registration and of the London Bills of Mortality. Attempts were made to estimate the omissions – Maitland's effort for the London Bills is noteworthy – and also to persuade Parliament to improve the registration system. In general these latter efforts failed. When changes were made in the system, they were largely for quite different reasons. The Hardwicke act of 1753, which prescribed that marriages should take place in churches or chapels and be preceded by banns or licences, was designed to prevent clandestine marriages.[1] The Act of 1783 aimed at raising revenue, and levied a stamp duty on the entries of all burials, marriages, births or christenings. It was extended in 1785 to cover Dissenters and this was done at the request of the Dissenters themselves, for they assumed that their registers would thereby be legally valid records of civil status. But legal equality was not achieved and there were widespread objections to the Act, which was said seriously to have reduced the effectiveness of parish registration in some areas.[2] The Act was repealed in 1794. The only other significant legislation before the transfer to civil vital registration was Sir George Rose's Act of 1812. This did aim to reform both the keeping and the maintenance of parish registers, but it was ineffective. Burn poured scorn on it, stating that it was a mutilated form of the Bill originally introduced in the House of Commons (with the most useful clauses removed by the House of Lords), and that it had 'ever since remained subject to ridicule, and without the power of enforcing any of its enactments, except that respecting forgery'.[3] Criticism of the Act went unchallenged in the House of Commons debate in 1833, which resulted in the appointment of the Select Committee on Parochial Registration. Sir George Rose's Act was, of course, primarily concerned with records of civil status, but it was passed when Rickman had already organized two censuses and had collected parish register returns on a national scale. Given these circumstances, as well as the growing interest in the measurement of mortality, it is not surprising that the Act also tried to satisfy this interest by prescribing that entries for burials should record ages at death. The 1831 census reports contained analyses of those ages from 1813, when the Act came into force, until 1830.[4] Other Bills for modifying the registration system were introduced – in 1824, for example, and in 1835 – but failed to be enacted.[5] Nevertheless, circumstances were influencing legislators in ways which soon made possible a break with the past. Several factors were involved.

The most important factor was related only in part to the problems of vital registration as such, namely concern with the civil disabilities of the religious groups outside the Established Church. Efforts had been made at the end of the eighteenth century to remove these disabilities, but they had failed. But when, in 1811, Lord Sidmouth attempted to reduce still further the existing area of religious freedom by narrowing the interpretation of the Toleration Act and imposing more stringent conditions on the licensing of preachers, the counter-agitation was so powerful that the Bill was withdrawn. And almost immediately afterwards a new organization was created – the Protestant Society for the Protection of Religious Liberty, under the leadership of John Wilks, MP for Boston. Spurred by this Society, further attempts to constrain religious liberty were blocked and, on the positive side, the Test and Corporation Acts were repealed in 1828 and an Act to remove Catholic disabilities was passed in 1829.[6]

It was John Wilks who, in the Reformed Parliament on 28 March 1833, proposed the appointment of a Select Committee to inquire into the state of parochial registration. In his speech he retraced the history of the system. He demonstrated the failure of the Rose Act, referring to the large number of parishes which had not sent annual returns to the bishops, to the errors and frauds in the parish registers themselves, and to the court cases which had ruled that a baptismal entry was not valid evidence of the age or legitimacy of a child. But he also stressed, in addition, the particular difficulties of Catholics and Dissenters under the existing system, to have to conform with which they would regard as offensive and unjust. He believed that there were no less than 4 million Dissenters in the country – nearly one third of the total population of Britain. 'That body included men not inferior in wealth or influence, in ingenuity, or learning, or industry, or worth, to the best and most favoured of the population. Of them, also, a considerable portion including many hundred congregations, disapproved of infant baptism, and must be specially precluded from all registers except registries of births. For that great portion of the people, no provision, by the existing laws, supplied the means of effective and legal registration, which their security – and the general welfare, inseparably involved in their security – imperiously demanded.' England was behind the age, in comparison with such countries as France, Holland and Flanders, which had civil registration. His idea was a system of civil registration, which must embrace all births, marriages and deaths; it might be operated by the established clergy, but it must be national and civil and not ecclesiastical or sectarian. A Select Committee should report on the existing system and on a general registration of births, baptisms, marriages, deaths and burials. And his proposal was supported by the Attorney General and by the Solicitor General. The latter also drew attention to the frauds currently practised, including making entries in Bibles 'to which the artifical appearance of venerable age was successfully imparted. Indeed there was a regular manufactory of Bibles for that purpose.' A Select Committee was accordingly appointed.[7]

A second factor which may have helped to account for the acceptance of the idea of civil vital registration, though it appeared to have no direct influence on the debates in Parliament, was the interest of the medical profession and of a number of statisticians in the use of existing data and in the provision of better data on mortality. This was referred to earlier, when the works of Fothergill, Black, Percival, Haygarth and Heysham were mentioned.[8] In the late eighteenth century the effect of variolation (inoculation) further stimulated this interest in statistics of mortality and morbidity;[9] and when vaccination took over from inoculation, that, too, became a subject for study, as also the possible replacement of smallpox by other diseases.[10] William Heberden Jr – his father had been responsible for an eighteenth-century collection of the London Bills of Mortality – tried to use the London Bills to assess the fall in mortality since the eighteenth century.[11] And though he appeared to commit a 'howler', his work, like that of Woolcombe on pulmonary tuberculosis,[12] was in keeping with the trend to quantification in medical inquiries, also finding expression in the publications of Bisset Hawkins and Thackrah.[13] In the 1830s statistical analyses of death and sickness appeared in the medical journals and in the *British Medical Almanack*. In *The Lancet*, T. R. Edmonds published a long series of articles, using in particular the parish register returns under the Rose Act, attacking Rickman's initially incorrect use of burial statistics, criticizing John Finlaison – actuary to the National Debt Office – and displaying his own 'law of mortality' and 'law of sickness'.[14] The *London Medical Gazette* was the vehicle for an equally long series of articles on mortality by John Rickman, and there were other contributors, including Villermé on mortality in the manufacturing districts and Francis Corbaux on marital fertility.[15] The discussions of mortality – often involving attempts to judge whether it had been falling since the eighteenth century – led to criticisms of the imperfections of the basic data and to proposals for their improvement. A fairly elaborate proposal, which took into account the earlier recommendations of Corbyn Morris, was put forward by a well-known doctor, George Man Burrows, in *The London Medical Repository* in 1818. His contribution was in fact a substantial digest of a pamphlet which he had published earlier that year, and commenting on the space given to the article and to the omission of other contributions to make room for it, the editor explained: 'We feel, however, persuaded that our readers will agree with us, that some sacrifice is due both to the writer and to the important nature of the paper... we shall receive with much gratification any remarks of correspondents on this momentous topic of investigation; which has not only a medical, but a moral and political bearing.'[16] The recommendations provided for details of causes of death by age and sex, with information on whether the cause was certified by a medical practitioner. In effect, these various contributions were preparing the medical profession for responsibilities which they came later to accept with much greater willingness than was the case in many other countries.

Another group which was being similarly prepared – though technically its members should have required little preparation – was that of the actuaries and statisticians involved or interested in annuities, life assurance and Friendly Societies. Although annuities had long been used by Governments to provide revenue, scientifically based schemes for annuities and assurance were of recent origin. To have an actuarial basis, accurate mortality statistics were needed and, in the case of Friendly Societies, accurate statistics of sickness. In principle, the basis of mortality calculation – the probabilities of dying or surviving – was visible in John Graunt's rudimentary life table, published in 1662, not too unrealistic for the early years of life, but conjectural and highly unrealistic for later ages.[17] The Huygens brothers wrote to each other in 1669 about this table, Lodewijk Huygens suggesting that it might 'even be useful for fixing annuities',[18] while Johannes Hudde, disagreeing with Graunt's figures, sent Christian Huygens in 1671 a mortality table based upon annuitants in Amsterdam.[19] Halley's 1693 table, derived from data for Breslau, was much more realistic and Halley himself showed its practical relevance.[20] In turn, De Moivre adapted Halley's work, introducing a 'law of mortality', and producing a set of annuity tables.[21] Nevertheless, until the middle of the eighteenth century, life assurance was still generally being conducted on the same basis as insurance on shipping, and for short periods only. The Royal Exchange and London

Assurance charged £5 per cent for ships and the same rate for the captain's life. And the Amicable scheme was really a share-out one, with no guarantee of a definite sum at death, and with entry refused after the age of forty-five. It is believed that because he was so rejected, James Dodson, master at the Royal Mathematical School, Christ's Hospital, and a former pupil of De Moivre, developed the framework of a mutual system of whole-life assurance, the risks being calculated in accordance with the mortality rates derived from the London Bills of Mortality.[22] Though Dodson did not have his scheme accepted, it formed the basis of the Equitable Society, established in 1762 under a Deed of Settlement drawn up by Edward Mores, who was also responsible for introducing the term 'actuary' into the assurance world.[23] It was at this stage, in 1768, that Richard Price began to be consulted about the affairs of the Society.

Price was generally interested in assurance and critical of the unsound schemes which were far from infrequent in the eighteenth century. His advice was sought and his criticism considered authoritative – so much so that when, after commenting adversely upon the Scottish schemes for the widows and children of the Scottish clergy and professors, he admitted that he had been mistaken, it was regarded as desirable to publish the correspondence between him and Alexander Webster.[24] He was also concerned to promote old age pensions financed through contributions to parish funds and later helped to draft a Bill for providing old age and sickness benefits through Friendly Societies. These attempts failed. In his association with the Equitable Society – which became closer when his nephew, William Morgan, was appointed assistant actuary in 1774 and actuary in 1775 – he gave sound advice on the accounting system, and on the need for a continuous record of mortality of the assured population and of a comparison of actual deaths with those expected according to the life tables on which the system was based. It was not Price's recommendations which gave rise to difficulties, but his life tables; and not in connection with the Equitable Society, but in their use by William Morgan when, in 1808, the National Debt Office began to offer life annuities as a means of reducing the public debt.[25]

In a later analysis of the history of British government life annuities Frederick Hendriks stressed the fact that the losses incurred by the government between 1808 and 1829 under the old annuity scheme could not be attributed solely to the use of defective life tables. He believed that there were 'graver defects of financial principle inherent in the life annuity plan'. But he recognized that, given the particular governmental scheme (of annuities without benefit of survivorship), the life tables chosen were far less suitable than would have been the two tables often used in older schemes, namely those of Kersseboom or Deparcieux. In his view, Price's Northampton life table was the 'worst adapted to the purpose', and it is necessary to consider how that table was arrived at.[26]

In his *Observations on Reversionary Payments*, Price had not only tried to show how life tables should be constructed and used, but also to present a life table based upon experience which might be considered reasonably appropriate for the country. London experience would clearly not be typical. Instead, Price chose Northampton, one of the towns for which Bills of Mortality were regularly collected and published. Two tables were constructed; one based on the deaths for 1735-70 and the other on the deaths for 1735-80, the latter being adopted by the Equitable Society in

To the WORSHIPFUL

RICHARD MEACOCK, Efq; MAYOR,

The Aldermen, Bailiffs, Burgeffes,

And the Reft of the Worthy Inhabitants

of the Town of NORTHAMPTON,

This yearly BILL of MORTALITY is prefented,

By their moft obedient humble Servant,

JOHN COX.

The BILL of MORTALITY within the Parifh of *All-Saints*, from the 21ft of *December* 1787, to the 21ft of *December* 1788; including Perfons (in Number 10) buried from the *County-Infirmary*; the Meeting in *College-Lane*, 19; the Meeting on the Green, 1; and the Quakers' Burying-Ground, 1.

DISEASES in the Parifh of *All-Saints*.

Abortive and Stilborn	4	Confumptions -	27	Fevers -	14	Jaundice -	1	Rupture - 1
Accidents -	3	Convulfions -	1	Fits -	21	Meafles -	4	Rheumatifm - 1
Aged -	13	Croop -	4	Inflammations -	5	Mortification -	2	Small-Pox 40
Afthma -	2	Dropfy -	9	Impofthume -	1	Palfy -	1	Suddenly 4

WHEREOF HAVE DIED,

Under Two Years old	47	Ten and Twenty -	10	Forty and Fifty -	17	Seventy and Eighty - 12
Between Two and Five	24	Twenty and Thirty -	11	Fifty and Sixty -	8	Eighty and Ninety - 2
Five and Ten -	6	Thirty and Forty -	10	Sixty and Seventy -	11	Ninety and an Hundred 0

The Ages of the other Parifhes, not included.

	CHRISTENED.			BURIED.		
	Males	Females	*Total.*	Males	Females	*Total.*
ALL-SAINTS. -	52	55	107	73	65	138
St. SEPULCHRE'*s.*	20	11	31	23	25	48
St. GILES'*s.*	14	17	31	24	38	62
St. PETER'*s.*	2	3	5	6	4	10
At the Meeting in *St. Peter's* Parifh -				5	3	8
In the whole Town.	88	86	174	131	135	266
Births among the Diffenters, not included.	Increafed - 20			Increafed - 98		

Buried of the Small-Pox.—All-Saints, 40. St. Sepulchre's, 7. St. Giles's, 7. St. Peter's, 3. Meeting in St. Peter's Parifh, 3.—Total 60.

Quod adeft memento
Componere æquus; cætera fluminis
Ritu feruntur. HORACE.
Improve the prefent Hour, for all befide
Is a mere Feather on a Torrent's Tide.

COULD I, from Heav'n infpir'd, as fure prefage
To whom the rifing Year fhall prove his laft,
As I can number in my punctual Page,
And Item down the Victims of the paft;

How each would trembling wait the mournful Sheet,
On which the Prefs might ftamp him next to die;
And, reading here his Sentence, how replete
With anxious Meaning Heav'n-ward turn his Eye!

Time, then, would feem more precious than the Joys.
In which he fports away the Treafure now;
And Pray'r more feafonable than the Noife
Of Drunkards, or the Mufic-drawing Bow.

Then, doubtlefs, many a Trifler on the Brink
Of this World's hazardous and headlong Shore,
Forc'd to a Paufe, would feel it good to think,
Told that his fetting Sun muft rife no more.

Ah felf-deceiv'd! Could I, prophetic, fay,
Who next is fated, and who next, to fall,
The Reft might then feem privileg'd to play;
But, naming *none*, the Voice now fpeaks to ALL.

Obferve the dappled Forefters, how light
They bound and airy o'er the funny Glade—
One falls—the Reft wide-fcatter'd with Affright,
Vanifh at once into the darkeft Shade.

Had we their Wifdom, fhould we, often warn'd,
Still need repeated Warnings, and at laft,
A Thoufand awful Admonitions fcorn'd,
Die felf-accus'd of Life all run to Wafte?

Sad Wafte! for which no After-Thrift atones':
The Grave admits no Cure of Guilt or Sin.
Dew-Drops may deck the Turf that hides the Bones;
But Tears of godly Grief ne'er flow within.

Learn then, ye Living! By the Mouths be taught
Of all thefe Sepulchres, Inftructors true,
That, foon or late, Death alfo is *your* Lot,
And the next op'ning Grave may yawn for *you*.

Northampton Bill of Mortality

1782. But the tables were based on deaths alone, a procedure appropriate only where a population is, and has long been stationary. In all other circumstances – and they are the real circumstances of life – life table construction requires both deaths by age and sex and population by age and sex. Price knew this and later obtained suitable data for Sweden from Wargentin. But these data could not be assumed to represent the situation in England and there were no suitable data for any English community available to Price at the time he was writing. Though Price attempted to make allowance for his inadequate data, the allowance was not appropriate.[27] His tables suffered from the basic defects in their construction. With an increasing population, a life table based on deaths alone underestimates the expectation of life. Annuities calculated in accordance with such a life table would give excessive value for money to their purchasers; those who sold them would make a loss. And this occurred in the case of the National Debt Office, for William Morgan – perhaps from devotion to his uncle's memory – used the Northampton tables, instead of taking into account the actual mortality experience of his own society. The defects of existing life tables were brought to wider attention when the government came to be interested in the spread of Friendly Societies and in the possible use of annuities – as suggested in the petition of Cadogan Williams – as a means of ensuring contributory old age pensions to a large section of the community.[28]

When civil vital registration had been in force for some years and William Farr, the distinguished demographer, had produced the first national life table for England and Wales, based on the data for 1841, he also carried out a full-scale analysis to show what would be the results of following the Richard Price approach, deriving a life table solely from the statistics of death. To make the illustration particularly sharp, the data for Northampton were used. In characteristic Farr manner, the exercise – published in the *Eighth Report of the Registrar-General* (for 1845)[29] – contained a good deal of other material: on the history and antiquities of Northampton, on apprenticeship and on occupations. The essential part, however, consisted of two life tables, both relating to the period 1838-44, one constructed solely from deaths, the other correctly from age-specific mortality rates. The first, or Price-type, table gave a mean expectation of life at birth of 24·88 years, the second of 37·57 years. As Farr put it (p.279) with respect to annuities, 'A society which receives deposits that will pay £25, and finds itself, in time, called upon to pay £37, will be insolvent, and ultimately fall to ruin'. The reverse would happen with life assurance; more premiums would be paid than necessary to produce the sum guaranteed at death. 'An excess of premiums in a proprietary life office would be profit. In a mutual insurance office, if the members paid 32 premiums on an average, when they were expected to pay 28, and only the sum that 28 would provide were paid to the heirs of those who died in the first stage of its existence, a large surplus would be left for the thrice-fortunate survivors.' In his letter to the Registrar-General, Farr said tersely: 'It is, I think, proved beyond doubt that Dr. Price's table is erroneous to an extent that deprives it of all value' (p.277). And Farr returned to the subject later, when he had produced the second national life table, based on the data for 1838-44. He quoted William Morgan as having acknowledged that deaths were 'one third less in the Equitable experience than the Table indicated'. He added: 'Great injustice has been done by the use of this Northampton Table; which, in mutual offices makes one member pay 40, 30, 25, 20, 10 per cent more than the premium which is required to secure a policy of the same value, and distributes the surplus thus acquired unequally. The old offices, which have used the Northampton Table, have a great difficulty in getting themselves right. By its use the proprietary offices have exacted enormous and unequal premiums from the portions of the community who happened to be ill-versed and ill-instructed in the intricate science of Life Insurance.'[30]

These comments were written after civil vital registration had yielded its first returns of superior national data. But even before that the evidence presented to the various Select Committees on Friendly Societies had provoked an increasing uneasiness about the Northampton tables and also in general about the basic data available for calculating the probabilities of mortality and sickness.

The 1825 report drew attention to the very great growth in the number of Friendly Societies since the original 1793 Act – by 1802 there were almost 10,000 societies and by 1815 almost a million members of the various societies. A 'very considerable relief' had been given to the parishes, and 'much additional comfort derived by individuals'. But the bases of the tables used had not been adequately investigated. Different associations used different tables, without specifying the reasons. Questions were raised about the Northampton tables of mortality and sickness, and it is not surprising that the committee showed some confusion. The actuaries, too, were far from united in their opinions, and at one point the committee asked the question: 'Who are professional actuaries or persons skilled in calculation? And in what way are the Justices to satisfy themselves that the persons by whom the Tables are signed, really answer to the discription of skilful calculators?' The committee concluded that 'the rate of mortality and sickness in England, is not at present sufficiently well ascertained to justify a Parliamentary enactment of any particular set of Tables. Even the generally received opinion, of the improvement in the value of life, is rejected by certain observers of much eminence. And it must be owned, that no extensive information has hitherto been collected, as to the duration of life among the lower orders; and it is obvious, that neither experience, drawn from the higher and middling classes, nor results taken from the army or navy, or from the London Hospitals, can be depended upon, in reference to the general mass of the Manufacturing or Agricultural population.'[31]

Doubts regarding the Northampton life tables were still more sharply expressed in the 1827 report, which was particularly concerned with superannuation and hence with the question of deferred annuities. Evidence was given by some of the best known actuaries and applied mathematicians of the day – Milne, Finlaison, Francis Bailey, Gompertz, Griffith Davies, Babbage and William Morgan, as well as by the Rev. John Becher, the founder of the Southwell Friendly Society. The committee reported: 'Of these gentlemen, no one, except Messrs. Becher and Morgan, recommends the Northampton tables as a safe basis for a deferred annuity.' A series of life tables had been examined, some based on Swedish data, and the evidence was strongly in favour of tables which gave an expectation of life higher than the Northampton tables. For general purposes, the committee believed that the Carlisle tables might be used. But at the same time it was made clear that: 'Your Committee cannot conclude their observations upon this part of the subject, without recommending to the House the adoption of measures for making an accurate and extensive collection of facts, whereby the solution of all questions depending upon the duration of human life, and the number of children born, may be facilitated.'[32]

As to the data available at the time, John Finlaison, the actuary to the National Debt Office, used the records of various government tontines and life annuities.[33] He rejected the idea of using the statistics of parishes or other communities, given their existing deficiencies, and doubted whether such statistics would ever be accurate. 'How can the facts A. and C., that is the census of the town, &c. at the commencement and the conclusion of the observation be accurately procured? The population, if they could all be discovered (not an easy matter), have no interest, certainly no inclination, to disclose voluntarily their exact ages. Many of them cannot or care not to tell how the fact is, and very few will be found anxious to state it correctly. How can the particulars B. and F. which, *mutato nomine*, imply the number of births, and also the number of incomers or settlers into the town, &c. with their several ages at the time, be procured?... Finally, are the particulars E. or the deaths at every age, accurately set forth in the municipal or parish registers? No one will affirm or believe such a thing... If it again be contended that observations on statistical bills of mortality furnish, nevertheless, sufficient approximations to the truth, I would beg leave respectfully to inquire whether any such approximation may not in fact be an approach to some ideal standard of truth existing only in the mind of the calculator, rather than to the truth itself, of which perhaps no certain criterion has heretofore been discovered.'[34] Forgetting for the moment Finlaison's pessimism as regards possible improvements in the vital and population statistics – he was similarly pessimistic in his evidence to the Select Committee on Parochial Registration – it is true that the only life table which approximated to the 'truth' for an English community was that constructed by Joshua Milne for Carlisle.

This table was based upon materials which John Heysham had collected and published, namely the Bills of Mortality for the town and the results of two enumerations, the first in 1780 and the second in 1787. The Bills of Mortality for Carlisle were not only unusually detailed but seriously attempted to cover the births and deaths of Dissenters. Whether they were covered completely is not clear, but what is evident is that the numbers of births recorded were considerably larger than those returned to John Rickman in connection with his census inquiries.[35] The correspondence between Milne and Heysham, as printed in Milne's *Treatise* and in Lonsdale's biography of Heysham, shows both that Milne was quite searching in the questions he asked about the statistics and about the nature of the town population; equally, it shows Heysham's efforts to answer these questions – as he had done earlier in reply to William Wales's quite different inquiries.[36] But it is not unlikely that the population statistics were less reliable than the vital statistics. The two surveys through which the population statistics were collected do not seem to have been equally closely controlled. In particular, the returns for the second survey are not given in nearly as much detail as those for the first. Further, the second survey was known by Heysham to have been incomplete initially; he himself then completed it, and he regarded the final result as satisfactory. But there is no direct and incontestable evidence that ages were actually collected in the second survey. The increase in population between the two enumerations is suspiciously 'neat', namely 1000 persons, and the complete absence of any change in age composition between 1780 and 1787 is also rather surprising.[37] It is thus possible that the second figure was an approximation and that the second age structure was 'estimated' from the first.[38] Milne did not appear to question these matters. Finally, the population statistics were not available by age and sex in combination. The life table had thus to be for 'persons' and not entirely correctly so. Nevertheless the resultant life table was a pioneer effort and became widely acknowledged as such, though there were criticisms of the imperfect graduation of the data and there were queries and doubts as to how far the table was representative of the country as a whole.[39] But the most striking fact was that the Carlisle table was the only one of its kind for Britain at the time. The unsatisfactory nature of the various tables had been noted by the Select Committee on Friendly Societies in 1827. Rickman's returns after the implementation of the Rose Act, though widely used, were known to be inaccurate; their use served to publicize the unreliability of the existing materials. The question was discussed in the influential *Reviews*, sometimes in connection with census reports, sometimes in commenting on the reports on Friendly Societies.[40] And statistics of mortality were also the subject of discussion at the newly established (1833) statistical section of the British Association for the Advancement of Science.[41] There was certainly no lack of information on the inadequacy of the data and on the imperfect estimates of the level and trend of mortality in Britain.

When the Select Committee on Parochial Registration set about its tasks, much of the information it received – and no doubt had requested – inevitably related to the gross imperfections of the existing system of parochial registration even for the members of the Established Church. And, as the Committee reported, if the present system were improved, it would still be by definition 'exclusive and intolerant'; it would 'practically punish' those outside the Established Church 'for claiming the rights of conscience and believing what their judgments direct'. And the punishment would also be inflicted on those who 'may purchase or derive property' from the Dissenters.[42] Considered simply as a system for providing valid records of status and descent, the various witnesses confirmed that the civil provisions in other countries were far superior. John Bowring put it emphatically in his evidence: 'I think I can state, however, as a general result, that I have never seen any satisfactory registry that has not been in the hands of civil functionaries, and that, generally speaking, the popularity of registration, its economy, its usefulness and its completeness, have increased in the very proportion in which it has been removed from the religious to the civil authorities.'[43]

But the committee also heard evidence on the demographic aspects. Dr George Man Burrows – author of the pamphlet proposing a full-scale reform of vital registration – was a witness and spoke of the demographic and other benefits of effective registration.[44] John Finlaison naturally referred to the importance of better registration in respect of mortality analysis, the construction of life tables and the calculation of the value of annuities and life assurance for each sex and at every age. But he ruled out the practical possibility of ascertaining causes of death. '. . . I should think that branch of inquiry is out of the question; at any rate, as the laws of population and mortality depend upon masses and not particular cases, whatever utility may result from a registry of disease [he meant cause of death], the objects of the calculator may, for the most part, be obtained without it tolerably well.'[45] But Dr Burrows did not share this view, while the annual meeting of the Provincial

Medical and Surgical Association (the forerunner of the British Medical Association) resolved that the secretary of the Association should tell the committee that 'great benefit might be expected to accrue to medical science, and consequently to the community at large, if arrangements were made for recording the *causes of deaths* in the local registers of mortality'.[46] The prize witness on the demographic side was Adolphe Quetelet, the Belgian statistician.[47] He described the system operative in Belgium, in which civil registration had to precede the religious ceremonies of marriage, baptism and burial, and commented on the accuracy of the results. Asked about England's defective data and lack of 'important political and economical knowledge', he said: 'Lately at the philosophical meetings at Cambridge [he meant the British Association meetings] it was a subject of discussion; I heard from several distinguished persons that there was a general complaint of the imperfection of elementary population documents in this country... It is indeed a subject of wonder to every intelligent stranger, that in a country so intelligent as England, with so many illustrious persons occupied in statistical inquiries, and where the state of the population is the constant subject of public interest, the very basis on which all good legislation must be grounded has never been prepared; foreigners can hardly believe that such a state of things could exist in a country so wealthy, wise and great.'[48] The committee evidently agreed. It recommended a national civil registration system, with a central office in London which would house duplicates of all the records. Effective registration of births and deaths would not be difficult to achieve, even if death registration were to include 'the malady and cause of mortality'. The question of who should be the registrars in the new system should be left to Parliament to decide.[49]

In the event, the Government brought in two Bills, introduced by Lord John Russell on 12 February 1836 – one for amending the laws regulating the marriages of Dissenters and the other for a general registration of births, marriages and deaths. The reasons for the delay in bringing comprehensive proposals before Parliament, given the urgent recommendation of the Select Committee, are not entirely clear; but Lord Russell's speech implied that it was associated with the reorganization of an important section of local government under the new Poor Law.[50] He said that hitherto there had been a problem of the kind of person who might operate the new system, but 'within the last year or two a change had taken place in the domestic policy of the country with regard to the Poor-laws, which seemed to open the way to the establishment of a civil registration, and which would not be attended with considerable expense'. With the spread of Poor-law Unions, there could soon be a sufficient foundation, and it was proposed that the local Poor-law Commissioners should have the power to appoint one of their officers, or any other suitable person to be the registrar. The question of the civil disabilities of the Dissenters under the existing system was again stressed, and Lord Russell went so far as to say that he had always been 'favourable to the opening of the Universities of Oxford and Cambridge to Dissenters; but he should be guilty of something like delusion if he held out any prospect of immediate relief in this respect'.[51]

Although there was a good deal of discussion, there was little in the way of basic opposition in the House of Commons. The matter was somewhat different in the House of Lords, where the leaders of the Established Church could more fully express their distaste for the new registration. The Archbishop of Canterbury,

Registration of Deaths.

CAUTION

To Persons burying, and omitting to give Notice thereof to

THE REGISTRAR.

William Edwards, Sexton of Bromley, Middlesex, was **summoned** before **Mr. Yardley,** at the Thames Police Court, on 20th February, 1850, to answer a Complaint preferred against him at the **instance of The Registrar General,** under the authority of **The Secretary of State,** for a violation of the twenty-seventh Clause of the Registration Act, in omitting to give Notice to the District Registrar of **Births and Deaths,** of the fact of his having, on the 7th January last, **buried,** as **Still-Born Children,** the dead bodies of two Male Infants, **who** had been **Born alive, and did not Die until several hours after their Birth.**

The facts of the case, as stated by **Mr. Bodkin,** Counsel for the Prosecution, were fully proved in evidence, whereupon **Mr. Yardley,** after commenting severely upon the Offence of which the Defendant **had** been guilty, **Convicted** him in the Penalty provided by the **Act, at** the same time intimating to him that, for any similar infraction of the Law, he would not only incur the pecuniary Fine of **Ten Pounds,** but render himself liable to a Prosecution by

Indictment for Misdemeanor.

EXTRACT FROM THE REGISTRATION ACT.
(6 & 7 *Wm. IV.,* Cap. 86.)

By Section 27, it is enacted, "That every Registrar immediately upon registering any death, or as soon "thereafter as he shall be required so to do, shall, without Fee or Reward, deliver to the Undertaker or other "person having charge of the Funeral, a Certificate under his hand, according to the form of Schedule (E) to this "Act annexed, that such death has been duly registered, and such Certificate shall be delivered by such Undertaker, "or other Person, to the Minister or Officiating Person, who shall be required to bury or to perform any religious "Service for the burial of the dead body, and if any dead body shall be buried for which no such Certificate shall have "been so delivered, the person who shall bury, or perform any Funeral, or any religious Service for the burial, shall "forthwith give notice thereof to the Registrar * * * * * ; and *every person who shall bury, or perform* "any Funeral, or any religious Service for the burial of *any dead body,* for which no Certificate shall have been "duly made and delivered as aforesaid, *and who shall not within Seven Days give notice thereof to the Registrar,* "SHALL FORFEIT AND PAY ANY SUM NOT EXCEEDING TEN POUNDS *for every such offence.*"

GENERAL REGISTER OFFICE,

February, 1850.

Registration warning

while anxious to relieve the hardships of the Dissenters, could not agree to any proposals which would deprive members of the Church of England of any advantages they now had. He was against the compulsory measures involved in the Bill, which would invade privacy and enforce compliance by grievous and ruinous penalties. He objected to the separation of baptism and registration. The Bill would not give security against the violation of the marriage laws. Why should a poor man care whether a birth was registered? 'It was required to gratify the statistical fancies of some few philosophers, in order that they might know how many were born in a year. If they wished to obtain that information they ought to pay for it, and not make the poor man pay for it, with a penalty... The system of registration as now proposed could never be carried into effect in this country.'[52] Nevertheless he did not oppose the marriage and registration Bills going into Committee and they did so, emerging with large numbers of amendments. In the House of Commons there was criticism of these amendments. But Lord Russell, while agreeing with this criticism, since he felt that the amended Bills were poorer than the originals, urged that as the main principles had been preserved, the amendments should be accepted. It could then be seen how matters would work out in practice. And so the Bills were passed on 17 August 1836, to come into operation 1 March 1837, reflecting the habit of compromise supposed to be characteristic of the British.[53]

Civil registration was ensured, but was not made an indispensible preliminary to religious rites. In the case of marriage, where registers were signed in churches and chapels, the quality of the information recorded continued to depend heavily on the clergy; marriage statistics in England and Wales are still far less satisfactory than statistics of births and deaths.[54] The period allowed for the registration of a birth was rather long – up to forty-two days, as compared with five days for a death – and the responsibility for registering births and deaths fell primarily on the registrars.[55] So far as parents, relatives or other persons in attendance were concerned, their responsibility was to give information to the registrar 'upon being requested so to do'. And the information requested was rather limited. For marriages, for example, the socio-demographic information consisted of: age (and initially this need not be more specific than 'full age' or 'minor'); previous marital condition; rank or profession of groom, bride (often not given), groom's father and bride's father. Residence at the time of marriage had to be stated, but might be artificial, taken up temporarily for the purpose of the marriage. For births: sex and father's rank or profession. And for deaths: sex, age, rank or profession and, notably, cause of death; the recommendation of the medical profession had, after all, been implemented, though it is not clear whether as a result of the direct influence of that profession.[56]

Considered from the point of view of their contribution to population analysis, the two Acts were by no means epoch-making. They did less than had been done by the Swedish system introduced almost a century earlier, or might have been done if the 1753 Bill had become law. But the need for a better knowledge of population trends was only one element in the situation. And even in respect of that element it is curious that, in the midst of the Malthusian era, and with the new Poor Law only recently introduced, it was to mortality analysis rather than to fertility analysis that the civil registration system contributed.[57] Whether it would have been practicable to prescribe that more information be given at the registration of marriages, births and deaths cannot now be estimated. Certainly, the implementation of the new system did not take place without protests.[58] There were religious protests, based on the fear that parents would use birth registration as a substitute for baptism. To do so would endanger the salvation of children and reduce the income of the clergy. There were inevitably protests at the invasion of privacy. A case at the Leicester Quarter Sessions in 1839 attracted attention in *The Times*. The wife of a day labourer had refused to give the necessary information about her new born baby to the local registrar when he called on her, telling him to get it from the parish register. 'Surely', wrote *The Times* correspondent, 'our countrymen will not be found prepared to submit, whatever may be the statistical advantages of a universal register, without remonstrance to the provisions of an Act of Parliament, if they shall be found capable of being ratified to such an extent as this under the authority of a court of justice.' And the article quoted Wat Tyler as an example of what the natural feelings of Englishmen might prompt them to do 'under a tyranny leading to the violation of the decencies of domestic life...' But there were also prosecutions by way of example, and this wife was prosecuted and was found guilty, though the prosecution did not wish to press for punishment, but only to make the law known.[59] There were stories of incestuous marriages taking place under the new system. And there were complaints about some of the registrars. One in particular was the subject of a Parliamentary question, on the grounds that he was a socialist, a Vice-President of the Socialist Society, a professed Owenite, reported to have used his offices for socialist assemblies as well as for registration.[60] Nevertheless, the new system got under way reasonably well and was accepted quite rapidly.

The products of the new system – the statistics of marriages, births and deaths – were used with great effectiveness under the hand of William Farr, appointed in 1839 as Compiler of Abstracts.[61] Farr was one of the outstanding vital statisticians of the nineteenth century. Like John Graunt, the founder of demography, Farr applied an instructed imagination to what were still not fully adequate data. But Farr had at his disposal techniques of analysis which, though visible in rudimentary form in Graunt's work, had been greatly extended in the eighteenth century. Relatively modern life table techniques were, so to speak, lying in wait for the comprehensive statistics produced by civil registration.[62] And, of course, the inadequacies of those statistics were minute in comparison with the gross errors and gaps of the seventeenth-century Bills of Mortality. Moreover, with the support of the first two Registrars General, Lister and Graham,[63] Farr was able to develop mortality analysis and, especially with the early collaboration of the medical profession, the analysis of cause of mortality by occupation.[64] The individual observations of Ramazzini and the small-scale inquiries of Thackrah were transformed, under Farr's direction, into the classic occupational mortality analysis of the Supplement to the *Thirty-fifth Annual Report of the Registrar-General*[65] and led to the social class analysis of the mortality of infants, men and married women later developed by T. H. C. Stevenson.[66] Until very recently, few countries could show mortality analysis of comparable scope and quality.[67]

Developments were less satisfactory in respect of marriage and birth statistics. Marriage statistics suffered, as was pointed out earlier, because they remained largely in the hands of the clergy. In 1870, for example, 90 per cent of marriages involved religious ceremonies; even in 1967 the proportion was 66 per cent. Control of the clergy was far less effective than control of the registrars. The recording of occupations on the marriage certificate was poor – and still is so – and the proportions of unstated ages were 75 per cent in 1848, and 30 per cent in 1870.[68] Birth statistics were not very informative and the indices of fertility relatively unsophisticated: the crude birth rate, the general, legitimate and illegitimate fertility rates and the ratio of births to marriages.[69] Swedish data were more useful, as Farr knew. Whether there was resistance to the improvement of marriage and birth statistics is not clear, but there was certainly less interest in those statistics than in the data on mortality.[70] One valuable contribution was Farr's estimates of the completeness of birth registration. These suggested that even in the period 1841-50 birth registration was about 93 per cent complete: but the estimates also provided a justification for the 1874 Act, which transferred the onus of registration from the registrar to the parents, or occupier of the house, or other persons in attendance or having charge of the child.[71] It is possible, too, that this Act benefited from Scottish experience, for the 1854 Act, which provided for civil registration in Scotland, defined the responsibility for registering births and deaths in terms comparable to those later adopted in England and Wales. After 1874 no major legislative change occurred until 1938,[72] though there were administrative changes of importance as well as census improvements which contributed directly to the study of fertility and which made possible a still more ample use of registration statistics. By 1938 the situation had changed and interest had shifted to fertility – to the long-period decline in the birth rate and to the apparent threat of a falling population in the near future. It was this interest which made possible the 1938 Population (Statistics) Act,[73] which very greatly extended the range of information demanded for statistical purposes – not to be recorded on the birth certificate – at birth registration. Taking into account subsequent modifications, consolidated in the 1960 Population (Statistics) Act,[74] birth registration now provides almost as much information as was specified for Scotland by the 1854 Act, while changes in the information required at death registration allow the construction of population estimates in the greater detail needed for calculating a wide range of far more meaningful fertility rates.[75]

Civil registration in Scotland came later than in England and Wales and under somewhat different auspices. Parish registration was reported to be much poorer in Scotland than in England and Wales. In the debates which led to the 1854 Act, introducing civil vital registration in Scotland, Lord Elcho reported estimates that, in 1850, probably only about 30 per cent of births and deaths had been registered. James Stark, from whom the estimates derived, had in fact written that since 1794, when the tax on registration was repealed, 'not a third of the births over Scotland have been entered on the parochial registers'.[76] The question had been discussed by the General Assembly of the Church in 1816, and from 1847 onwards several Bills were introduced, though without success.[77] But the pressure for change was increasing. The General Assembly, in 1853, asked for a comprehensive system of vital registration, and there was a memorial during the same year from the Lord Provost, magistrates and town council of Edinburgh. There were also petitions from the Royal College of Surgeons of Edinburgh and from the managers of the Life Assurance Offices of Scotland. Finally, Lord Elcho brought in a comprehensive Bill, strongly influenced by the continental registration system which had been set up under the *Code Napoléon*.[78] The Bill was passed, to come into operation 1 January 1855, and provided for registration of births within twenty-one days and registration of deaths within eight days. Marriage statistics were covered more satisfactorily than in England by prescribing that a comprehensive schedule had to be completed either in advance of the marriage or in the presence of the Minister and that the completed schedule had to be delivered within three days to the registrar for the parish concerned. In addition, both at death registration and at the registration of births, the information to be supplied was much more extensive than was required in England and Wales – so extensive, indeed, that it was collected for only one year.[79] The collection proved far too laborious for the existing arrangements, and in 1856 the scope was narrowed so that the questions asked were similar to those in England and Wales.[80] Even the data collected in 1855 were not fully analysed until much later, and not by the Registrar General. Matthews Duncan used the material on births for Edinburgh and Glasgow for his study of fertility; while in the early twentieth century Lewis and Lewis tabulated the birth information for the country as a whole.[81] It was through the Population (Statistics) Act of 1938 that the range of registration data was again expanded, though it was still not quite as wide as had been prescribed in 1854.[82]

NOTES

1 J. S. Burn, *History of the Fleet Marriages*, London 1834.

2 According to J. S. Burn, *The History of Parish Registers in England*, 2nd edn, London 1862, pp.35 & 217. There appears to have been some variation in the way the 1783 Act was interpreted locally and hence in the effect of the Act on registration. Mr R. E. Jones, who has analysed a large number of parish registers for Shropshire, has found no evidence in them of deterioration in registration following the Act.

3 *The History of Parish Registers*, p.35.

4 The summary for England and Wales is given in the *Parish Register Abstract*, London 1833, p.486.

5 The 1835 Bill concerned the marriages of Dissenters and was introduced by Sir Robert Peel. See *Hansard*, 3rd series, Vol.31, 1836, col.381.

6 See W. L. Mathieson, *England in Transition 1789-1932*, London 1920, ch.5, and B. L. Manning, *The Protestant Dissenting Deputies*, Cambridge 1952, Part 3, chs.1 & 2.

7 *Hansard*, 3rd series Vol.16, 28 March 1833, cols.1209-1222. Judging from the report, John Wilks appeared to be the dominant member of the committee.

8 Thomas Short was another doctor who made use of vital statistics and collected them for a number of parishes (see T. Short, *New Observations... on City, Town and Country Bills of Mortality*, London 1750).

9 See G. Miller, *The Adoption of Inoculation for Smallpox in England and France*, Philadelphia 1957. References to studies in Colonial America are given in J. H. Cassedy, *Demography in Early America*, Cambridge, Mass., 1969, esp. pp.132-147. See also N. M. Karn in *Annals of Eugenics*, 1931, pp.279ff. The effect of inoculation

in England is examined in detail by P. E. Razzell, 'Population change in Eighteenth-Century England', *Economic History Review*, Vol.18, No.2, August 1965. He believes that inoculation contributed very powerfully to the decline in mortality; I find the case 'not proven'. In estimating the effect of inoculation in the eighteenth century, some difficult questions have to be answered; and it is unlikely that the poor statistics of the eighteenth century would enable them to be answered.

10 See R. Watt, *Treatise on Chincough, with Inquiry into the Relative Mortality of the Diseases of Children in Glasgow*, Glasgow 1813. Watt believed that smallpox had been replaced by measles and that infant and early childhood mortality in total had remained unchanged. But Roberton pointed out, correctly, that Watt was drawing his conclusion from the numbers of deaths and not from the mortality rates. The level of mortality had fallen; with the elimination of smallpox, the proportionate contribution of measles was bound to rise; especially as measles attacks tended to be at somewhat higher ages than smallpox. See J. Roberton, *Observations on the Mortality and Physical Management of Children*, London 1827, Sections 5 & 6; also the review of Roberton's book in *Edinburgh Medical and Surgical Journal*, Vol.29, 1828, pp.373-385.

11 *Observations on the Increase and Decrease of Diseases*, London 1801. Heberden assumed that 'griping in the guts' was dysentery and did not notice that the apparent diminution in deaths from this cause really involved their transfer to 'convulsions', which Creighton reasonably equated with infantile diarrhoea, a major factor in infant mortality, especially in the summer. For Creighton's comments, see C. Creighton, *A History of Epidemics in Britain*, reprinted London 1965, Vol.2, pp.747-758.

12 W. Woolcombe, *The Frequency and Fatality of Different Diseases, particularly on the Progressive Increase of Consumption...*, London 1808.

13 F. Bisset Hawkins, *Elements of Medical Statistics*, London 1829 (his book was based on the Gulstonian lectures which he gave at the Royal College of Physicians) C. T. Thackrah, *The Effects of Arts, Trades, and Professions, and of Civic Status, and Habits of Living, on Health and Longevity*, London 1832 (reprinted, ed. A. Meiklejohn, Edinburgh & London 1957). On the general subject of quantification in medicine, see G. Rosen, 'Problems in the application of statistical analysis to questions of health: 1700-1880', *Bull. Hist. Med.*, 1955, 29, pp.27-45.

14 See *British Medical Almanack*, 1837, pp.13-139. In essence, Edmonds 'rediscovered' Gompertz, though he did not regard his work in that light.

15 L. H. Villermé, *London Medical Gazette*, Vol.15, 1835, pp.804-808; F. Corbaux, *loc. cit.*, Vol.15, 1835, pp.735-736. Like Edmonds, Corbaux also put forward various 'laws' of population. See his book, *On the Natural and Mathematical Laws concerning Population, Vitality, and Mortality*, London 1833.

16 George Man Burrows, 'On the uses and defects of Parish Registers and Bills of Mortality, with the outlines of a plan for rendering them of greater public utility', *The London Medical Repository*, 1 October 1818, pp.265-294. The pamphlet was entitled: *Strictures on the Uses and Defects of Parish Registers and Bills of Mortality... with Suggestions for Improving and Extending the System of Parochial Registration*, London 1818.

17 On Graunt, see my paper, 'John Graunt and his *Natural and Political Observations*', *Proc. Royal Society*, Series B, Vol.159, No.974, 10 December 1963.

18 F. Hendriks, 'De Witt and actuarial science in Holland', *Journal of the Institute of Actuaries*, Vol.34, January 1899, p.387.

19 Société Néerlandaise d'Assurances sur la Vie et des Rentes Viagères, *Mémoires pour Servir à l'Histoire des Assurances sur la Vie et des Rentes Viagères aux Pays-Bas*, Amsterdam 1898, pp.77-81.

20 For Halley's 1693 life table, see the modern reprint, E. Halley, *Degrees of Mortality of Mankind* (ed. L. J. Reed), Baltimore 1942. Halley's technique is discussed by R. Böckh, 'Halley als Statistiker', *Bulletin de l'Institut International de Statistique*, Vol.7, 1893; the source of his data is examined in J. Graetzer, *Edmund Halley und Caspar Neumann*, Breslau 1883.

21 A. de Moivre, *Annuities upon Lives*, London 1725. De Moivre's 'law' was that, from the age of thirty, the probabilities of surviving decrease in arithmetical progression: 'the decrements of life considered from the Term of Thirty, are constantly equal' (p.10). A modern Swedish actuary regards De Moivre's 'law' as not a bad measure of the mortality of the times (K.-G. Hagstroem, *The Swedish Actuarial Society: Fifty Years*, Stockholm 1954, p.20). De Moivre may have been the originator of the term, 'expectation of life' (see G. M. Low 'The history of actuarial science in Great Britain', *Troisième Congrès International d'Actuaires*, Paris 1901, p.851).

22 J. G. Anderson, *The Birthplace and Genesis of Life Assurance*, London 1937, pp.38ff.

23 M. E. Ogborn, 'The actuary in the eighteenth century', *Proceedings of the Centenary Assembly of the Institute of Actuaries*, London 1950, Vol.3, pp.357-383; and idem., *Equitable Assurances*, London 1962, pp.48ff.

24 *A letter from the Rev. Dr. Webster, of Edinburgh, to the Rev. Dr. Price, of London, and Dr. Price's Answer*, Edinburgh 1771. Details of the Scottish scheme are given in [Anon.], *An Account of the Rise and Nature of the Fund Established by Parliament, for a Provision for the Widows and Children of the Ministers of Church, and of the Heads, Principals and Masters in the Universities, of Scotland*, Published by Order of the Trustees, Edinburgh 1759. Price's influence extended abroad. In France, for example, when the *Compagnie Royale d'Assurances* was authorized by the King in 1787, it appointed Duvillard as its mathematician and claimed in its prospectus that it had followed Price's recommendation in attaching a mathematician to its administration (see A. Quiquet, 'Notes pour une histoire de l'actuariat en France', *Troisième Congrès International d'Actuaires*, p.997).

25 There were earlier schemes for raising new funds – annuities and tontines. But the 1808 scheme was in keeping with Pitt's sinking fund idea for redeeming perpetual governmental indebtedness through conversion into terminable annuities.

26 F. Hendriks, 'On the financial statistics of British Government life annuities (1808-1855), and on the loss sustained by government in granting annuities', *J.R.S.S.*, Vol.19, December 1856, pp.325-384, esp. pp.331, 337, 343 & 345. Kersseboom's tables will be found in W. Kersseboom, *Essais d'Arithmétique Politique*, Paris 1970. For Deparcieux's tables, see A. Deparcieux, *Essai sur la Probabilité de la Durée de la Vie Humaine...*, Paris 1746. An article quoted at length from a letter from John Finlaison to Herries, 30 April 1827, reporting on the losses incurred by the Government's annuity scheme (*Westminster Review*, Vol.IX, April 1828, article 5, p.406: in his discussions with B. W. Richardson, *The Health of Nations*,

London 1887, Vol.1, p.xxvii, Chadwick acknowledged the authorship of this article in the Benthamite journal).

27 In essence, Price assumed that the excess of burials over christenings in some years was attributable to immigration into Northampton of persons twenty years of age, and that in fact the numbers of indigenous christenings and burials could be regarded as equal. Hence Price subtracted from the burials a number which he assumed would represent the deaths of immigrants. But the population of Northampton was increasing, and an excess of burials over christenings was more probably the result of differential omissions in the registering of births and deaths.

28 W. Sutton ('On the method used by Dr. Price in the construction of the Northampton mortality table', *J.I.A.*, Vol.18, January 1874, pp.107-122) suggests that 'it seems by no means improbable that the success of that Society [the Equitable] was one of the reasons which led the Government, in the Life Annuity Scheme passed in 1808, to make the Northampton Table the basis of the annuity rates, entirely ignoring the fact that what is profitable to the buyer of annuities will be unprofitable to the seller. No doubt Dr. Price's acknowledged ability and reputation carried great weight with Mr. Pitt's Government, but Dr. Price had been dead some 17 years, and it is by no means unlikely that could he have been consulted, he would have advised against the adoption of the Northampton Tables' (p.108). The evidence does not give much support to this latter hypothesis. What is, however, clear is that some of the officials associated with Friendly Societies in the 1820s did not seem to understand the basis of the Northampton tables, and that several of the actuaries who appeared before the Select Committees on Friendly Societies made statements of very doubtful validity. The petition of Cadogan Williams resulted in the appointment of a Select Committee. See *Report from the Select Committee on Life Annuities*, London 1829. In his evidence to the committee, John Finlaison, actuary to the National Debt Office, referred to the overstatement of mortality by the Northampton tables (*Report*, pp.29-30).

29 London 1849.

30 *Twelfth Annual Report of the Registrar-General* (for 1849), London 1853, p.v. (Appendix).

W. Sutton (*op. cit.*, pp.113-114) showed that the results in Price's second Northampton table (which was *the* Northampton table) could be reproduced almost exactly by assuming that Price attributed 13 per cent of the deaths in the period 1735-80 to immigrants who entered Northampton at the age of twenty years. But even if this assumption had been correct, the exclusion of the deaths would not have resulted in a realistic life table.

31 *Report from the Select Committee on the Laws Respecting Friendly Societies*, London 1825, pp.6, 7, 12 & 16-18.

32 *Report from the Select Committee on the Laws Respecting Friendly Societies*, London 1827, pp.4, 8 & 11. The reference to 'the number of children born' is in relation to the question of maternity benefits. The 1825 report had been concerned with this question and had contained data – collected by Dr A. B. Granville and analysed by John Finlaison – on the reproductive histories of 876 'poor married women delivered in their own houses' in London, by the 'charitable assistance of the Benevolent Lying-in Institution and the Westminster General Dispensary'. See *Report*, pp.134-135.

33 Finlaison himself did not escape censure. The annuities based upon his tables were used for speculation by purchasers who appointed nominees and could thus choose selected lives. According to Rickman, Finlaison had urged that the annuities should not be given beyond the age of sixty-five, save where they were for the personal benefit of the nominees, but that this was not done until later. So 'physicians were dispatched to supposed healthy counties, at no small expense, to form opinions of preferable old men (or old women) on whose lives annuities might most hopefully be purchased'. (J. Rickman, *London Medical Gazette*, Vol.16, 1835, pp.592-593). Hendriks ('On the financial statistics', p.351) agreed that there had been much speculation (with profit to the speculators and loss to the government) on 'selected lives, generally in the humbler ranks of life, and resident in healthy agricultural and Highland districts, or belonging to families whose hereditary longevity is beyond the average. Such nominees have usually received a fraction of the annuity, to keep alive their beneficial interest and to preserve them in a better condition to sustain a prolonged vitality.' The nominees selected were 'particularly at advanced ages, at which the correctness of the Government tables is very doubtful. . .' According to John Francis (*Annals, Anecdotes and Legends : a Chronicle of Life Assurance*, London 1853, pp.206-212), a payment of £100 for a man of ninety would yield an annuity of £62 per year; if the nominee lived fifteen months, the purchase money would have been paid back and the payments thereafter would be pure profit. 'The desire to speculate on nonagenarian lives soon became a mania. Barristers with a few thousands pounds, – ladies with a small capital, – noblemen with cash at their bankers, availed themselves of the mistake. It is difficult to say to what extent it would have proceeded, had not Mr. Goulborn availed himself of a clause in the act, to cease granting annuities which might prove unfavourable to government' (p.212). But the only statistical analysis I have seen is in a note contributed by W. T. Thomson, an Edinburgh actuary, to *The Assurance Magazine*, 1851, pp.29-31*, based on a small number of lives selected at ages seventy-five to eighty-one. The analysis suggests that the recorded average duration of life up to age eighty-seven was higher than that indicated by either the Government tables or that derived from the experience tables of seventeen life assurance companies, computed in 1843.

34 *Report of John Finlaison, Actuary of the National Debt, on the Evidence and Elementary Facts on which the Tables of Life Annuities are Founded*, pp.8 & 9 (appended to *Report of the Select Committee on Life Annuities*, London 1829).

35 Dr J. T. Krause told me several years ago, that he found some – though not many – vital events relating to Dissenters not included in Heysham's counts. Both Heysham's and Rickman's returns of baptisms and burials are summarized in Milne, *op. cit.*, Vol.2, p.409. A comparison yields the following ratios of Heysham's totals to Rickman's:

	Baptisms	Burials
17 years ending 1796	1·23	1·02
31 years ending 1810	–	1·03

Heysham himself drew attention to the fact that in his earlier Bills the statistics of christenings excluded a number of Dissenters (see the 1779 Bill, Table 6a) as well as private baptisms (see the 1780 Bill, Table 3). But from 1781 onwards, he believed, the coverage was much better – Dissenters being shown separately from 1782.

36 But Milne's questions were concerned mainly with matters other than – or subsequent to – the life table for the period 1780-87. The Carlisle table was essentially based upon the data published in 'An Abridgment of Observations on the Bills of Mortality in Carlisle, from the year 1779, to the year 1787, inclusive' (see W. Hutchinson, *The History and Antiquities of the City of Carlisle and its Vicinity*, Carlisle 1796, pp.85ff.), the statistics of deaths and population being graduated separately by a graphical technique. (On this technique, see G. King, 'On the method used by Milne in the construction of the Carlisle table of mortality', *Journal of the Institute of Actuaries*, October 1883, pp.186-211.) Although the table was realistic, in the sense that deaths were related to population in the corresponding age-groups, it is unlikely that the results give a 'true' picture of mortality in Carlisle. It is possible that infant and early childhood mortality was overestimated, for at ages under five the rates were calculated by relating deaths to the enumerated population, without allowance for the under-enumeration usually found at those ages. (Modern life tables usually relate infant deaths – under one year – to live births in the appropriate period.) As against this, it is of course possible that deaths were under-registered; infants dying in the first few days of life may have been omitted from the returns of deaths and of births. Nevertheless, the Carlisle table was certainly better than any other life table available for England at the time. On the correspondence between Heysham and Milne, see H. Lonsdale, *The Life of John Heysham, M.D.*, London 1870, and J. Milne, *op. cit.*, Vol.2, ch.11.

37 The Heysham manuscripts contain the returns by sections of the city for the first survey, giving age and (though not in combination) sex and marital status. There are no returns in that detail for the second survey among the manuscripts.

38 Professor Kruskal drew my attention to the rounding of the total increase and to the constancy of the age structure.

39 Farr referred to the imperfect graduation – *Twelfth Annual Report of the Registrar-General*, p.iii. Edmonds believed that Milne had overstated mortality in the first five years of life and that he had subsequently in part admitted this error – *The Lancet*, 1835-36, Vol.1, p.694.

40 For example: in *The Westminster Review*, Vol.9, April 1828, pp.384-421, reviewing publications on Friendly Societies and William Morgan's account of the Equitable Society; in *The Edinburgh Review*, No.97, March 1829, pp.1-34, ostensibly reviewing an anonymous pamphlet (*Proposals for an Improved Census of the Population*, London 1829, of which I have been unable to find any copy); and in *The Quarterly Review*, Vol.LIII, February 1835, pp.56-78, reviewing British and Irish reports on the 1831 censuses and L. R. Villermé's study of the population of Great Britain. The article in *The Edinburgh Review* gave a short but informative account of the second stage of the eighteenth-century population controversy and also commented on the value of a 'generation' life table – if it could be constructed – arrived at by following a representative and large number of children from birth to death (pp.11 & 12).

41 The section established a committee, with Babbage as chairman and Drinkwater as secretary – both of whom were interested in the provision of accurate data on mortality (*Report of the Third Meeting of the British Association*, London 1834, p.483). The Statistical Society of London (later to become the Royal Statistical Society)

was founded in 1834 as a result of that meeting. At the 1834 meeting of the British Association, the committee of the medical section set up two sub-committees, one in London and the other in Edinburgh, to 'communicate with' the statistical section or with the new Statistical Society 'relative to a registration of deaths, comprising particulars of a medical nature, with the view that if any legislative measure should hereafter be adopted as to registration, such suggestions may be offered by the Association as may seem best fitted to attain the requisite information for this desirable object' (*Report of the Fourth Meeting of the British Association*, London 1835, p.xxxix). Bisset Hawkins was a member of one of the sub-committees. The resolution concerning the appointment of these sub-committees was repeated in 1835 – *Report of the Fifth Meeting*, London 1836, p.xxxii, which volume also contained a report by the Edinburgh sub-committee (pp.251-255) recommending the inclusion of cause of death at death registration.

42 *Report*, p.9.

43 *Ibid.*, p.101.

44 *Ibid.*, p.51. But he thought that, with effective registration, the expense of a census would be diminished, if not almost superseded.

45 *Ibid.*, pp.59-63. He believed that, after an 'improved registry had been kept a considerable number of years, the population could be determined with accuracy from the results presented by the register, far better than by any census'.

46 *Ibid.*, p.174. The Provincial Medical and Surgical Association held its first annual meeting in Worcester in 1832 and its second in Bristol in 1833. After the establishment of various branches, the Association changed its name in 1856 to the British Medical Association (there had previously been an Association under that name, and William Farr had been a member of its council; but the activity had ceased by about 1846). In 1833 the Provincial Association had 316 members on its roll of whom some 250 attended the Bristol meeting. From the start, members were interested in medical topography and effective vital registration; indeed, there was strong pressure for the registration of disease as well as of deaths. (See E. M. Little, *History of the British Medical Association 1832-1932*, London n.d. [1932], esp. pp.16-30 & 119-122.)

47 Quetelet played a very important part in the international development of statistics and, in agreement with Farr and Babbage, helped to initiate the series of international statistical congresses, the first of which was held in Brussels in 1853. He, too, was concerned with the formulation of statistical 'laws', especially in relation to social phenomena, but they were not the kind of 'laws' or 'theories' in which sociologists (or other social scientists) are now primarily interested; and Sarton's claim that Quetelet, rather than Comte, should be regarded as the founder of sociology is not well argued. It is true, however, that Quetelet's main social science contribution – *Sur l'Homme et le Développement de ses Facultés ou Essai de Physique Sociale*, 2 vols, Paris 1835 – created a great deal of interest, as well as much controversy. It was soon published in various translations – the English translation in 1842 was one of the numerous didactic publications issued by William and Robert Chambers. A copy of the second edition, presented by Quetelet to Florence Nightingale and extensively marked up by her, carries on the title page the expression of her belief in 'the sense of infinite power – the assurances of solid certainty – the endless vista of improvement – from the principles of Physique Sociale if only

found possible to apply on occasions when it is so much wanted'. See G. Sarton, Preface to *Isis*, Vol.23, 1935.

48 *Report*, pp.119-122.

49 *Ibid.*, pp.8-11.

50 Less comprehensive Bills were introduced after the report of the Select Committee, but were not passed. See *Westminster Review*, Vol.XXI, July 1834, article 14, pp.214-220. The 1836 Bills were attacked in *Blackwood's Edinburgh Magazine*, May 1836, Vol.XL, pp.601-606. Sir Robert Peel's Bill was introduced in the Commons in March 1835 and in May was handed over to the new government. In June, however, Lord John Russell explained that he would not proceed further with the Bill, because the Dissenters wanted substantial amendments. John Wilks called for national civil registration – in accordance with the recommendations of the Select Committee on Parochial Registration – and Russell replied that this would be proposed during the next session.

51 *Hansard*, 3rd series, Vol.31, 1836, cols.367-380.

52 *Ibid.*, 11 July 1836, cols. 82-89.

53 *Ibid.*, 11 August 1836, cols.1121-1125.

54 'An Act for Marriages in England', 6 & 7 William IV, c.85; 'An Act for registering Births, Deaths and Marriages in England', 6 & 7 William IV, c.86. *Acts*, William IV, Vol.28.

55 An Amending Act in 1837 (1 Victoria c.22) imposed a penalty of £10 on all persons not transmitting certified copies of registers of births, deaths and marriages, as required by the 1836 Acts.

56 The inclusion of cause of death in death registration is usually attributed to the intervention of Edwin Chadwick, and is so stated in the publication of the General Register Office, *Registration and Vital Statistics in England and Wales*, London, revised 1969, p.3. The evidence, however, consists of material written after the event and is not completely clear-cut. The most consistent account is that given by B. W. Richardson, based upon discussion with Chadwick, possibly long after the event. According to Richardson (*op. cit.*, pp.xliv-xlv), 'in his anxiety to get a clause into the new Act for certifying causes of mortality, Mr. Chadwick applied to Lord John Russell, who, of the leading politicians of the time, was most impressed with his labours. For some reason, probably from preoccupation, Lord John could not in this instance be roused to exertion. He could not, to use Mr. Chadwick's words, "be got to take hold of the idea." In this strait, Mr. Chadwick wrote to Lord Lyndhurst, who soon became deeply interested in the project, and not only introduced it into the Bill in the Lords, but carried it through the Upper House with so much success that it passed the lower house with easy transit.' It has not so far been possible to find any relevant correspondence with Lord Lyndhurst in the Chadwick Collection (at University College London), while Chadwick's long letter to Russell (3 July 1836) was concerned primarily with the appointment of registrars and with Chadwick's strong desire to prevent the appointments from being in the hands of the Boards of Guardians. The sole reference to the technical aspect of the new system relates to the role of the Registrar General, who, 'presuming always that he is a competent person who as an actuary or otherwise is conversant with getting sound returns should be made mainly responsible...' (f.16 & 17). (The letter was written some two weeks before the cause of death amendment was

proposed in the House of Lords committee – 21 July 1836 – when it was also accepted. On 28 July the Lords approved the amended Bill but added some further amendments. The revised Bill was then returned to the Lords and accepted on 12 August.) As for the 'easy transit' in the Commons, Russell had urged that, although he did not agree with all the amendments, it would be better to accept them and get the Bill passed.

Dr Michael Cullen, who has examined the development of a statistical approach to the study of social problems in Britain, with particular reference to the period 1830-1850, has kindly allowed me to read the chapter in which he discusses in detail the origins and passage of the 1836 Acts. He deals with the other references usually cited in support of Chadwick's claim – namely Chadwick's draft letter to Lord Ellenborough and Ellenborough's letter to Chadwick, both dated 27 October 1841, and Chadwick's letter to Dr T. Laycock, dated 13 April 1844. There is at least a confusion over names – perhaps a failing memory converted Ellenborough into Lyndhurst when the information was given to Richardson. Unfortunately, the Ellenborough-Chadwick correspondence could not be found in the Chadwick collection at the time of writing – the collection is being catalogued and some of the documents may well have been displaced. But the Chadwick-Laycock letter is completely explicit. Chadwick wrote: 'When the registration was proposed as a boon to the dissenters I objected that it should be put on a [widely?] different footing. I got the "causes of death" inserted in spite of the manager of the bill or rather Lord Ellenborough adopted the suggestion' (Copybook III, letter 19, Chadwick to Laycock).

This would appear to settle the argument. But there is another claimant to the responsibility for the cause of death column, namely F. Bisset Hawkins. His claim was urged by William Munk (*The Roll of the Royal College of Physicians*, 2nd edn, London 1878, Vol.3, p.303). Bisset Hawkins, whose work was referred to earlier, was Professor of Materia Medica at King's College (he resigned his chair in 1835) and also, in 1833, Factory Commissioner and later Inspector of Prisons and Metropolitan Commissioner in lunacy. Munk wrote: '. . .Dr. Bisset Hawkins was instrumental in obtaining the insertion of a column containing the names of the diseases or causes by which death was occasioned.' I have not come across any supporting evidence, though it is true – as was noted earlier – that Bisset Hawkins was a member of the Edinburgh sub-committee (of the Medical section of the British Association) which recommended that insertion.

As for the substantive question of the reporting of the cause of death, this was one of the items mutilated by House of Lords amendments, which allowed burial without a certificate from the Registrar or an order from the Coroner. Moreover, no provision was made for certification of the cause of death (this was prescribed by the 1874 amending Act). However, the successful appeal to the medical profession by the Registrar General undoubtedly helped to overcome this defect. The interest of the profession is shown by the fact that, out of 2193 Registrars appointed up to 30 September 1838, 527 were medical men. But the numbers then fell off, and by 1917, according to the then Registrar General, had practically reached vanishing point (see B. Mallet, 'The organization of vital registration and its bearing on vital statistics', *J.R.S.S.*, Vol.80, Part 1, January 1917).

57 In addition, data on the probability of marriage and on the frequency of births

of various parities were relevant to the evaluations of the level of subscriptions to Friendly Societies, and were discussed by the Select Committees concerned with these societies.

58 Reactions to the new system are referred to by S. E. Finer, *The Life and Times of Sir Edwin Chadwick*, London 1952, p.125, and also in the *First Annual Report of the Registrar-General*, London 1839, pp.21-22. However, estimates of the extent of under-registration in even the early years of the new system make it clear that, in spite of some adverse reactions, civil vital registration soon became far more effective than parochial registration had been. See Appendix 4 to the present chapter.

59 *The Times*, 7 January 1839.

60 *The Times*, 25 January & 7 February 1840. The registrar, Mr Pare, was defended by the Marquis of Normanby but subsequently resigned his appointment.

61 N. A. Humphreys (ed.), *Vital Statistics*, London 1885, pp.vii-xxiv. See also M. Greenwood, *Some British Pioneers of Social Medicine*, London 1948, chs.6 & 7. Generally on the development of medical and vital statistics, see M. Greenwood, *Medical Statistics from Graunt to Farr*, Cambridge 1948.

62 There was, understandably, criticism of Farr's initial life tables. Alexander Finlaison drew attention to the mis-statements of age in the 1841 and 1851 censuses – reported by Farr himself – and at death registration, and also to the fact that whereas the census included men in the armed forces and the merchant marine, their deaths were only covered by registration if they died at home. All this was true. But even allowing for these errors, Farr's tables were the best early *national* tables – the first national tables based upon *relatively* reliable population and vital statistics. Finlaison, of course, was not really interested in overall national life tables, but in tables for those sections relevant to tontines and annuities. He would have wanted separate tables for the 'wealthy, middling, and the indigent' classes. For his purposes he preferred to use tables derived from the experience of government annuitants. See *Copy 'Of the Report and Observations of Mr. Alexander Finlaison, Actuary of the Commissioners for the Reduction of the National Debt, relating to Tontines and Life Annuities, and to the Duration of Life among Nominees'*, House of Commons, 25 August 1960, pp.50-59.

63 T. H. Lister was the brother-in-law of Lord John Russell. Farr's appointment was attributed by Humphreys (*op. cit.*, p.xii) to the physician, Sir James Clarke, whose book on consumption Farr had helped to revise. But according to B. W. Richardson (*op. cit.*, p.xlv), Farr's name was suggested by Chadwick, who had also proposed Babbage for the post of Registrar General. According to Chadwick (in his letter to Laycock, 13 April 1844), Farr's name had been suggested by Dr Arnott as 'the only medical man whom he knew as having paid attention to vital statistics...' The relationship between Farr and Chadwick was not, however, an easy one. Farr took an independent view and Chadwick resented some of his actions. Two relevant letters are printed in full in Appendix 1 as throwing some light on the attitudes of two of the most important figures in the public health movement in nineteenth-century Britain.

64 It is clear that the resolution sent to the Select Committee on Parochial Registration by the Provincial Medical and Surgical Association reflected the general interest of the medical profession in cause mortality analysis. After the passage of the 1836 Act the Registrar General was able to obtain the immediate and full

support of the leaders of the profession. In May 1837 they (the Presidents of the Royal College of Physicians and the Royal College of Surgeons and the Master of the Society of Apothecaries) issued a circular which stated '. . .having authority from the several bodies whom we represent, [we] do resolve to fulfil the intentions of the Legislature in procuring a better Registration of the causes of Death, being convinced that such an improved Registration cannot fail to lead to a more accurate statistical account of the prevalence of particular diseases from time to time' (*First Annual Report of the Registrar-General of Births, Deaths, and Marriages in England*, London 1839, pp.77-78; see also pp.86ff. for Farr's first analyses of cause mortality).

65 London 1875.

66 See *Seventy-Fourth Annual Report of the Registrar-General* (for 1911), London 1913. The analysis of the mortality of married women by the socio-economic status of their husbands was undertaken in connection with the 1931 census.

67 One very important change, an administrative one, involved the 'transfer' of births and deaths to place of usual residence. This change, which occurred in 1911, was essential for the study of local variations in fertility and mortality (see *Seventy-Fourth Annual Report of the Registrar-General* (for 1911), London 1913, p.viii).

68 In large numbers of the marriage entries only 'full age', 'minor' or 'under age' were recorded.

69 The crude birth rate was 'invented' by Gregory King at the end of the seventeenth century, and the ratio of births to marriages by John Graunt.

70 The situation might perhaps have been different if Farr had become Registrar General. But in spite of his international reputation, this was not to be. He retired in 1880 when he was not appointed to the vacant post of Registrar General. Nevertheless, it would be untrue to conclude that his services were entirely unrecognized by the government. He was Assistant Commissioner at the censuses of 1851, 1861 and 1871 and his salary in 1874 was £1100 per year, exceeded only by the Registrar General's at £1200. The point is that, in characteristic English tradition (Scottish tradition has been less rigid), the Registrar General has always been a lay administrator. In spite of the recommendation of the Royal Commission on Population, there was no move to change the tradition. It should also not be forgotten that Farr must have been given full and positive support by the Registrars General under whom he served, though this evidently did not compensate for his failure to achieve the top public position in his field.

Apart from the discussion by the Statistics Committee of the Royal Commission on Population (*Reports and Selected Papers of the Statistics Committee*, Papers of the Royal Commission on Population, Vol.2, London 1950, pp.21-25), the structure of the General Register Office seems rarely to have been considered by official bodies. The only nineteenth-century report I have found is that of a Treasury Committee in 1855 (*Report on the General Register Office*, London 20 July 1855). The report gives a succinct statement of the functions of the General Register Office, namely: 'The primary object of the Department is to record all the Births, Deaths, and Marriages in England and Wales, without distinction of class or religious persuasion, in order to furnish the means of tracing the descent of property, of calculating the expectation of life and the laws of mortality, and of ascertaining the state of disease and the operation of moral and physical causes on the health of the people and the progress of population' (*Report*, p.1.). But there is no discussion of how those functions might best be carried out.

Somewhat later (about 1872), Farr produced a statement of the duties of the Statistical Superintendent. Since, as far as I know, this was not published, it is worth recording here. It is given in Appendix 2 to this chapter.

71 'An Act to amend the Laws, relating to the Registration of Births and Deaths in England...' 37 & 38 Vict. c.88. Similar conditions applied to death registration. Between the 1840s and the 1870s there was considerable discussion of the merits and defects of civil registration. For some references to this discussion, see H. W. Rumsey, *Essays and Papers on Some Fallacies of Statistics concerning Life and Death, Health and Disease*, London 1875. The growth of the public health movement accounts in part for this discussion; and public health provisions not infrequently were made in advance of the development of statistics which might have helped to evaluate their effect.

72 An Act of 1926 provided for the registration of stillbirths – an example of the delay referred to in note 71 (see Births and Deaths Registration Act, 1926, 16 & 17, Geo. 5, c.48).

73 1 & 2 Geo. 6, c.12. On the background of this Act, passed explicitly to provide data needed for the study of fertility trends, see Appendix 3.

74 8 & 9 Eliz. 2, c.32.

75 At birth registration the information covers ages of father and mother, occupation and place of birth of father, place of birth of mother, date of marriage, whether mother married more than once, number of live born and stillborn (separately) children borne by mother. At death registration, marital condition and, if married, date of birth of surviving spouse are required. Before the 1938 Acts the vital events covered were events registered rather than events which had occurred in a specified period; for births, for which the registration period was long and might in practice vary considerably over time, this caused some difficulties of interpretation. (Marriages are registered immediately after they have taken place, and the delay in registering deaths is usually only two or three days. See General Register Office, *Registration and Vital Statistics in England and Wales*, revised edn, London 1969, pp.18-19.) The scope of fertility indices now published includes: age-specific total, legitimate and illegitimate fertility rates; age-at-marriage and duration-specific marital fertility rates by calendar year of marriage; marital fertility by numbers of children ever born. But information on birth intervals is not available and is a serious gap, especially as, given the permeation of the society by birth-control practice, the timing of births may change rapidly in response to changes in economic circumstances.

76 James Stark, 'Contribution to the vital statistics of Scotland', *Journal of the Statistical Society of London*, Vol.14, March 1851, p.48. Accounts of the defects of parochial registration in Scotland are also given in G. Seton, *Sketch of the History and Imperfect Condition of the Parochial Records of Births, Deaths and Marriages in Scotland*, Edinburgh & London 1854. Many years later Bisset-Smith, Registration Examiner, reviewed the material for a few areas and argued that about 46 per cent of births were recorded before the introduction of compulsory registration, the proportion falling in the later years towards 1850 (see G. T. Bisset-Smith, 'A statistical note on birth registration in Scotland previous to 1855; suggested by inquiries as to veri-

fication of birth for old age pensions', *J.R.S.S.*, Vol.72, September 1909, pp.621-622).

77 See Seton, *op. cit.*, pp.102-112. One bill – Lord Rutherfurd's Bill of 1847 – was discussed in detail by a committee of the London Statistical Society (see *Journal of the Statistical Society of London*, Vol.11, August 1848, pp.282-287).

78 *Hansard*, 3rd series, Vol.132, 6 April 1854, cols.569-578. For a discussion and criticism of an earlier Bill, see *Blackwood's Edinburgh Magazine*, Vol.66, September 1849, pp.263-276.

79 Thus at death registration the questions included: where born and how long in this district; occupation; age; names and occupations of parents; if married, to whom and issue in order of birth and ages (age at, and date of, death if dead); cause of death and how long the disease continued. The questions asked at marriage included: date and place of marriage; ages and occupations; relationship of bride and groom; if married previously, children by each former marriage; names and occupations of parents. At birth registration the following questions were asked: father – age, occupation, birth place, date and place of marriage, issue living and deceased; mother – age, birthplace, parity of present birth. The Act is 'an Act to provide for the better Registration of Births, Deaths, and Marriages in Scotland', 17 & 18 Vict. c.80 (see Schedules A, B & C).

80 In 1861 the date and place of marriage, which had been excluded from birth registration after 1855, was reintroduced. The question on relationship of bride and groom (at marriage) was excluded on the grounds of the difficulty experienced in obtaining the information. A minute from the Registrar General to the Privy Council (13 August 1860) stated that 'no statistical deductions of the slightest value, relative to the consanguinity of the persons married since the Act came into operation, can be drawn from the Duplicate Register Books which have been transmitted to this Department'. This has been confirmed by an analysis kindly undertaken by Mr Robert McLeod, Deputy Registrar General for Scotland, of two 1859 marriage registers – one for Dundee and the other for North Uist. Of the 328 entries examined, no information was given in 295 cases; 'no relationship' in 30; and a relationship in 3 cases (1 niece, 1 cousin, 1 second cousin). Where there was no relationship, the registrars were apparently not required to state that, though some obviously did so. The difficulty is that of not knowing whether no entry meant no relationship.

The question of consanguineous mating was obviously of some concern to Scottish statisticians. Stark (*op. cit.*, pp.61-62) discussed the matter with reference to the frequency of 'idiocy' and 'insanity' in Scotland, and wrote: 'There is one peculiarity in the social condition of the people of Scotland which appears to me to be quite adequate to explain the excessive tendency to insanity and idiocy among its population, that is, the prevalence of the intermarriage of blood relatives.' He pressed for the inclusion of a question on blood relationship in the marriage schedule in England and Wales and no doubt would have been equally anxious to have the question included in any Scottish schedule. Information of this kind has been used in France, the Netherlands and Italy to study changes in the frequency of consanguineous mating over time, differences between various regions, and the association of consanguineous mating with infant mortality. Ideally, however, in the absence of effective record linkage sytems, information on blood relationship of spouses should also be given on the birth certificate and on the infant's death certificate.

As to the reduction in the range of data after 1855, the Registrar General, in a minute to the Treasury (27 June 1855), noted that the revised forms would be 'as nearly as possible in accordance' with those is use in England and explained that the Registrars had had 'the greatest possible difficulty in procuring the information prescribed by the previous schedules. Given this difficulty, the likelihood that the information was unreliable was greatly increased.'

I am indebted to Mr Robert MacLeod, Deputy Registrar General for Scotland, for copies of the relevant minutes and for many helpful comments on the Scottish registration system.

81 J. Matthews Duncan, *Fecundity, Fertility, Sterility and Allied Topics*, 2nd edn, Edinburgh 1871; C. J. Lewis & J. N. Lewis, *Natality and Fecundity*, Edinburgh & London 1906. Unfortunately, the Lewis & Lewis tabulations were undertaken at a time when the study of fertility had not made much progress and thus omit various analyses which would today be found desirable. There might well be a case for a new set of analyses of the 1855 data on births (at least on a sample basis) as well as of those on marriages and deaths.

82 The structure of the registration system is defined in detail in the Registration of Births, Deaths and Marriages (Scotland) Act of 1965 (1965, c.49).

APPENDIX 1

Two letters from the Chadwick Collection and a correspondence between Chadwick and Farr

The letters which follow have been included here for several reasons. First, the letter from Chadwick to Laycock contains an explicit claim that Chadwick was responsible for the insertion of 'cause of death' in death registration under the 1836 Act. Secondly, the letter from Farr shows his antagonism to any suggestion that the Poor Law Commission might be associated with vital registration. Thirdly, both Farr's early analysis of deaths and Chadwick's use of death statistics are brought into question in the Chadwick-Laycock letter. It is only these latter questions which will be considered here.

Chadwick told Laycock – almost in so many words – that Farr had incorrectly attributed a number of deaths to starvation, and that the Poor Law Commissioners, on examining the cases, had found that very few of the deaths were the result of starvation, and even these were 'either accidental or suicidal'. The reference in question was to Farr's analysis of mortality in England and Wales during the first half-year of civil vital registration, published in the *First Annual Report of the Registrar-General* (London 1839). Farr had written (p.106): 'It will be seen with regret that in the half-year the deaths of 63 individuals were ascribed (principally at inquests) to starvation; this is almost 1 annually to a population of 111,000. The want of food implies the want of everything else – except water – as firing, clothing, every convenience, every necessary of life, is abandoned at the imperious bidding of hunger. Hunger destroys a much higher proportion that is indicated by the registers in this and in every other country; but its effects, like the effects of excess, are generally manifested indirectly, in the production of diseases of various kinds. The privation is rarely absolute; the supply of food is inadequate to supply the wants of the organization, which requires daily animal or vegetable matter containing not less than nine ounces of carbon.'

John Graunt, the founder of demography, was also interested in the frequency of deaths from starvation, though his comments show a rather different perspective. 'My first Observation is, That few are *starved*: This appears, for that of the 229250 which have died, we found not above fifty one to have been *starved*, excepting help-less *Infants* at Nurse, which being caused rather by carelessness, ignorance, and infirmity of the Milch-women, is not properly an effect, or sign of want of food in the Country, or of means to get it' (*Natural and Political Observations made upon the Bills of Mortality*, London 1662, Willcox edition, Baltimore 1939, p.33). The frequency suggested by Farr's comment was higher – 63 deaths out of a total of 148,701 registered in the half-year. But Farr had not examined the deaths by age and his figure included 'helpless infants'. Moreover, his claim that most of the deaths so ascribed had been done so at inquests by Coroners was not correct. The claim was an incautious one, since death from starvation may result not only from depri-vation caused by poverty, but also from causes not so associated – for example, from congenital pyloric stenosis in the case of infants, from carcinoma of the pylorus, from malnutrition and liver damage in the case of chronic alcoholics, to name a few possibilities.

Chadwick was very prompt to take up the matter, and the resultant correspondence, originally published in the *Official Circulars* issued by the Poor Law Commissioners, is reprinted in this Appendix. It is clear that, so far as some of the details are concerned, Farr was wrong. Of the 63 cases, 36 were infants; of the remaining 27 cases, only 13 had been attributed by Coroners or registrars to 'hunger or want of proper food'. But his general point of view regarding the role of poverty in mortality was sound, though it was not until 1911 that the combined census and vital registration statistics were used to show the strong relationship between socio-economic status and mortality; and not until Charles Booth's survey of London that the high frequency of chronic poverty was shown in a sufficiently objective way to help to bring to an end the Malthusian policy of dealing with the poor. Farr's comments were those of a pioneer of social medicine; Chadwick's criticism reflected a narrower view of the factors affecting mortality.

The second point in the letter to Laycock related to Chadwick's use of mean ages at death as indicators of differential mortality. He did this frequently and in a variety of contexts, especially in *A Supplementary Report on the Results of a Special Inquiry into the Practice of Interment in Towns*, London 1843, pp.239-266. For example, he referred to deaths in the working class parish of St Margaret's, Leicester (p.241), in which the mean age of death in 1840 was 18 years. In the streets which had been drained, the mean was $23\frac{1}{2}$ years; in the partially drained streets $17\frac{1}{2}$ years; and in the undrained streets $13\frac{1}{2}$ years. He also gave the mean ages at death of individuals in various socio-economic categories, namely, gentlemen, tradesmen, labourers and paupers, both including and excluding deaths of children under ten years of age. And in the main report, similar statistics were presented for a variety of areas, socio-economic groups and occupations (*Report. . . from the Poor Law Commissioners, on an Inquiry into the Sanitary Condition of the Labouring Population of Great Britain*, London 1842, esp. pp.153-170). Technically, he was of course wrong in using these indicators, and contemporary criticism was justified. The age structure of the population exposed to risk had not been taken into account, and this age structure was influenced not only by the level of fertility but also by the social factors associated with selection into and out of occupations. Farr was, at least by implication, one of the critics (*Fifth Annual Report of the Registrar General* (for 1841), 2nd edn, London 1843, pp.38-45), and there was detailed criticism by Neison in the *Journal of the Statistical Society* (Vol.7, pp.40-69, F. G. P. Neison, 'On a method recently proposed for conducting inquiries into the comparative sanatory condition of various districts. . .'; this was in reply to Chadwick's paper in the same volume, pp.1-40, 'On the best modes of representing accurately, by statistical returns, the duration of life, and the pressure and progress of the causes of mortality amongst different classes of the community, and amongst the populations of different districts and countries'). But, as in the case of Farr's technical error, there is the question whether Chadwick was wrong in the wider sense. And the answer, as Greenwood pointed out, is not categorically 'Yes', for Chadwick was essentially right in stressing the role of environment in producing wide differences in mortality levels; though it was not until later that this could be shown with greater authority (see M. Greenwood, *Some British Pioneers of Social Medicine*, London 1948, pp.53-58).

Dr W. Farr to Edwin Chadwick:

February 13th 1837.

Dear Sir,

Is your inquiry to be retrospective or prospective? If the former the replies will be general, vague, and I fear of little value; and to make the prospective inquiry more satisfactory, would require some provision, which should combine accuracy in the observers with their apparent interests.

I do not think that there should be any special Registry for Epidemics; they should be entered in the same General Registry as other diseases, although special questions may be put to the medical men such as are exemplified in Dr. H's note, on any particular emergency.

The accompanying form of Registry would furnish answers to the most important questions that could be asked; and keeping it would cause little trouble.

"Occupation" is omitted because all your patients are paupers; but it may be added after Residence.

After the simple observations have been collected, they should be reduced into order, at the central districts.

But I am afraid that at your offices you are too much occupied, and have too little acquaintance – practical acquaintance – with the subject – to do much in medical statistics; although you may render much valuable assistance to a National Board of Health – if such an establishment existed – and great light may by your means be thrown on the health of the lowest classes.

I enclose a scurrilous publication — the British Annals of Medicine – in which the unparallelled Registration job is set in unfavourable, but I fear true light. The sentiments of the article are very generally felt although they have yet for obvious reasons been expressed in few quarters. Why does the present Ministry destroy itself in the minds of its best friends by such transactions?

The Poor Law Commissioners should have nothing whatever to do with the Registration of Births, Deaths and Fatal Diseases; although it is quite natural in them to desire the addition to their patronage and power.

Have you published the paper on Great Dietaries in its present complete state? Would you send me the number of the Annales d'Hygiène I left with you some time ago?

I enclose Dr. Hodgkin's notes; it would perhaps be well to have the queries he has proposed, printed, and distributed among the Unions. They would furnish much useful Medical information.

I remain Dear Sir,
Yours truly,
William Farr

Annual Report of P.L.C.

PS. The Table No.3.b. [?] is badly done, and must be very inaccurate. What is meant by the "Average number of Paupers attended per month" – the number constantly ill, or the number of attacked per month? The latter I suppose!

[Source: Farr Folder]

Edwin Chadwick to Dr T. H. Laycock :

April 13 1844

My dear Sir,

The unsettling of insurance tables by the doctrine that every place has its own circumstances and that these circumstances govern the mortality, has annoyed the actuaries. One of them read a paper on the night after mine at the Statistical Society to shew that both average ages and proportions of deaths were erroneous where they did not take into account the distribution in ages of the living population. The Counsel of the society not very handsomely printed this paper without allowing me an opportunity of reply. I have in a few copies intended for private distribution printed a few sentences in reply. You will find them in the last pages of the number herewith sent.

When the registration was proposed as a boon to the Dissenters I objected that it should be put on a widely different footing. I got the "causes of death" inserted in spite of the manager of the bill or rather Lord Ellenborough adopted the suggestion. When the bill was carried I got the Poor Law Commissioners to go out of their way to recommend the appointment of medical men as registrars expecting that here and there some one would be found to take an interest in the subject and notwithstanding the defects of the machinery shew the important account to which it might be turned. I recommended the last government to appoint a person of special qualifications as a Registrar General. Lord John however chose to appoint his brother in law to the post of £1000 a year: a very good novelist but who cared nothing for the subject and was the least fitted to deal with it. I next urged Mr. Lister to appoint a qualified clerk and I recommended to his notice Mr. Farr who had been recommended to me by Dr. Arnott as the only medical man whom he knew as having paid attention to vital statistics and Mr. Lister was adduced to give Mr. Farr the appointment. I was busy attending to other matters in forgetfulness of Mr. F. and the registration when my attention was called to some attacks made [illegible] in the Lancet on some tables in which I had shewn as the returns I got did undoubtedly shew that where the amount of prison diet was the highest, in any large number of prisons the amount of sickness was the greatest. I was somewhat surprised by the information that these attacks were made by Mr. Farr to whom I had shewn the tables in question before the results were made public and he gave me his assent that they were correct, as in fact they were notwithstanding the subsequent attack upon them. Of this I took no notice. The next thing I found however was representations in the registrar general's returns of a number of deaths from starvation (a subject which I had very carefully examined under the poor law) and which unless there had been a vast alteration in the condition of society I knew could not be true. I got the commissioners to call for the original registries and in the third number of the official circular you will see what the examination displayed in respect to Mr. Farr's statistics and his integrity. Since then the alleged cases of starvation have been regularly examined or nearly so, with the same general results that is to say some two or three per cent of the cases registered as deaths from privation are cases of death from the privation of food and those either accidental or suicidal. I have not paid attention to Mr. Farr or his animosities or petty jealousies but I am sorry to say that it is not the only instance in which in looking into some covert from whence an insidious attack on my labours have proceeded I have found someone behind to whom I have rendered some special service. .

Yours very truly
E. Chadwick.

[Source: Copybook III, letter 19]

The Farr-Chadwick correspondence on deaths from starvation in the *Official Circular* issued by the Poor Law Commissioners dated 9 March and 18 May 1840 is reprinted below.

RELIEF OF DESTITUTION

Correspondence of the Poor Law Commissioners with the Registrar-General on the subject of a passage in a Letter addressed to the Registrar-General by Mr. Farr, and published in the Appendix to the Registrar-General's First Annual Report.

Poor Law Commission Office,
Somerset House,
September 30, 1839

Sir,

I am directed by the Poor Law Commissioners, to state that their attention has been drawn to the following passage in the letter from William Farr, Esq. on the registered causes of death, which is published in the appendix to your First Annual Report, p.106.

"It will be seen with regret that in the half year the deaths of sixty-three individuals were ascribed (principally at inquests) to starvation; this is almost 1 annually to a population of 111,000. The want of food implies a want of everything else, except water; as firing, clothing, every convenience, every necessary of life, is abandoned at the imperious bidding of hunger. Hunger destroys a much higher proportion than is indicated by the registers in this and in every other country, but its effects, like the effects of excess, are generally manifested indirectly, in the production of diseases of various kinds."

The statement that so many persons have in the course of six months perished of actual hunger, if left unexplained, appears to the Commissioners calculated to produce a belief that the provisions of the law, which are intended to bring relief within the reach of every one needing it, are either inadequate to their object or improperly administered; and I am therefore to request that the particulars of the cases on which such a statement is founded, may be communicated to them, in order that, if on inquiry, it should appear to be correct, some remedy for the evil may be provided, and if erroneous, means may be taken to remove the impression which it might otherwise serve to create.

The Commissioners also desire me to point out that in a subsequent passage of the same letter, p.111, it is stated that the "Poor Law Inquiry, and Successive Parliamentary Committees, have shown that the families of agricultural labourers subsist upon a minimum of animal food, and an inadequate supply of bread and potatoes."

The Commissioners are not aware that there is any reason whatever for the belief that the agricultural labouring classes in this country are suffering from the want of an adequate supply of food, nor that the evidence taken by the Commissioners of Poor Law Inquiry, or before the Parliamentary Committees, would lead to such a conclusion, and they are desirous, therefore, of being informed of the particular portions of evidence on which the allegation contained in the passage above cited rests.

I have, &c.

Edwin Chadwick, *Secretary*

J. H. Lister, Esq. &c.

The Poor Law Commissioners received from the Registrar-General, a copy of the registries described as those of the sixty-three cases above referred to, and also sixteen other additional cases, together with the following copy of a letter from Wm. Farr, Esq.

General Register Office,
29th November, 1839

Sir,

I have examined the passages in my letter to which the attention of the Poor Law Commissioners has been directed, and submit to you "the particulars of the cases" which have been referred to the head "Starvation" in the abstracts.

It was considered that "starvation" would include the terms in the registers which imply death by privation, the want of warmth, and of proper food at all ages. It must not be understood to imply merely hunger.*

The passage in my letter (p.106) states that sixty-three is not to be considered the true number of deaths from starvation, and that the want of proper food is generally accompanied with a want of all the other necessaries of life. To render the sense of the passage which Mr. Chadwick has quoted complete, the concluding sentence of the paragraph should have been given: – "*The privation is rarely if ever absolute;* the supply of food is inadequate to supply the wants of the organization, which requires daily animal or vegetable matter containing not less than nine ounces of carbon." Few die from the absolute want of food, while many die, or drag on a miserable existence upon insufficient, innutritious diet.

The effects of want vary at different ages, and in different circumstances, such as cleanliness, ventilation, and the extent to which the starvation is carried. But from the structure of the teeth and stomach, from all the experiments and facts, it appears that man requires a certain amount of *animal* and *vegetable* food; that the nature of this should be varied, and that the privation of proper food, according to the extent to which it is carried, produces death directly or indirectly by giving rise to diseases of various kinds.

---

* To starve, from the Anglo-Saxon, *starfan;* German, *sterben,* to die, to be destroyed, has the following acceptations according to Johnson: –

1. To perish.
2. To perish with hunger.
3. To be killed with cold.
"Have I see the naked *starve* for cold." – Sandys.
"From beds of raging fire to *starve* in ice." – Milton.
4. To suffer extreme poverty.
"Sometimes virtue *starves* while vice is fed" – Pope.
5. To be destroyed with cold.

In the present state of our knowledge it may be assumed that the quantity of food required by animals of every species, including man, is the average quantity of plain food that they consume in ordinary circumstances when the supply is not limited. The rations in the public service afford a fair standard. The English soldier's daily ration is bread, 16 ounces; beef or mutton, 12 ounces – 16 ounces; besides vegetables, sugar, coffee, &c. The French soldier has bread, 26 ounces; meat, $8\frac{1}{2}$ ounces. The carbon and nitrogen in the food represent its nutritive power (Prout, Bridgewater Treatise); the nitrogen should amount to $1\frac{1}{2}$ ounces – 3 ounces, the carbon to 11 ounces. The carbon is converted into carbonic acid, is burnt, in fact; sustains the temperature of the body at blood heat, and escapes in respiration. The quantity of food should by proportional to the intensity and quantity of labour; the harvest-man will consume twice the amount of the soldier's ration, and twice as much as he requires in the short winter days. The human machine in this respect bears some resemblance to the steam-engine. But there are reservoirs of nutritive matter in the body, and a deficiency of a half or three-fourths, rarely produces any serious effect in less than 30 or 90 days, particularly if the place of nutritive matter be supplied by earth, &c., as it is in parts of America.

From a very able memoir, by Dalton, in the "Memoirs of the Manchester Philosophical Society," it appears that he consumed, on an average of 14 days, 23 ounces of bread, oatcake, and pastry; 2 ounces of potatoes; 4 ounces of butchers' meat; 9 ounces of cheese; 31 ounces of milk; 22 ounces of tea; and beer daily. The whole containing $11\frac{1}{2}$ ounces of carbon, $1\frac{1}{2}$ ounces of nitrogen, nearly the same as the rations in the public service.

Assume, as we may very fairly, that full diet would contain carbon, 11 ounces; nitrogen, 2 ounces, $= 13$ ounces avoirdupois. Then the workhouse dietaries of the Poor Law Commissioners contain about $9\frac{3}{4}$ of these elements (8·7 ounces carbon, 1 ounce nitrogen), and the workhouse dietary is $= 0·75$ of full diet. Dr. Kay states that the average expense of maintenance in the workhouses of Norfolk and Suffolk would be "18s. a-week, or about 50l. a-year" for a man, his wife, and four children; and he found that of 120 families, whose number of children averaged 3·7 to a family, the annual income, including the earnings of the wife and children, was, 35l. 9s. If the diet of the families out of the workhouses is in the same proportion or $= 0·8$ of the workhouse dietary, it will follow that the families of agricultural labourers, in the employment of the great agriculturists of Norfolk and Suffolk are upon but little better than half diet, $= 0·6$ of full diet. The gross income is 4d. a-day per head; and this furnishes the rent, firing, clothing, &c., as well as food.

From a series of facts before me, if appears that full diet cannot be procured by adults for less than 10d. a-day. Reduce it to 6d. for children, and the cheapness of coarse food, then the result will differ little from that stated above. The calculation proves to demonstration that the agricultural labourer can purchase scarcely any animal food. This appears to be the case, the family subsists upon potatoes, salt, bread (a limited quantity), and a small quantity of bacon.

In my letter, I state that "the food of the inhabitants of towns is as substantial as that of the agricultural labourer. The Poor Law Inquiry, and successive Parliamentary Committees, have shown that the families of agricultural labourers subsist upon a minimum of animal food, and an inadequate supply of bread and potatoes."

The "portions of evidence on which this allegation rests," will be found in the

Appendix to the Poor Law Inquiry, answers to the question 29; whence it appears that the rate of labourers' wages is 5s. 10d., and seldom exceeds 9s. a-week. The labourers' family consists of about five individuals on an average; and the earnings of the wife and children can scarcely be estimated at 3s. a-week, if, indeed, they counterbalance with the harvest wages the labourers' loss of time by sickness and irregular employment.

The Parliamentary Papers furnish abundant evidence on the subject. It will be sufficient to refer to the evidence of the agricultural labourers themselves (probaby the best judges), to Dr. Kay's valuable tables (14th Report, Appendix G.), to Mr. Turner's tables, and to those of Mr. Pearce and Mr. Marshall in the volumes of evidence taken in the last and previous sessions of Parliament.

> I have the honour to be, Sir,
> Your obedient Servant,
> William Farr

To the Registrar-General, &c., &c. &c.

> *Poor Law Commission Office,*
> *Somerset House,*
> *February,* 1840

Sir,

The Poor Law Commissioners have had under their consideration the copy of a letter received by you from Mr. Farr, in explanation of his statement of the number of deaths which he reported to you as having been caused by starvation. They have also examined a copy of the particular cases on which he founds his statement. It appears to the Commissioners that the statement (in the sense in which it must have been understood by the public), is entirely unsustained by the facts from which it purported to be deduced. Mr. Farr, in his explanatory letter, says that the word "starvation," as used in the passage, "It will be seen with regret, that in the half-year, the deaths of 63 individuals were ascribed (principally at inquests) to *starvation*," – "includes the terms in the register which imply death by privation, the want of warmth, and proper food at all ages. It must not be understood to imply merely hunger."

Although the word "starvation" may perhaps be considered to have the double sense of the privation of warmth as well as of food, Mr. Farr had himself supplied a definition which (whatever might be his own meaning), appears to the Commissioners to have restricted it to the understandings of others to cases of death caused by the inability to procure food.

"The want of food implies a want of everything else, except water; as firing, clothing, every convenience, every necessary of life, is abandoned at the imperious bidding of hunger. Hunger destroys a much higher proportion than is indicated by the registers in this and in every other country; but its effects, like the effects of excess, are generally manifested indirectly, in the production of disease of various kinds."

This description is further confirmed by the addition of the concluding sentence of the paragraph, which he states should have been given to render the sense of the paragraph complete. "The privation is rarely if ever absolute; the supply of food is inadequate to supply the wants of the organization, which requires daily animal and vegetable matter, containing not less than nine ounces of carbon."

On an examination of the particular cases the Commissioners observe, that instead of the sixty-three deaths having been ascribed "principally at inquests" to starvation, in only sixteen cases does it appear that any inquests were held; and it further appears that in the majority of the sixty-three cases the deaths were not ascribed in the registries to starvation, either in the sense of the privation of food, or the privation of warmth as usually understood. Not less than thirty-six of the cases appear to have been the cases of infants, of whom two were under the age of one week, seven under one month, eleven under two months, six under three months, and the rest under nine months, nearly all of whom died from various causes of mortality prevalent amongst the children of all classes, *e.g.*

Helen Elizabeth Thompson, aged three weeks, (condition of parent, a gentleman) died at No.20, Whitmore-road, Hoxton. Cause assigned in the registry, "*Owing to malformation about the mouth, the child was incapable of deglutition, and gradually perished from want of sustenance.*"

Frederic Browning, aged eight months, father a woolcomber, died at Exeter workhouse. Cause assigned in the registry, "*Starved from malformation.*"

George Pugh, aged nine days, father a miller, died at Sutton-lane, Shrewsbury. Cause assigned in the registry, "*For want of nourishment after the death of the mother.*"

Edward Dopson, aged 19 days, father a carter, died at Stone-lane, Oxford, Ramsbury. Cause assigned in the registry, "*Want of proper nourishment, the mother having died in giving him birth.*"

Margaret Dalton, aged six weeks, parents' condition not stated, died at Aylesbury. Cause assigned in the registry, "*Brought up by hand, the mother died in childbed.*"

George Chamberlain, aged three months, father a tailor, died at Mount Pleasant, Gosport. Cause assigned in the registry, "*Pined away for want of the breast; the mother died 16th of July, the child 23rd of August.*"

Henry Roberts, aged one month, parents' condition not stated, died at 16, Bury-street, Bloomsbury. Cause assigned in the registry, "*For want of the nourishment usually supplied by the mother.*"

The following are further exemplifications: –

Ellen Wombwell, aged six weeks and three days, the condition of parents not stated, died at West Hackney. Cause assigned in the registry, "*Atrophy from want of the breast-milk.*"

Andrew Austin, aged 14 weeks, father a shoemaker, died at West Hackney. Cause assigned in the registry, "*Atrophy from want of the breast-milk.*"

Thomas Ebenezer Edmonds, aged nine months, parents' condition not stated, died at 14, Albion-place, Newington. Cause assigned in the registry, "*Atrophy from weaning.*"

Sophia Browne, aged 16 weeks, parents' condition not stated, died at 33, Carnaby-street. Cause assigned in the registry, "*Occasioned through weaning.*"

John Owen, aged three weeks, parents' condition not stated, died at 9, United-buildings, Mary-le-bone. Cause assigned in the registry, "*Loss of the breast.*"

Of the remainder of the thirty-six cases of infants, the causes of death, in twelve cases, are ascribed simply to "inanition;" the deaths of two others are occasioned "through weaning;" seven "from the want of the nourishment usually supplied by the mother;" one, "probably, from want of proper food;" four to "atrophy for want of breast milk;" two others as follow: –

Ann Alcock, aged eight weeks, father a labourer, died at Swaffham. Cause assigned in the registry, "*Weak child, and had no breast-food.*"

Charlotte Clayden, aged seven months, father a shopkeeper, died at Henham. Cause assigned in the registry, "*Wasting away without fever after weaning.*"

The public could not have understood that cases such as these, casualties incidental to infant nurture, were denoted by the terms in which they and the whole of the sixty-three cases (including the thirty-six cases of infant mortality) are characterized as arising from one all-pervading cause, "the want of food:" and that "firing, clothing, every necessary of life" were abandoned by these infants "at the imperious bidding of hunger." The Commissioners are equally at a loss to comprehend the application of the following terms: –

"The privation is rarely, if ever, absolute; the supply of food is inadequate to the organization, which requires daily animal or vegetable matter, containing not less than nine ounces of carbon." To these thirty-six cases of infants whose natural food is stated to be a pint or a pint and a half of milk daily, containing, perhaps, one or two ounces of carbon in the whole quantity, and whose deaths in such cases as the following –

Harriet Parkin, aged 10 weeks, father a spectacle-frame maker, died in New George-street, Eccleshall Bierlow. Cause assigned in the registry, "*Weakness from want of natural sustenance from the mother.*"

— Nash, aged six weeks, condition not stated, died at Croom's Hill, Greenwich. Cause assigned in the registry, "*Want of breast-milk.*"

might be ascribed, with more probability, not to the want of food, but to the extreme ignorance in administering proper nutriment to infants, which physicians represent as too often found in the labouring classes, many of whom, on the loss of the mother, offer broth, or even gin, instead of milk, as means of sustenance.

In such cases as those last cited of infant deaths, and also in such cases as the following of adults –

Susannah Waddington, aged 18 years, died at Halifax. Cause assigned in the registry, "*Inflammatory fever from exposure to cold,*"

there is nothing to show that indigence was a primary cause. So far from "privation", either of food or shelter being generally assignable in all the cases in which the term "starvation" is used, excess is distinctly assigned in several, as in the following, which are sent as cases of starvation in addition to those comprised in the sixty-three cases in question.

Charles Allen, a beggar, aged 46 years, died at the house for farmed poor, Lombard-street, St. George the Martyr. Cause assigned in the registry, "*Natural death, accelerated by intemperance and exposure to cold.*"

Sarah Page, a married woman, aged 50 years, died at Buxton. Cause assigned in the registry, "*Found dead; exposure to cold all night in a state of intoxication.*"

Benjamin Ollerinshaw, slater, aged 50 years, died at Longnor. Cause assigned in the registry, "*Intoxication and exposure to cold.*"

Gerrard Potter, shopkeeper, aged 89 years, died at Adlington. Cause assigned in the registry, "*Surfeit from exposure to cold, as sleeping in a wood.*"

Benjamin Dawson, woolcomber, aged 46 years, died at Warley. Cause assigned in the registry, "*Died from excessive drinking, and exposure to the weather.*"

On examination of the registered causes of the deaths of adults it appears that in a large portion of the remainder of the cases, death was ascribed, not to hunger, but to the exposure to cold from casualties such as wayfarers or persons of the labouring classes are exposed to from accident or want of caution, without reference to indigence, *e.g.*

William Cookham Ellis, a seaman, aged 19 years, died at Stockton on Tees. Cause assigned in the registry, *"Inclemency of the weather."*

John Jones, farmer's servant, aged 14 years, died at Holywell, Verdict *"Found dead on the highway about 9 o'clock in the morning of the 21st of December, 1837, being starved in consequence of the very boisterous night of the 20th instant, in the parish of Yscei-fiog."*

Edward Marvin, a Chelsea pensioner, by trade a carpenter, aged 45 years, died at Deeping. Cause assigned in the registry, *"Found dead; died from natural cause, and from being exposed to the weather."*

Male person, unknown, died at Brentwood. Cause assigned in the registry, *"Died in consequence of exposure to cold."*

Dorothy Thorpe, a widow, aged 77 years, died at Boroughbridge. Cause assigned in the registry, *"Died from starvation, in consequence of exposure to the inclemency of the weather."*

The Commissioners are glad to find that of the cases investigated before coroners' juries, in but one case is any blame attached by the verdict to the administrators of relief, and that that case had been brought to the notice of the Commissioners, and made the subject of a special inquiry, and of the application of such remedy for the prevention of the future occurrence of such cases as then appeared available.

Charlotte Leonard, pauper, aged 71 years, died at the workhouse, Bethnal-green, Middlesex, 26th of October, 1837. Cause assigned in the registry, *"Died from want, occasioned by the gross neglect of the parochial authorities of St. Luke, Middlesex, and St. Matthew, Bethnal-green."*

Of the seven other cases classed as arising from hunger, and the voluntary abandonment of food, but ascribed by coroner's juries to various causes, one case is a case of murder:

Elizabeth Breadman, a bastard, aged two days, died at Kingsclere, Hants, 1st of September, 1837. Cause assigned in the registry, *"Pressure and exposure; verdict against the mother, 'Murder.'"*

and another is a case of manslaughter:

Benjamin Broadway, apprentice, aged 18 years, died at the workhouse, Islington, Middlesex, 10th of August, 1837. Cause assigned in the registry, *"Starvation; Manslaughter against Wm. Smith."*

The Commissioners have directed inquiries to be made as to the particulars of several of the cases when the causes of death have been ascribed by coroner's juries to starvation in the sense of the privation of food; and they have received statements of evidence respecting them, from which it appears that no blame is justly imputable in the cases either to the parish or to the union officers, nor any defects in the administration of relief which has not always been sought by the deceased where it was available. On the face of the registry it appears that the deaths of several were either voluntary or wilful, or suicidal, *e.g.*

Benjamin Miller, late a soldier and pensioner, aged 46 years, died at Tuxford, Nottinghamshire, 24th of July, 1837. Cause assigned in the registry, *"Want and exposure, arising from insanity."*

Of this class of cases are the two following:

Jane Morris (condition of life not stated), aged 47 years, died in the House of Industry, Oswestry, Salop, 18th of September, 1837. Cause assigned in the registry, *"For want of the common necessaries of life, refusing the protection of the house."* Esther Beaumont (condition not stated), aged 57 years, died at Sheffield, Brightside Bierlow, Yorkshire, 31st of August, 1837. Cause assigned in the registry, *"Want of the common necessaries of life."*

The answer made to the inquiries of the Commissioners in this case by the clerk of the Union is as follows:

"Esther Beaumont resided in Brightside Bierlow, and was settled in Ecclesfield, from which parish she has been in the habit of receiving a small weekly allowance. Some time previous to her death (August, 1837) this allowance was discontinued by the overseers, who gave an order for the workhouse, from a desire to benefit the woman, but which she refused to accept. Her situation was not known to any of the officers of this Union until it was too late to render any assistance, and no blame was attached either to them or to the officers of Ecclesfield, which at that time was not in Union."

What may have been the influences which governed the two individuals, in the two last cases, the Commissioners have no means of knowing; but the false and mischievous statements propagated respecting the new modes of administering relief, which have in some instances occasioned the refusal of bread offered as out-door relief – refusals made on the supposition that it was poisoned, have prepared the Commissioners to expect the occurrence of such instances, as the natural effects of such statements upon weak and ignorant minds.

In respect to the use of the ambiguous term of "starvation" by coroners' inquests, the Commissioners find that it is applied on very uncertain conjecture, especially where the body is not opened and carefully examined. For example, in the following case:

Thomas Kitchen, formerly a servant, aged 43 years, died in the parish of St. Giles-in-the-Fields, and St. George, Bloomsbury, Middlesex, 8th of November, 1837. Cause assigned in the registry, *"Visitation of God, being at the time in great want of the common necessaries of life."*

The Commissioners are informed that the deceased was a man who got his living by selling tracts; that on the night before his decease he left a beer-house in Drury-lane, where he had been drinking in company with two others with whom he took up his abode in the attic of a house occupied by some labouring people, and in the course of the forenoon he was found dead on the floor. He had some halfpence in his pocket, and had made no application for relief. He had been previously ill, and it was believed from a letter in his pocket that he had been the subject of medical examination. He was believed to be a common beggar of the description frequenting that neighbourhood. The neighbourhood where the death occurred is one inhabited by some of the most wretched of the population in the metropolis, and it is stated by the officer employed to collect evidence for the inquests in that neighbourhood, as well as by other witnesses, that such an occurrence as a death, proved to have arisen from the absolute privation of food, or from the inadequacy of the common necessaries of life, or from the inadequacy of legal relief which is known and open to all the destitute, has not occurred within that district, or been alleged on any coroner's verdict, during the last ten years.

In the following case:

Robert Laycock, a pauper, printer, aged 28 years, died at the workhouse, St. Sepulchre's, London, 30th of December, 1837. Cause assigned in the registry, *"Consumption and destitution."*

the indefinite terms of the verdict would admit of various interpretations, but the evidence upon it is characteristic of the causes:

"Jordan Lynch, of King-street, Snow-hill, surgeon, says, 'I made a post-mortem examination of the body of the deceased to-day; I found him in an extreme state of emaciation; there were spots of secondary veneral disease on the legs, and I found the bones of the nose and larynx to have been moved by disease; I found the liver to have been diseased by drinking ardent spirits; I found the stomach small and contracted from want of food; I found the lungs in a high state of inflammation, and that was the approximate cause of death; want had diminished the powers of life, and exposure to the cold air was prejudicial to him; the inflammation of the lungs was the case of his death; I think any relief in that stage was unavailing."

The Commissioners observe upon these last cited cases as exemplifications of their grounds for believing that the correct course is to restrain the inferences from such statements below the terms which happen to be used, rather than to extend them beyond their ordinary meaning. Thus instead of the returns proving the existence of one all-pervading cause of mortality, hunger, when examined, and so far as they serve as data, they prove the reverse. Of the 63 cases, it appears that there are, of the various casualties of

Infant mortality, malformation, inanition, weaning, inability to take proper nourishment, &c.	36
Murder	1
Manslaughter	1
Starvation, ascribed to cold by coroners' juries	6
—, by the Registrars	6
—, ascribed to hunger or want of proper food by coroners' inquests	7
—, by the Registrars	6
	—
	63

In respect to the several cases of death from hunger which are not accounted for, the Commissioners find that from the great length of time which has elapsed since their occurrence, and from the administration of relief in the places where they occurred having been imperfectly organized, there was no probability of obtaining sufficiently correct results to repay the trouble of a special inquiry into them. But even as they appear on the face of the registries they do not sustain, but rather rebut, any inference as to the want of food having been a prevalent cause of death. Any cause of hunger or destitution equally pervading a whole class of the population at the same time and place must be attended with effects as extensive as the cause.

Now the cases of death which are ascribed to the want of food (which want may possibly have arisen from indigence) will be seen to have occurred almost singly in different and distant places at various times, and that almost every individual who has so died is of a distinct class or occupation.

Taking these cases last specified to be cases where the want of food has arisen from accidental, isolated, and individual causes, the Commissioners, nevertheless, deem them the subject of very serious consideration. Whilst they consider it a duty to remove, as far as may be in their power to do so, false and exaggerated impressions as to the frequency of death by hunger, they would not diminish the feeling of anxiety on the occurrence of any single case of death arising from absolute want amidst a community in which so heavy a tax is paid for the prevention of such casualties. They conceive that, for the maintenance of the care for life and social feelings of anxiety for the relief of suffering, which characterize a civilized people, every such case should be the subject of a careful inquiry, with the view to the adopting of any available measures for the prevention of the recurrence of similar casualties. They are concerned to find, so far as appears from the copies of the registries you have supplied to them, that nearly as many cases of death from the want of the necessaries of life have passed without inquiry as have been the subject of inquiry before coroners' juries, *e. g.*

Mary Harkness, an itinerant vender of thread and tapes, aged 62 years, died at the Workhouse, Church-street, St. Paul, Deptford, Kent, 18th of December, 1837. Cause assigned in the registry, *"Frostbitten and want."*

Joseph Copley, husbandman, aged 44 years, died at Armley, Yorkshire, 26th of July, 1837. Cause assigned in the registry, *"No particular disease; a want of proper support."*

Rebecca Baker, lodging-house-keeper, aged 27 years, died at St. Botolph, Lincoln, 27th of October, 1837. Cause assigned in the registry, *"Said to die from want."*

William Croupe, beggar, aged about 50 years, died at Garstang, Lancashire, 16th of December, 1837. Cause assigned in the registry, *"General debility and insufficiency of food and lodging."*

Mary Bryant, a widow, age not stated, died in the Poorhouse, Swansea, Glamorgan, 13th of December, 1837. Cause assigned in the registry, *"Debility, occasioned by want of food."*

RELIEF OF DESTITUTION

Further Correspondence of the Poor Law Commissioners with the Registrar-General on the subject of a passage in a Letter addressed to the Registrar-General by Mr. Farr, and published in the Appendix to the Registrar-Generals First Annual Report.

In compliance with the request of the Registrar-General, the Poor Law Commissioners have directed the insertion of the subjoined letter from Mr. Farr, in vindication of the statement made in his letter of the 29th November, 1839.

The Commissioners see no grounds for altering the opinions they expressed in their first letter, with relation to the statement in question. They conceive that the inferences that the deaths of infants from inanition was occasioned by the destitution of the mothers, is entirely gratuitous as respects the cases cited. The Commissioners do not assert the impossibility of a death having occurred from the destitution of the mother in any of the cases of infant mortality, but no such cause was assigned on the face of the returns or appeared in evidence with relation to those cases, and the assumption could not, as it appears to them, be justified by any facts as to infant mortality having been occasioned by destitution in other cases occurring at other times and places, supposing the facts to be so. The Commissioners observe that Mr. Farr, on a gratuitous assumption that reference was made by them to the amount of deposits in the savings banks in 1837, which was 16,578,849*l*., denies the correctness of that part of their letter wherein it is stated that "the increasing amount of upwards of 20,000,000*l*. of deposits in the savings banks, almost wholly from those of the labouring classes who are frugal, attest the amount of means at their disposal beyond a bare subsistence." The reference was made in round numbers, not to returns of past years, but to what they were informed was the then present amount, which they believed was increasing. On inquiry which they have directed to be made at the National Debt Office as to the precise fact, they are informed that the balance due to the savings banks on the 20th of November, 1839, was 23,583,365*l*.

On the question raised by Mr. Farr as to the accuracy of the statement in respect to the amount expended by the labouring classes on spirits, the Commissioners observe that the data were stated in the letter, and that no one could be misled by the expression "two thirds more", or be led to understand otherwise than that the duty of eight millions formed one third of the cost of twenty-four millions to the consumer. The Commissioners do not feel themselves called upon to enter further into the examination of any of Mr. Farr's statements on the subject, but will feel it a duty to avail themselves of the facilities which the Registrar General may afford for the investigation of any cases of alleged starvation caused by destitution, which in future may be brought to their notice, and they trust that the investigation will be made in a manner as satisfactory to the public as to themselves.

"General Register Office, March, 1840

"Gentlemen,

I have the honour to transmit to you the enclosed copy of a letter from Mr. Farr, in reply to the comments on his previous letters, contained in that which was addressed to me by your direction in the past month. As the preceding part of this correspondence has been published, while yet unfinished, in your Official Circular issued early in the present month, I trust you will give equal publicity to his reply, a copy of which I now enclose.

"I entirely concur with you in the belief you express 'that the new registration may be made to serve as a new and valuable additional security against the omissions of due inquiry in the class of cases in question' (namely, of deaths alleged to have been caused by want), 'as well as in others;' and I beg leave to assure you that it is my earnest desire to aid, by my co-operation, in the furtherance of that important object, and to take such means as shall enable you to be furnished with early information of every registered case of death which shall appear to have been caused by destitution.

"I have the honour to be, Gentlemen,

"Your obedient servant,

(*Signed*) "T. H. Lister

"*To the Poor Law Commissioners.*"

"(Copy.)

"March 17th, 1840

"Sir,

"I have read, at your request, the letter of the Poor Law Commissioners dated 24th February, 1840. It contains remarks on two passages, published in the Appendix to your Report,* on the cases of starvation, registered in the year 1837, and on my letter of the 29th November. 1839: and it is intended to show that the passages in the first letter 'are entirely unsustained by the facts.' The question under dispute is starvation, considered as a cause of death; and the importance attached to the subject will justify me in discussing, more fully than I have hitherto done, its more important bearings.

"The 148,701 statements in the column, headed 'cause of death,' in the registers, were classed in the first abstract by me, without distinction of age, profession, or any other circumstance, except the sex, the registered cause of death, and the districts. The passage in my letter (Appendix, p.106) was written with the tabular results of the abstracts before me, the facts under discussion having constituted rather more than 4 ten-thousandths of the number of entries. The 63 cases, ascribed to starvation, have since been extracted from the registers, with the time and place of death, the age, sex, rank, or profession, the cause of death as described in the registers, the names of the persons, and the names and descriptions of the informants. I stated, parenthetically, that the cases were ascribed to the cause in question, 'principally at inquests.' This is an error. I wrote from memory and was mistaken in the proportion of inquests. The coroner was not the 'informant', or at least did not sign the registers, in the majority of instances; for, as the Poor Law Commissioners remark, it appears on the face of the registers that in the year 1837 'nearly as many cases of death, from the want of the necessaries of life, have passed without inquiry, as have been made the subjects of inquiry before coroners' juries.' With this exception, the passage in my letter is substantially correct.

"It is quite true that 36 of the cases were 'only infants' under one year of age; that 12 of them died 'simply of inanition;' and that the remaining 24 died for want of their natural nourishment – the mother's milk, or an adequate substitute for milk.

"From your Report, Sir, it appears that in the year ending June 30th, 1838, 71,888 infants died under one year of age, the greater part of them the children of the lower classes, and many of them the offspring of paupers. Is it not probable that out of these a much higher proportion than twice 36 were starved in the cold nights of winter, and on the coarse, innutritious, inadequate subsistence of impoverished parents?

"The Poor Law Commissioners profess their inability to understand how 'firing, clothing, every necessary of life, were abandoned by these infants at the imperious bidding of hunger.' They can have no difficulty in understanding that, if the mothers are ever reduced to extremities, the children will share and suffer their fate. In a recent work Dr. Alison supplies an illustration. 'During the inclement weather of the spring of 1838,' says this benevolent and scientific physician, 'I saw three young women with natural children on the breast, who were out of work,

---

*Report of the Registrar-General, 1839, 8vo. Appendix, pp.106, 111.

11

161

in a miserable state of destitution; after some weeks of severe suffering, *the children all died, certainly from the effects of cold and imperfect nourishment.'**

"If infants die of starvation, the deaths will generally be ascribed in the registers to the want of the mother's milk. The informants are not likely to state that the want of the strong diet of adults was the cause of death in their cases.

"Infants are starved (1) on the thin milk of ill-fed mothers; or (2) in cases where the mother does not suckle the child, and the artificial food is coarse, and such as nature never intended for the food of infants.

"The experience of Foundling Hospitals shows that the want of the mother's breast is more fatal to infants than the want of sufficient food is to adults. The Abbé Gaillard states† that at Parthenay 54 of 153 foundlings died in the year after birth, or 35 out of 100 born. At X—— 197 out of 244 born, or 81 per cent., perished in the first year.

"He ascertained that as much care was taken of the children at X—— as at Parthenay; but at X—— the children were all brought up by hand (*au biberon*), and it is to the want of milk (*au défaut seul d'allaitement*) that the Abbé and the managers of the hospital ascribe the excessive mortality. The same fact is deduced by M. Villermé from three extensive returns, which he procured from the Foundling Hospitals of Rheims, Lyons, and Paris. In ordinary circumstances, when the children are suckled by the mother, the deaths in the first year out of 100 born alive, are 15 to 20; a proportion which, as has been seen, increases to 80 in the 100 when the children are deprived of milk. The privation of milk is the privation of food, and is equivalent to the starvation of adults.

"It is only when the child is deprived of milk and the event can be traced to no disease, that the death of infants is ascribed to starvation; and it will be perceived, upon the slightest reflection, that the 'want of nourishment usually supplied by the mother, weaning,' &c. &c., can be referred to no other head in the *abstract* than 'starvation.' 'Want of breast milk' is not a disease, but it is a cause of death. It is, in the strictest scientific sense, 'starvation.'

"I must notice one passage in the letter of the Poor Law Commissioners on this subject. It is this: 'Not less than 36 of the cases appear to have been the cases of infants, nearly all of whom died from various causes of mortality prevalent amongst the children of all classes, *e.g.* Helen Elizabeth ——, aged three weeks (condition of parent a *gentleman*), died at ——. Cause assigned in the registry, *Owing to malformation about the mouth, the child was incapable of deglutition, and gradually perished from want of sustenance.* Frederick ——, aged eight months, father a woolcomber, died at Exeter workhouse. Cause assigned in the registry, starved from malformation,' &c. &c. &c. &c.

"It is somewhat remarkable that neither of these two cases is included in the 36, or in the 63 cases, to which the Poor Law Commissioners say they belong, and of which they give them as examples. They were classed under 'malformations'

---

*Cited by the Editor of the Medical Gazette, February 28, 1840, in a series of articles on the diet of the poor, written in an excellent spirit.

†Résultats du défaut d'allaitement des nouveaux nés par M. L'Abbé Gaillard – Annales d'Hygiène, tome 19, p.39.

in the abstract, and are not in the classified list of 63 cases, which the Poor Law Commissioners have forwarded to you as an appendix to their letters.*

"Twelve deaths were ascribed to cold. It will be seen, upon reference to the long list of cases in 1838, that 'death by starvation' has been understood by the registrars, informants, coroners, and juries, all over the country, in the sense that it has in the English classics, and as it has been defined by the lexicographers. It denotes death by cold, death by hunger, death by cold and hunger, accidental death, by cold and hunger, death by want the result of destitution, or death by cold and hunger the result of destitution. The senses run imperceptibly into each other as the facts do in nature. The deaths by want the result of destitution, make the strongest impression on the mind; they are, perhaps, the most frequent. Hence the accessary idea of destitution is often called up by 'starvation.'

"In the rigorous winters of this latitude, the human race requires artificial heat, and fuel in parts of England is so expensive, that very little fire can be procured by the poor. The 'tables of mortality' for the metropolis show that 997 persons died in the coldest week in January, and only 813 in the last mild week in February. Is it, then, extravagant to assert that of 148,701 deaths, 'a much higher proportion' than 12 had their source in starvation by cold, in too many instances unmitigated in intensity when it penetrated the bare chamber, gathered round the desolate hearth, and froze the veins of the infant, the sickly, or the old?

"Medical practitioners meet with many distressing cases of starvation in this metropolis. I will mention one. In the winter of 1838 I was requested, in the middle of the night, to see a woman, who, it was said, was dying for want of help. I followed the messenger through a labyrinth of narrow passages, near Fitzroy market, and found in the corner of an attic a young woman, thinly clad, lying on a straw bed spread upon the floor. She had given birth to a child, then at her feet. Three children lay on the same bed, under a single rug. It was intensely cold. She had no fire, no candle, no food, and, if I recollect right, had not more than three half-pence in money to meet the exigencies of child-birth. The lodgers in the room below had been aroused by her groans.

"The Poor Law Commissioners discuss, at great length, the question whether blame attaches to them and to the administration of the new Poor Law, in connection with the deaths of 14 adults, ascribed in the registers of the half year more specifically to starvation, in the sense of 'privation of food.' This may be a question well deserving investigation; but it is a question with which, as it appears to me, I have here nothing to do. In my letter I brought no charge against the administration of the new Poor Law, and neither mentioned nor alluded to the Poor Law Commissioners. The passage has never been made the handle of an attack by their enemies. It refers to a 'cause of death' existing 'in this *and in every other country*,' and it forms part of a *paragraph*, addressed almost exclusively to members of the medical profession, on deaths from intemperance, gout, debility, tumours, cancer, scrofula, mortification, abscess, inflammation, and hœmorrhage.†

"The abstract was a classification of the causes of death, and had no reference to the remote, incidental, or accessary circumstances in which the direct cause of

---

*The list was not published in the Official Circular.
†Registrar-General's Report, App., p.106.

death originated; for the reason that this would have led to endless subdivisions of the several heads, and could have yielded few satisfactory results. Thus every case of death by drowning was classed under 'Violent deaths;' yet drowning might either be suicide, accident, murder, or manslaughter. The same observation applies to deaths by blows, hanging, burns, wounds, poisons, &c. &c., which, after careful consideration and consultation with you, Sir, it was deemed advisable, in the present state of registration, to refer to one generic head, 'violent deaths.'

"Whether starvation occurred therefore in infants, or in the aged; whether it was accidental, inevitable, or the result of negligence, the fact itself remained unchanged; it was still starvation; and, unless other causes were mentioned, could only be referred to one head in the classification. In determining the connexion and origin of the facts, more particularly in tracing the circumstances of starvation with the view of criminating, or of exculpating, any class of individuals, it would be necessary to examine all the statements in the registers with this object in view. A list of the particulars of 79 cases, which appeared calculated to assist the Poor Law Commissioners, was transmitted to their secretary; and several of the cases referred to other heads in the abstract, are, perhaps, as interesting and as important for the purpose which they professed to have in view, as the 63 cases.

"Of the cases in addition to the 63, the Poor Law Commissioners have cited (incorrectly) the case of Helen Elizabeth ——, and another instance in which starvation was occasioned by 'malformation;' also four cases of intoxication, and death by exposure to cold. Of a pauper, aged 50 years, the registered cause of death was *mortification of the feet – starved with hunger and cold*. This case was entered in the abstract under 'mortification;' the cases of intoxication and starvation, by cold, under 'intemperance;' the starvation of insane persons under 'insanity.' Each case could be entered under only one head; and it was considered that intemperance, insanity, and malformation were the prior causes, although starvation was the direct cause of death. Mortification is a well defined disease; and the case was classed under it, although the mortification was the effect of 'hunger and cold.'

"When the starvation is not absolute it generally gives rise to disease. The informant may then either specify the starvation or the disease, as the cause of death; and it is often difficult to determine the influence of several concurring causes on that event, so that the registers can only be considered to indicate an approximation to the real number of deaths from starvation. In all statistical observations of this uncertain character there are errors on both sides; errors of omission and insertion. To correct the errors of the registers the investigation should not be restricted to one class of causes. Deaths from other causes may be included in the 63 ascribed to starvation; it is still more probable that cases of starvation were registered under the remaining 141,544 specified causes, or included in the 7,094 cases in which the cause of death was not stated.

"The following list of cases of starvation in the year 1838, in number 123, has been extracted, in continuation of the list which was furnished to the Poor Law Commissioners, and which they published in the *Official Circular* so far as it illustrated their views. It will be seen that the number of cases in the Appendix to your First Report was not above the average. All the entries have been extracted in which the death was ascribed to starvation by hunger or by cold; but no attempt has been made to distinguish the cases of death from destitution, hunger, or want of shelter and fuel (which apparently constituted the majority), from the accidental deaths in storms; or the death of the houseless outcast, from the deaths of persons in good circumstances. The list is exclusive of infants under one year of age, as the Poor Law Commissioners have objected to the inclusion of such cases under the head of starvation.

[The List of Cases is omitted.]

"It is difficult to say what proportion of the mortality in England should be ascribed to insufficiency of food. If the quantity of provisions and the supply of food to the great mass of the population could be augmented, the mortality would be reduced; but every improvement in the means of the working classes leads to ameliorations in their habits, clothing, dwellings: so that the effect of better food is mixed up almost inextricably with other elements. I believe that the amount of subsistence exercises a less *direct* influence upon the diseases, epidemics, and general mortality of the population than Mr. Malthus imagined. The Poor Law Commissioners have, however, directed Mr. Chadwick to inform you that my letter contains 'the representation that the registers assign the *mortality to one all-pervading cause – hunger.** They repeat the words three times, with little variation, and reserve them for the peroration of their letter. It might be inferred from this, that the greater part of my letter had been devoted to the 'all-pervading cause' in quest, niowhereas it was only incidentally referred to in two passages of 40 lines. I stated that according to the registers 63, or less than *one hundred-thousandth* of the people, die annually of starvation; and added, 'Hunger destroys a much higher proportion than is indicated by the registers in this and every other country; but its effects, like the effects of excess, are generally manifested indirectly in the production of diseases of various kinds.' Upon this ground, and this sentence, which they quote, they assert in their letter to you that I 'assign *the mortality to one all-pervading cause – hunger.*' If 63 died of starvation, what did the words 'a much higher proportion' imply? Fifty per cent. would be 'a much higher proportion;' doubled, the number would be 126; decupled 630; and the reader could scarcely have extended the sense of the expression further. Now 148,701 deaths were registered in the half year, and if 630 deaths had been distinctly ascribed to the 'all-pervading cause,' 148,071 would have remained to be ascribed to other causes.

"A passage in the Appendix to your Report distinctly expresses my opinion as to the influence of external causes on the mortality.†

"'Different classes of the population experience different rates of mortality, and suffer different kinds of diseases. The principal causes of these differences, besides the sex, age, and hereditary organization, must be sought in three sources – exercise in the ordinary occupations of life, the adequate or inadequate supply of warmth and of food, and the different degrees of exposure to poisonous effluvia and to destructive agencies.'

"It is subsequently shown, that the number of deaths in 25 cities was 47,953; and in country districts, containing nearly the same population, 29,693. The low diet of agricultural labourers was adduced as evidence against the doctrine, that the high mortality of cities is to be ascribed to the deficiency of food, and not to the

---

*Official Circular, No.11, p.10; also pp.9, 11.
†Registrar-General's Report, Appendix P, p.108.

impurity of the air. I am quite at a loss, therefore, to understand, why the Poor Law Commissioners reiterate three times, that my letter ascribed the mortality of the people of England to 'one all-pervading cause;' the all-pervading cause being nothing more than a cause which indirectly produced a much higher proportion than 63 in 148,701 deaths.

"I have shown from the facts registered in 1837 and in 1838, that the number of deaths from starvation in any of its senses was not exaggerated; that the classification of the cases was accurate; and that the passage which has called down animadversion is substantially correct. I admit, without any hesitation, that it *may* have been misunderstood; and I may add that the meaning of the term 'starvation' was not well understood by the public: its complications at different ages, with hunger, cold, destitution, and human agency, could scarcely have been conjectured, much less well known, by persons who had thought but casually on the subject, before they were made acquainted with the facts that have been extracted from the registers by your direction.

"The ascertained low rates of wages in agricultural districts refute the observations in the Poor Law Commissioners' letter 'on the *surplus means* of the *great mass* of the labouring population.' This is an extensive question, and cannot be satisfactorily discussed here. I may nevertheless remark in passing, that the arguments drawn from the savings' banks, and the sale of spirits, are inaccurately stated and fallacious. The Report referred to England and Wales, during the half year ended December 31st, 1837. The amount of deposits in the savings' banks was 16,578,849*l.* on November 20th, 1837, and not 'upwards of 20,000,000*l.*' The number of depositors was 547,910. The population was about 15,880,000; so that only 3½ per cent. of the total population, or 7 per cent. of adults, above the age of 20, were depositors in the savings' banks: 93 adults in 100 held no deposits, which is surely no proof that the 'great mass' of the agricultural labourers had 'surplus means.' The Poor Law Commissioners enter into a calculation to show that the labourers of England and Wales expend from 40,000,000*l.* to 50,000,000*l.* a-year in 'comforts and luxuries.' The proof is arithmetical. 'A sum of 8,444,800*l.*;' they say, 'is annually paid as duty on gin, whiskey, rum, and other spirits, the ultimate cost of which to the consumer cannot (the Commissioners believe) be less than *two-thirds* more, or nearly 24,000,000*l.* per annum.* The duty on tobacco, malt, and hops is 7,000,000*l.*, the cost of which commodities and of beer to the consumer will be scarcely less than the cost of spirits; making an aggregate of not less than between 40,000,000*l.* and 50,000,000*l.* per annum.' Now 8,444,800*l.*, and the 'two-thirds of that sum,' namely, 5,629,867*l.* make 14,074,667*l.*, which, when multiplied by 2, gives as the product 28,149,334*l.*

"From the data supplied by the Poor Law Commissioners it is evident that they have committed an error in the calculation of from 12,000,000*l.* to 22,000,000*l.* per anuum; and this in a letter urging an accusation of inaccuracy and exaggeration in an affair of 63 in 148,701 facts.

"I do not believe that a knowledge of the fact, that a certain number of persons die from starvation can lead to evil, if it have the effect of stimulating the vigilance and charity of the English public.

---

*Official Circular, p.11.

"The Poor Law Commissioners state, that 'for the maintenance of the care for life and social feelings of anxiety for the relief of suffering which characterize a civilized people, every case of death from want should be the subject of a careful inquiry.' They deem the cases in the registers 'a subject of very serious consideration.' They engage to institute inquiries themselves, 'and to ascertain if any, and what, remedies may be applied *for the future.*' They will apprize the clerks of Guardians that the cases of 'starvation will form the subject of special inquiries,' and will request the Guardians to make due inquiries as to the cause of death, and whether 'any and what blame attaches to the parish or Union officers, or whether it is ascribable to any and what defects in the administration of relief.'

"The measures which the Poor Law Commissioners propose to adopt 'for the future' will probably be viewed with satisfaction by the public; and I shall not regret that the facts in the registers, and the few lines in the letter, which you did me the honour to publish, in the Appendix to your Report, suggested inquiries which may ultimately diminish the chance of death from starvation. If there should be one death the less, 'for the future,' I ask no other vindication.

"I have the honour to be, Sir,

"Your very obedient and humble Servant,

(*Signed*) "William Farr

"*To the Registrar General.*"

William Farr's descriptions of the duties of the Statistical Superintendent of the General Register Office

Farr Collection, Vol.2, British Library of Political and Economic Science

DUTIES OF STATISTICAL SUPERINTENDENT

1. The Statistical Superintendent has to plan, and to superintend the abstracts which are prepared and published by the Registrar General accompanied with the required Commentaries and Reports. The Reports relate to the Population – to Marriages, Births, Deaths, and Causes of Death and the facts by which these are more of less directly influenced.

2. The assisting of the Registrar General in taking the Census and the Statistical analysis of the results have since 1851 constituted part of the work carried on under the supervision of this Officer and I conceive should continue to be.

3. He has to keep himself informed of the Statistics of other States – to keep up a correspondence with the heads of Foreign Statistical Departments – and be prepared to work in concert with them on International Statistical Inquiries.

4. He has to give evidence before Parliamentary Committees on Statistical subjects, and to serve when required on Commissions.

   (Dr Farr, for instance, was called upon to serve on the Royal Indian Sanitary Commission under the Presidency of Lord Herbert, and afterwards Lord Derby to supply Tables, and to contribute to the Report.)

5. The Registrar General's Annual, Quarterly, and Weekly Reports – The English Life Table in one Volume, and the Reports on Cholera, which are occasional Reports, will show better than anything else – the nature of the work of the Department and the consequent duties of the Statistical Superintendent.

6. It will be seen from those publications that three Kinds of acquirements are required for the efficient discharge of the duties.

   1. Knowledge of Medicine and the Collateral Sciences.

   2. Practical Mathematical Knowledge of some range.

   3. A fair acquaintance with at least the French, Italian and German languages.

7. Dr. Farr takes the liberty of adding that he joined the department at the age of 31, and that up to that age he had been pursuing medical and scientific studies – in the English and French Hospitals – in the University of Paris, and in the University of London. Unless he had expended his time – and money – on these preliminary studies – he does not conceive that he could have filled the duties of his Office to the satisfaction of the Registrar General, or to the advantage of the Public Service. And he would venture to suggest that his successor should possess more than his qualifications if not more than his advantages in order to keep pace with the progress of science, and with the public requirements in connection with the Economy and the Health of the Country.

8. The Office is necessarily of a Professional and an Administrative character, and a future Candidate should probably possess the Diploma of State Medicine – which has been suggested and will probably ere long be instituted.

9. Dr. Farr has had during his 35 years office the invaluable assistance of Mr. Hammick and Mr. Clode in supervising the work of the Clerks of the Department and submitting the returns to the Registrar General. On the promotion of Mr. Clode – Mr. Thoreller has filled his place.

10. The Office being of a distinct character, should, Dr. Farr submits, in future be designated by a distinct **Title**, as a good title is part of the pay of all branches of the public service; and induces men to enter it in preference to other fields of employment, and this is necessary as successful and eminent medical men get incomes ranging from £2000 to £10,000 a year.

The background of the Population (Statistics) Act of 1938

The earlier discussion has shown that it is often very difficult **to** infer from the available historical materials which factors and which individuals were responsible for particular changes in census taking and vital registration. In view of these difficulties, and given the fact that the Population (Statistics) Act of 1938 effected the first major change in the scope of vital registration in Britain since 1836, I thought it might be useful to set down the circumstances leading to that Act. Members of my own committee – the Population Investigation Committee – were involved in pressing for the changes brought about by the Act and I have been able to draw upon unpublished documents of my committee, and the recollections of my colleagues, as well as on the files of the Office of Population Censuses and Surveys.[1]

It is, however, necessary to begin rather earlier than the Act itself and to indicate some of the factors associated with the change in attitude to population trends in the 1930s. Of course, the continuing decline in the birth rate in most Western societies during that period – that is up to and including 1932 and 1933 – was fully visible from the published statistics. But the possible implications of the continuing decline upon the size and structure of the population were not generally realized until wide use had been made of the indices of replacement developed independently by R. Boeckh and R. R. Kuczynski on the one hand and by A. J. Lotka on the other.[2] Boeckh's contribution, which involved the application of life table concepts to the analysis of net replacement, was made at the end of the nineteenth century. Subsequently, Kuczynski used an intermediate stage of the calculation to provide a measure of fertility, and the two indices, known respectively as the net reproduction rate and the gross reproduction rate, were displayed in the writings of Kuczynski, and particularly in the two volumes entitled *The Balance of Births and Deaths*, (Vol.1, New York 1928; Vol.2., Washington, DC, 1931) as well as in *The Measurement of Population Growth* (London 1935), written after Kuczynski had left Germany and was at the London School of Economics in Professor Lancelot Hogben's Department of Social Biology. The work of Lotka derives in essence from his early studies in 1911, but the significance of this work was not widely appreciated until the appearance of two articles published by Dublin and Lotka in 1925 and 1930.[3] Lotka's work was both more fundamental and more rigorous than the work of Boeckh and Kuczynski, but being based on a sophisticated mathematical analysis it had less immediate impact on the outside world. By contrast, Kuczynski's many calculations of gross and net reproduction rates received considerable attention and were in effect adopted by the League of Nations in the sense that, when the League's *Statistical Year Book* was edited by G. Frumkin, these rates appeared regularly for as many countries as had data suitable for their calculation. By 1936 Kuczynski was deservedly well known in Britain, and his book, *The Measurement of Population Growth*, still remains an extremely interesting introduction to the study of fertility and replacement trends.

The Department of Social Biology, where Kuczynski continued his studies, was

one of the few centres in Britain concerned at the time with demographic inquiries. Professor Hogben regarded demography as one of the bases of a new political arithmetic.[4] And Dr Enid Charles had already published her striking volume, *The Twilight of Parenthood* (London 1934)[5] and had followed this with a series of widely quoted population projections.[6]

Kuczynski's work was focused upon quantitative replacement – the replacement of total populations. The Eugenics Society, on the other hand, was much more interested in qualitative replacement – that is, especially in differential fertility. Influenced at least in part by R. A. Fisher, who had put forward the hypothesis that social mobility in a competitive society reduced the fertility of the upwardly mobile,[7] the Society decided to investigate the possible use of family allowances as a means of modifying the pattern of differential fertility. In Britain the Family Endowment Society, inspired by Eleanor Rathbone, was promoting the adoption of family allowances as instruments of social justice.[8] In France and Belgium, where family allowance systems were already widespread, the allowances – which originally had aimed at providing a just 'family wage' – were increasingly being used as measures in a pro-natalist population policy. The Eugenics Society offered me a research grant to study the nature and consequences of family allowance systems in France and Belgium, and I was given an entirely free hand in doing so. My initial studies led me to extend the work to a more general consideration of pro-natalist population policies, including those in Fascist Italy and Nazi Germany. The result was a book entitled *The Struggle for Population*, published in September 1936.

In the meantime, Dr C. P. Blacker, who, as Secretary of the Eugenics Society, had been very largely responsible for my research grant, had himself become increasingly interested in the possible consequences of the decline of the birth rate. On a journey to Bangor, to address a branch of the Fabian Society, he read and was impressed by Enid Charles's book, *The Twilight of Parenthood*. Feeling that too little study had been made of the causes of decline in the birth rate and of the demography of the West in general, he believed that the time was appropriate for the establishment of some autonomous institution which would enable more attention to be given to the subject. To launch the idea he persuaded Professor (later Sir Alexander) Carr-Saunders to give the Galton Lecture in 1935 and to devote that lecture to the decline in fertility.[9] The interest aroused by that lecture in turn made it possible to persuade the Eugenics Society to provide funds to help in establishing an independent academic body which would concern itself more thoroughly with demographic matters. This body was the Population Investigation Committee, which held an introductory meeting on 8 January 1936 and its first formal meeting on 15 June of that year. At this formal meeting the committee recommended that I be appointed Research Secretary, a position which I held until the outbreak of World War II and again for some time from the end of the war. Carr-Saunders was Chairman of the committee and remained so until he retired in 1959, when I was elected to succeed him. Dr C. P. Blacker was – and still is – the Honorary Secretary.

During 1936 three books on population questions were being prepared for publication. Carr-Saunders had been invited by the Oxford University Press to write a general book on the subject, and it appeared under the title of *World Population – Past Growth and Present Trends*. Kuczynski was writing on aspects of the population of the British Empire, and his book, published by the Oxford University Press, was entitled *Population Movements*. The Oxford University Press also agreed to publish my own book, *The Struggle for Population*. These three books were reviewed in two articles in *The Times* on 28 and 29 September 1936 under the title of 'The Dwindling Family'.

The review was somewhat emphatic. The reviewer wrote '. . . there is no evidence that the British race will maintain its numbers in the future. Far from it, its numbers will certainly fall, perhaps catastrophically, during the next 50 years' (*The Times*, 28 September 1936). And *The Times*, in a leader on 29 September, asked if it was too much to hope that, 'before the next Budget speech inquiry will have begun into the nature of the problem, the possibility of remedies, and the lessons of foreign experience'. Taking the opportunity given by these articles, Carr-Saunders prepared an account of the aims and programme of the Population Investigation Committee, and this was published in *The Times* of 5 November 1936. He also wrote to the Minister of Health, suggesting that representatives of the Ministry and/or the Registrar General should be appointed to the committee. A reply received on 21 December stated only that the proposal was being given attention.[10]

Early in the following year (10 February 1937), Ronald Cartland, MP for King's Norton, introduced a motion in the House, calling upon the government to institute an inquiry into the prospective decline of the population, and an extensive debate followed (*Hansard*, House of Commons, 10 February 1937, cols.484-539). Cartland suggested that the government should collaborate with the Population Investigation Committee. The government spokesman, R. S. Hudson (Parliamentary Secretary, Ministry of Health), would not accept the proposal. 'We do not propose to set an inquiry on foot, because the subject is continuously under inquiry in my Department. We propose to intensify that inquiry. We shall welcome any assistance, but we think it is essentially a matter for the Government and not for outside societies' (col.534).[11]

In fact the Minister of Health, Sir Kingsley Wood, did appear to be interested in 'outside assistance', for on 11 February he wrote to Carr-Saunders, asking him to get into touch with the Registrar General and to discuss possible co-operation between the Population Investigation Committee and the General Register Office.[12] Several meetings were held, the first on 2 March. The Registrar General (S. P. Vivian, later Sir Sylvanus Vivian), told us that he hoped to include age at maternity in the birth registration provisions in the near future; this was one of the items necessary for the more effective study of fertility trends and the Eugenics Society had already proposed its inclusion in 1928. At least two more meetings took place and I prepared a memorandum for discussion with the Registrar General, indicating lines of research based upon existing census and registration data and suggesting additional questions to be asked at birth registration.[13] So far as the latter questions were concerned, I stressed the need to have date of marriage and birth parity reported at birth registration. These suggestions were entirely in keeping with the views which had been developed independently in the General Register Office. In addition, it was desirable, for the study of infant mortality, to have infant deaths tabulated by calendar year of birth. Kuczynski had drawn attention to the importance of this latter information in removing the need to estimate 'separation factors' in the calculation of infant mortality rates.[14]

Further reference was made in Parliament to the 'population question' later in February (25 February, *Hansard*, col.2182), when F. W. Pethick-Lawrence asked the Minister of Health whether the committee of inquiry had had its attention drawn to the restrictions imposed by some companies on the marriage of junior staff. But a much fuller reference to government intentions was given by Sir Kingsley Wood in the debate on Ministry of Health Estimates (*Hansard*, 8 June 1937, cols.1610-1611; 18 June 1937, col.794). Sir Kingsley explained that two inquiries were in progress – one by the Registrar General and the other by the Population Investigation Committee. But it was clear that inquiries by these bodies (or by a Royal Commission, if there were one) were handicapped by inadequate statistics. 'I regret to say that our methods of obtaining and keeping important vital statistics are unsatisfactory and incomplete. Further information is undoubtedly necessary in connection with fertility.'[15] And in winding up the debate he stressed the importance of extending the coverage of our vital registration (rather than attempting to collect relevant information through the census, which, in any case, was not due to be taken for another four years). But it would be necessary to treat as confidential information on date and duration of marriage and number of children born previously – to use the information for statistical purposes only. To do this would go beyond the existing powers of the Registrar General and new legislation might be needed.[16]

New legislation was found to be required. It was referred to in the King's speech on 26 October (*Hansard*, 26 October 1937, cols.8-9), and the Population (Statistics) Bill was introduced by Sir Kingsley Wood on 28 October (*Hansard*, 28 October 1937, col. 259). There was a further meeting of members of the Population Investigation Committee with the Registrar General, after which it was reported that the committee's representations had been taken into account in the preparation of the Population (Statistics) Bill (minutes of committee meeting, 9 November 1937).

For the rest, the progress of the Bill in Parliament is documented in the *Hansard* reports. There was opposition to the Bill, but it was not completely on Party lines. It is true that the main support for the Bill came from the Conservatives, some of whom were alarmed by possible depopulation in the future. Perhaps, as Sir Francis Freemantle declared during the debate on the Address, they were opposed to 'unilateral depopulation' (*Hansard*, 27 October 1937, col.194). (The Primrose League political school, at a meeting on 25 June 1937, had passed a resolution which, among other things, asserted that 'the present tendency of our population to decline constitutes a grave menace to our standard of life and to our security...' And on 7 October Duncan Sandys, on behalf of the Norwood Conservative Association, had put forward a resolution congratulating Sir Kingsley Wood on having decided to institute a special inquiry into the birth rate problem – CB 10/1, p.79.) Labour members not surprisingly expressed more concern with the condition of the existing population than with the question of future numbers, and some were in any case opposed to attempts to encourage a 'population race'. But, as Sir Kingsley Wood pointed out during the debate on the second reading, in 1930 a deputation to the Registrar General from the Science and Public Health Advisory Committee of the Labour Party had pressed for a considerably wider range of information on fertility, covering both census and vital statistics.[17] Criticism of the Bill was based partly on opposition to 'prying inquiries' and 'governmental inquisitions' – the Bill was widely referred to outside the House as the 'Nosey Parker Bill'[18] – and partly on the belief that the proposals were inappropriate, being more suitable for censuses, or would serve no useful purpose. The debate was perhaps unique in that A. P. Herbert (MP for Oxford University) wrote a 'poem' specially for the occasion, attacking the Bill for what he regarded as its essential irrelevance. The final stanza argued that:

'The world, in short, which never was extravagantly sane,
Developed all the signs of inflamation of the brain;
The past was not encouraging, the future none could tell,
But the Minister still wondered why the population fell.'

During its passage through Parliament, the Bill was modified in several ways. Nevertheless, the Population (Statistics) Act greatly extended the range of relevant information on fertility collected through birth registration – very much in line with the recommendations which William Farr had put forward in the 1860s. In his speech in the debate, Aneurin Bevan had referred to Carr-Saunders as 'probably the author of this Bill' (*Hansard*, 29 November 1937, col.1776). This was not the case.[19] But the Population Investigation Committee, under the chairmanship of Carr-Saunders, had certainly helped to promote the new legislation, advocating more comprehensive vital registration statistics for the purpose of adding to our knowledge and understanding of the trend and pattern of fertility, and thereby providing a better basis for policy decisions. And it was in large measure that aim which was described in the financial memorandum on the Bill: 'the object of this Bill is to extend the scope of the particulars which can at present be asked for upon the registration of a birth, stillbirth, death or marriage, and by this means to provide the statistical evidence needed for the practical consideration of the problems in regard to the future population of Great Britain to which the decline in the birthrate has given rise.'[20]

Exactly how important was the support given by the committee it is neither possible nor necessary to determine. No doubt Vivian was justified when he wrote to Blacker – who apparently accepted the validity of Vivian's comment – that he would make Blacker 'a present of the implication... that the value of fertility statistics in this connection was first brought to the notice of an innocent department in the memorandum submitted by the Committee, although in fact the department had so long ago as 1911 included a fertility enquiry in the Census, and had had more recently negotiations and discussions upon the subject with the Eugenics Society' (29 October 1937, CB10/III, p.365).[21] But the General Register Office had envisaged synchronizing a change in registration with a projected 1936 census, which did not materialize. If such synchronization had continued to be regarded as indispensable, no change in registration could have been achieved in practice until 1951. And there is nothing in the three volumes of papers relating to the Population Bill to suggest that, prior to the new wave of publicity in 1936 and 1937, the General Register Office had abandoned the idea of synchronization. On the other hand, the new wave of publicity in 1936 was not directly engineered by the Population Investigation Committee, but was in large part prompted by the prominence given in *The Times* to three books which, fortuitously, had appeared within a very short period. The committee seized the opportunity to publicize its existence and aims. The population question became a topic of public discussion partly because there were new books on the subject and partly because the gradual lessening of the economic depression in Britain made it possible for the question to be looked at in other than Malthusian terms. And the committee and the General Register Office were in agreement that the first priority should not be the appointment of a Royal Commission, but the improvement of the basic data required for the study of fertility trends. When sufficient concern had been shown in the House of Commons to offer a substantial prospect of a change in vital registration, the General Register Office had necessarily to take the primary responsibility. But, as the discussion has shown, the committee worked closely with the General Register Office to secure the desired change.[22]

NOTES

1 Formerly known as the General Register Office. There are three volumes of papers, entitled *Population (Statistics) Act 1938. Bill Files.* These papers, now accessible for study, will be transferred to the Public Record Office. Their present reference number is CB10/I-III.

2 There had been a (private) National Birth Rate Commission, set up in 1913 by the National Council of Public Morals, which had issued a number of reports. The Commission was reconstituted in 1918. But in general the effect of World War I was to raise Malthusian fears, and it was not until later that the declining birth rate again gave rise to concern.

3 L. I. Dublin & A. J. Lotka, 'On the true rate of natural increase as exemplified by the population of the United States, 1920', *Journal of the American Statistical Association*, Vol.20, 1925; and *idem.*, 'The true rate of natural increase of the population of the United States, revision on the basis of recent data', *Metron*, Vol.8, 1930. Lotka's contributions to the analysis of replacement are summed up in his later publication, *Théorie Analytique des Associations Biologiques*, Part 1, Paris 1934; Part 2, Paris 1939.

4 The Department of Social Biology was indeed one of the few centres in Britain engaged in substantial empirical social research. The results of much of that research were summarized in *Political Arithmetic*, edited by Professor Hogben, which appeared (London 1938) when the department had ceased to exist, following Professor Hogben's transfer to the Regius Professorship of Natural Philosophy at the University of Aberdeen. The department had very little impact on the London School of Economics as a whole, but a very considerable influence on many of those who worked directly with it. I was a member of the department in 1936 and continued to work there in 1937, after I had been appointed Research Secretary of the Population Investigation Committee. My own approach to social research was very considerably affected by discussions with Professor Hogben.

5 When this book was first published it was rumoured that public libraries were reluctant to buy copies since the title suggested that it might be a birth-control manual. I do not know whether that was actually the case. But it is true that when the book was reissued the title was changed to *The Menace of Underpopulation*.

6 E. Charles, 'The effect of present trends in fertility and mortality upon the future population of England and Wales and upon its age composition', *London and Cambridge Economic Service*, Special Memorandum No.40, 1935; and also 'The effect of

present trends in fertility and mortality upon the future population of Scotland and upon its age composition', *Proc. Royal Soc. Edinburgh*, Vol.56, Part 1, 1935-36.

7 R. A. Fisher, *The Genetical Theory of Natural Selection*, Oxford 1930, esp. ch.11. The hypothesis, derived in part from earlier work by J. A. Cobb, is in a sense only another way of looking at the theory of 'social capillarity' put forward by Arsène Dumont as an explanation of the decline in fertility in France (see his *Dépopulation et Civilisation*, Paris 1890). One of the investigations which I subsequently designed and which was undertaken by the Population Investigation Committee, aimed at testing the Fisher hypothesis. See J. Berent, 'Fertility and social mobility', *Population Studies*, March 1952.

8 Eleanor F. Rathbone, *The Disinherited Family*, London 1924. See also *idem., The Ethics and Economics of Family Endowment*, London 1927.

9 'Eugenics in the light of population trends', delivered 16 February 1935 (*Eugenics Review*, April 1935).

10 The letter was inevitably passed to the Registrar General of England and Wales, S. P. Vivian (later Sir Sylvanus Vivian), whose initial reaction was not enthusiastic. He wrote (to Sir G. Chrystal, Ministry of Health, 22 January 1937) that one of the research proposals – a complete survey of the main features of the history of the population of England and Wales since 1870 – was a 'colossal' one, and suspected that 'the present invitation is largely prompted by the desire to get our departmental assistance in the preparation of the requisite tables' (CB 10/III, p.211). (That interpretation was unjustified. The invitation was a natural one, in view of the role of the General Register Office in the collection and analysis of demographic statistics. The committee wished to benefit from the advice of representatives of the General Register Office. Of course, the committee hoped to be able to suggest further relevant analyses of official demographic data, but as a matter of general interest and not for the purpose of obtaining such analyses for its private use.) He suggested, as a basis for discussion, the idea of a liaison committee between the Population Investigation Committee and the Departments, to settle which inquiries would be of special interest to the G.R.O. and the 'extent of the departmental co-operation in them'.

11 In briefing the Minister of Health for the debate on the Cartland motion, the G.R.O. stated that an undertaking had been given to the Eugenics Society in 1930 'to make the necessary alteration in the birth register on the first convenient occasion', and that it had been intended that the change should 'synchronise with the figures of the then expected 1936 Census'. Though the census had not been taken, preparations for the change were being made and were far advanced. As for the Population Investigation Committee (reported to have invited Ministry of Health and G.R.O. co-operation 'on more than one occasion' – a report which must have derived from confusion regarding the Eugenics Society itself, since the Population Investigation Committee had only very recently been established), if the matter were raised in the debate 'it will be difficult to disregard altogether a Committee which comprises persons such as Professor R. A. Fisher and Professor Carr-Saunders' (R. A. Fisher was not a member of the Population Investigation Committee). It would be possible to say that 'we proposed to enter into consultation with the Committee with a view to some form of co-operation, (CB10/III, pp.226-227).

12 Vivian wrote to Carr-Saunders, 16 February; his letter crossed one from Carr-

Saunders, dated 17 February. In a subsequent letter to Blacker (29 October 1937) Vivian explained that the decision to write to Carr-Saunders had been reached before, and had not been inspired by, the debate on Cartland's motion (CB10/III, pp.364-366).

13 At the meetings Dr Blacker referred to a proposed inquiry into the practice on birth control (and abortion) to be sponsored by the Population Investigation Committee and for which he had designed a questionnaire. There followed some correspondence with the G.R.O. (and especially with Dr Percy Stocks) on the inquiry, but, apart from some pilot surveys, nothing substantial was done. It was not until the appointment of the Royal Commission on Population that a full inquiry was launched, under the direction of Dr E. Lewis-Faning, the questionnaire then used drawing very considerably on Dr Blacker's earlier version (the inquiry was sponsored by the Medical and Biological Committee of the Royal Commission; both Dr Blacker and I were members of that committee).

14 I also visited the General Registry Office, Edinburgh, to discuss possible analyses of Scottish vital and census statistics. The aim was not to make independent and unco-ordinated approaches to the two sources of official population statistics, but rather to see how far the special provisions of the Scottish system could be used to fill gaps in the English data. In particular, analyses of births by marriage duration would have been possible for Scotland, but not for England and Wales. In addition, both in England and in Scotland, there were relevant questions which could be answered by further tabulations of the vital statistics – for example, age at first marriage by groom's occupation, a tabulation which had been carried out for England and Wales in the late nineteenth century but had not been repeated subsequently.

15 There had been some pressure for the appointment of a Royal Commission – for example from Sir James Marchant, who had been Secretary of the earlier National Birth Rate Commission, Lord Bledisloe and Geoffrey Faber (letter in *The Times*, 23 March). The question had been discussed on 20 April at a meeting of the Royal Statistical Society ('On the value of Royal Commissions in sociological research, with special reference to the birth rate', *J.R.S.S.*, Part 3, 1937), at which Vivian argued that it was necessary to have the relevant data available before a Royal Commission could be of use. And further publicity had been given to the 'population question' by the publication in March of Dr G. F. McCleary's book, *The Menace of British Depopulation.*

16 By the time of the debate there had already been considerable activity by the General Register Office, and on 12 April Vivian had sent Sir George Chrystal (Ministry of Health) a memorandum, indicating the information which might be obtained through vital registration (CB10/I, pp.50-52). Later a draft Cabinet memorandum was sent to Sir George Chrystal (on 7 July; *loc. cit.*, pp.66-70). Estimates of additional costs were made by V. P. A. Derrick, the Chief Civil Statistician at the General Register Office (19 July, *loc. cit.*, pp.75-76). A Cabinet paper (CP229(37)) of 7 October by the Minister of Health and the Secretary of State for Scotland sought agreement on the introduction of legislation to provide particulars, to be obtained confidentially for statistical purposes only, at the registration of births, deaths, stillbirths and marriages. This was followed by a memorandum to the Home Affairs Committee on the draft Population Bill (HA39/37,

22 October) and the committee subsequently accepted the draft and recommended its introduction in the House of Commons forthwith (HAC 12th Conclusions (37), 26 October – conclusions of meeting 25 October).

17 Three Labour MPs – C. Atlee, F. W. Pethick-Lawrence and C. Ede – had tabled a motion that 'this House, while recognizing that the collection of some additional facts regarding the population may be desirable, cannot assent to the Second Reading of a Bill which instructs the registrars to elicit confidential and intimate information not urgently required for statistical purposes' (CB10/I, p.472). There were certainly misunderstandings – as regards the reasons for wanting the additional information, the confidentiality of that information, and the extent to which comparable information was already being collected in other countries.

In briefing the Minister it was also noted that the 1910 Census Bill, which had provided for detailed information on fertility to be collected at the 1911 census, was introduced by that 'Labour Party Stalwart', John Burns (CB10/I, p.471).

18 On the whole, the Press was friendly. But there was a violent attack in *The Sunday Express*, 7 & 28 November, (CB10/I, pp.390 & 476). The initial article was entitled: 'Scheme to deliver us all over to the Nosey Parkers'; the second was entitled 'Bill that could drag out all your secrets'.

19 Vivian was understandably ambivalent about the role which Carr-Saunders might play in connection with the Bill. In a letter to S. F. Hearder (Ministry of Health), 4 December 1937, he wrote: 'It might be undesirable to allow the idea to be strengthened that Carr-Saunders is the parent of the Bill and the dictator of its precise contents' (CB10/II, p.123). But he was anxious to have Carr-Saunders's public support of the Bill and its specific proposals. At one time he considered the possibility of a joint statement with Carr-Saunders, which the Minister might issue as a White Paper. This fell to the ground when he learned that Carr-Saunders had agreed to write an article for *The Observer*, and he then became concerned to make sure that the article would not be in conflict with the official proposals and with Vivian's view as to what questions were 'indispensable to the promotion of any serious statistical inquiry into the causation of the decline in the birthrate...'
Carr-Saunders and I discussed this with Vivian on 3 December and Vivian asked me to see him again 4 December and to confirm that *The Observer* article, which appeared on 5 December, would cover all the essential points. (Vivian believed that I had written the article. But I have no recollection of doing so and it is not in keeping with my experience of Carr-Saunders that he would attach his name to an article written by someone else. At most I helped only by providing some initial notes.) Subsequently Carr-Saunders wrote to S. F. Hearder (16 December), setting out for use by the Minister the reasons why the various questions proposed in the Bill were essential. He also wrote to Pethick-Lawrence to explain why it was most important to ask at birth registration for the date of marriage (CB10/II, pp.187-196).

20 The financial memorandum also referred to research – a 'programme of inquiry and research at present regarded as necessary and sufficient to elucidate the special birthrate problems above-mentioned'. The expenses of administration and research were estimated as not exceeding £7000 a year.

As was mentioned in the earlier discussion, changes in birth registration also involved consequential changes in death registration, in order that estimates of the appropriate base populations could be constructed. Marriage registration, however, was not changed to meet the needs of demographic analysis, and the reporting of occupations on the marriage certificate (four occupations are reported – those of the groom, the bride, the groom's father and the bride's father) is still unsatisfactory. The Population Investigation Committee had hoped that, in respect of reporting occupation at birth registration, the 1938 Act would specify the same detail as is required by the census. This was not done, but the committee was told (by the Registrar General) that the same object would be achieved by means of instructions to registrars. (In the debate on the Bill by a committee of the whole House, 1 February 1938, Sir Kingsley Wood had stated that this was possible under Section 4 of the 1874 Registration Act – *Hansard*, 1 February 1938, cols.105-106).

21 In fact, in earlier periods the General Register Office had obviously given considerable thought to the question of improving the vital statistics of the country. The subject was discussed in detail in 1916 by the then Registrar General, Sir Bernard Mallet, in his presidential address to the Royal Statistical Society (B. Mallet, 'The organization of registration in its bearing on vital statistics', *J.R.S.S.*, Vol.80, Part 1, January 1917). Mallet wished vital registration to show family linkages – for example by including on the birth certificate sufficient information to enable it to be linked with the marriage certificate of the child's parents – and was in favour of a national registration system. He stressed the need to register stillbirths and argued that, for statistical purposes, it was desirable that birth registration should provide much more information. More specifically he recommended that the additional particulars obtained at registration of birth should include: dates and places of parents' birth and marriage; number of children born to and surviving of the marriage; whether the mother had any occupation other than domestic duties and, if so, whether outside the home. At death registration, the additional particulars should cover the industry in which the deceased had worked and the length of time he had followed the occupation in which he was employed at the time of his death; the number of children alive or dead; for deaths of children, mother's occupation. However, he did not appear to be very hopeful that the changes would be made. He said '...we cannot, unfortunately, expect, however urgent our representations may be, that legislation will be framed solely with a view to obtaining the best possible statistics, and all that usually remains for statisticians is to make the best use they can for their own purposes of such opportunities as legislation throws in their way'.

It is probably true that, generally, the government was not greatly interested in improving demographic statistics and, as a result, the General Register Office tended to be regarded as an 'orphan child'. But between the wars, at least, it appeared to have acquired an 'orphan child' attitude and did not seem to press with very much vigour for improvements. The importance of the population debate initiated in 1936 was that it persuaded the government to place a much higher than customary emphasis on the value of more comprehensive vital statistics and thus to provide the kind of opportunity which Mallet had had in mind.

22 As for the question of collaboration between the General Register Office and the committee – the question which, in effect, initiated the discussions which led to the 1938 Act – there was little immediate practical opportunity. Although I

personally received much help from V. P. A. Derrick, the Chief Civil Statistician at the General Register Office, my research in 1938 and 1939 was largely concerned with developments on the Continent – and especially in France, Belgium and Germany – while Dr Grace Leybourne, who was appointed in 1937 to undertake research for the committee, was primarily interested in the relationship between the costs of education and the decline in family size (the results of her research were published in her book, G. G. Leybourne-White & K. White, *Education and the Birth-rate: a Social Dilemma*, London 1940). The war then intervened. The situation changed markedly with the appointment of the Royal Commission on Population, to which several members of the committee were attached. In particular, Carr-Saunders was Chairman of the Statistics Committee, while Kuczynski, Sir George Maddex (the Government Actuary) and I were members of that committee, along with V. P. A. Derrick, P. Stocks (the Chief Medical Statistician of the General Register Office) and J. G. Kyd (the Registrar General of Scotland). The Statistics Committee met frequently (there were sixty-two meetings of the full committee and many meetings of sub-committees) and there was close collaboration on various projects, several of which directly involved the General Register Office. In addition, the Population Investigation Committee itself, on the basis of a substantial grant provided by the Nuffield Foundation, undertook two major studies of direct relevance to the work of the Royal Commission. The collaboration which developed in the Statistics Committee continued after the work of the Royal Commission had been completed, and the link between the General Register Office and non-governmental specialists is certainly very much closer now than was the case in the 1930s.

Supplementary note

After this book was already in page proof, Mr R. E. Jones, who had been helping me with some research into the history of infant mortality in Britain, came across an important item in the Newsholme Collection in the library of the London School of Hygiene and Tropical Medicine. The item is a confidential but printed document, produced by the General Register Office and dated March 1915, entitled *Memorandum on the Registration Acts (Births, Deaths, and Marriages) with Proposals for their Reform.* This printed memorandum was clearly the basis of Sir Bernard Mallet's address to the Royal Statistical Society in 1916 and contains a detailed account of the limitations of the existing registration system as well as the proposals for reform indicated in Mallet's presidential address.

Vital registration in Britain during the nineteenth century

When civil vital registration was introduced in England and Wales in 1837 the situation was more favourable than is the case in many developing countries today. There was already in existence an ecclesiastical system which, even though it was known to be defective, still covered the bulk of vital events. But the new civil system was itself imperfect. Some of its deficiencies derived from the 1836 Act, which, as was pointed out in the earlier discussion, was 'mutilated' during its passage through the House of Lords. Other deficiencies were the result of the 'state of the art' in the nineteenth century. Cause mortality analysis, for example, was imperfect because of the contemporary limitations in the understanding and diagnosis of disease. The improvements made during the nineteenth century in the classification of causes of death were the result both of the systematic international co-operation of medical statisticians, stimulated especially by William Farr and Marc d'Espine, and also of the progress of medicine itself. It was not until 1900 that an international classification of causes of death was first approved. In addition, looking back with the experience of modern demographic analysis, we can see that in a number of respects the analysis of the available vital statistics was too restricted. It is worth commenting on these various limitations – on the first categories because they affect the interpretation of trends and levels and on the last because, with the growing interest in historical demography, some of the gaps may be filled by retabulating, on a sample basis, the records of earlier years.

One consequence of the 'mutilation' of the 1836 Act was the incomplete registration of births and deaths. Farr was fully aware of this, pressed for a revision of the requirements (achieved in the 1874 Act, which reallocated the primary responsibility for registering a birth to the parents, the occupier of the house in which the child was born or the persons attending the birth or having charge of the child)[1] and made several estimates of the degree of incompleteness. But Farr did not provide an explicit account of the way in which his estimates had been constructed. Because of that, some years ago I produced new estimates, which compared well with Farr's. The 'inflation ratios' required to convert the official statistics of live births into estimates of the 'true' numbers are summarised in Table 1, together with the official and 'corrected' crude birth rates and infant mortality rates. These estimates were based on the assumption that, save for the period 1841-45, death registration was complete. For 1841-45, however, a deficiency of 2 per cent in death registration was assumed, the whole of that deficiency being attributed to infant deaths.[2] Similar tests applied to the statistics for Scotland suggested that, from 1861 onwards, birth registration was virtually complete.

It should, however, be emphasized, that the estimates very probably understate the deficiencies of birth registration. They assume that the censuses gave complete child coverage – save for children under two years of age – from 1841 onwards. Since there were no post-censal surveys, direct tests of completeness of enumeration are not available. Nor can a 'balancing equation' be used because that would involve

Table 1: England and Wales: 'Inflation ratios' and crude birth and infant mortality rates

Period	'Inflation ratios'	Crude birth rate (per 1000)		Infant mortality rate (per 1000)	
		Based on registered births	Based on 'corrected' births	Based on registered births	Based on 'corrected' births
1831-37	1·33			–	–
1837-38	1·15		36·6	–	–
1838-39	1·14		(1831-40)	–	–
1839-41	1·12			–	–
1841-45	1·094	32·2	35·2	148	147
1846-50	1·064	32·7	34·8	158	148
1851-55	1·051	33·8	35·5	156	149
1856-60	1·034	34·3	35·5	152	147
1861-65	1·024	35·0	35·8	151	148
1866-70	1·016	35·1	35·7	157	154
1871-75	1·010	35·4	35·7	153	152
1876-80	1·004	35·2	35·4	145	144

Source: D. V. Glass, 'A Note on the Under-Registration of Births in Britain in the Nineteenth Century', *Population Studies*, July 1951; and *idem.*, 'Population and Population Movements in England and Wales, 1700 to 1850', in D. V. Glass & D. E. C. Eversley, *Population in History*, London 1965

assuming the full reliability of the statistics of immigration and emigration as well as of deaths. When, under the hundred-years rule, the enumerators' transcripts for the censuses of 1871 and 1881 become available for research, it should be possible to check, on a sample basis, the birth registration entries of individuals born during the period 1837-80 and listed in the censuses. This would provide an approximation to a direct birth registration test[3] and would thus facilitate a better estimate of the incompleteness of death registration.

The estimates summarized in Table 1 assume that death registration was complete, save in 1841-45. In so far as this was not the case, the 'corrected' birth rates should be higher, especially for the 1840s and 1850s, when the new registration system was still being 'tried out', so to speak, and was thus especially liable to error. It is not unlikely, for example, that some infants who died soon after birth were treated as stillbirths and escaped recording in both the birth and death registers. Until the 1874 Act it was not necessary to obtain a certificate before the burial of a stillborn child, and even after that Act stillbirths were notified but not registered (the official series of stillbirth registration statistics began in 1927 in England and Wales and in 1939 in Scotland).[4] Infanticide, though very probably uncommon, was by no means unknown, especially in respect of illegitimate births. William Acton obtained from the Registrar General a detailed analysis of deaths by violence among infants (under one year of age) in England and Wales in 1856. Taking only the most obvious categories – poisoned, drowned, strangled, suffocated (not by bedclothes or by food and not overlaid), murdered and infanticide – 365 cases were reported out of a total of 846 deaths by violence. And some of the other cases may also have constituted infanticide – for example, some of the deaths from opium, laudanum and Mother Godfrey's Cordial and by suffocation from bedclothes or from being overlaid (in the eighteenth century this latter category in the London Bills of Mortality was believed to conceal cases of infanticide).[5] At least those deaths were recorded, even if there was doubt whether the violence was deliberate. But where a 'stillbirth' concealed the death of a live-born child, neither the birth nor the death would have been recorded, and this would have been more likely to occur with illegitimate births.[6] The certification requirements of the 1874 Act did not entirely eliminate doubts concerning stillbirths, since many were certified by persons who had no medical qualifications. A parliamentary return in 1891 reported 17,335 stillbirths interred in 1890 (in 1335 Burial Board cementries), of which 4562 (26 per cent) had been buried without medical certification.[7] The Select Committee on Death Certification – which recommended the compulsory registration of stillbirths[8] – claimed that 'the facilities that exist for the disposal of the bodies of children said to be still-born without the production of scientific evidence of still-birth affords opportunities for easily getting rid of the bodies of children who have lived and have met their death by foul means. There is reason from the evidence to think that a great number of cases of crime are concealed under statements that children are still-born.' Further, 'in the case of illegitimate children the fact that a still-birth has not to be registered, coupled with the desire for secrecy, is an inducement to a certain class of midwives to ensure that the child be still-born.' There was also a financial incentive in the fact that 'a considerable saving in funeral fees may be effected by burying a child as still-born'.[9] But there was some compensatory falsification – the registering, for the purpose of defrauding assurance companies, of deaths which had not taken place or which had been attributed to non-existent individuals.[10]

The significance of these deficiencies for the overall vital statistics should not be exaggerated. Taking the nineteenth-century civil registration system as a whole, it is probable that the 'corrected' estimates given in Table 1 are not far from the truth.[11] The 'true' crude birth and death rates were likely to have been somewhat higher than those shown in the estimates – and especially in the 1840s and 1850s – but not markedly so, for the elements of most doubtful reliability in the new system were small in relation to the main universe of vital events.[12] Where those doubtful elements would have a substantially greater effect would, of course, be in connection with more specialized studies. For example, behind the relatively modest estimates of incompleteness of birth registration at the national level, there may have been considerable local variation, with the deficiencies being especially large in respect of the population living in urban slums. Contemporary, room-by-room descriptions of the conditions of existence in some of those urban slums suggest that the populations involved could not have had any powerful incentives to register their vital events.[13] No fully satisfactory corrections can be made on that account. Until 1911 vital events were not, for statistical purposes, transferred back to the usual place of residence of the individuals concerned; there are no independent statistics of internal migration; and the use of census statistics on birthplace to estimate intercensal migration would involve assumptions which, at the local level, would conceal part – or perhaps all – of the registration deficiency. It might nevertheless be worthwhile to estimate *regional* differences in registration completeness, since the bulk of internal migration probably took place within regions.[14]

No less – and probably rather more – problematic would be studies relating to illegitimacy and particularly in the period prior to the implementation of the 1874 Act, when certification of stillbirths was introduced. This applies both to the question of the relative level of infant mortality among legitimate and illegitimate births and to that of the level and trend of illegitimacy itself.

On the first question, infant mortality rates by legitimacy for twenty-four districts in England and Wales in 1875 (twelve districts with high infant mortality and twelve with low) were published in the *Thirty-eighth Annual Report* of the Registrar General. The ratio of illegitimate to legitimate infant mortality ranged from two to one to nearly four to one.[15] The statistics for 1875 were probably relatively reliable as a result of the 1874 Act. Even so, they were not entirely free from significant errors, as may be seen from the evidence gathered by the Select Committee on Death Certification. The rates would have been artificially depressed by the exclusion of infants who, dying shortly after birth, had been falsely certified as stillbirths or whose birth and death had both been concealed. Since this would have been more frequent among illegitimate than among legitimate births, the real ratios of illegitimate to legitimate infant mortality would have been even higher than the published statistics suggested.

The question of the level of illegitimacy in the mid-nineteenth century is also difficult to resolve, given the defects in the statistics. Illegitimacy was a matter of practical concern, especially during the first half of the century, in connection with the Poor Law and the parish support of unmarried mothers and their children. With the fall in illegitimate birth rates, interest also declined, but it has increased again with the rise in the rates since World War II. In addition, demographers have been studying the history of illegitimacy as part of the general history of fertility and of the 'demographic transition',[16] while historians who have been broadening their field to cover more sociological questions have been looking at extra-marital pregnancies and births as indicators of the 'sexual revolution' and of changes in the status of women.[17] The general impression given by studies in England and France – the studies so far have a rather limited territorial coverage – is that both pre-marital conceptions and extra-marital births increased during the eighteenth century. And the Swedish statistics show a marked increase in illegitimacy rates – from 12·2 per 1000 unmarried women aged 20-44 years in 1751-60 to 35·2 per 1000 in 1851-60 and still rising thereafter.[18] The question at issue is how far the illegitimacy rate in England and Wales increased during the nineteenth century.

The official statistics of illegitimacy in England and Wales are summarized in Table 2.[19] Shorter suggests that civil registration, under the 1836 Act, brought with it the 'collapse' of illegitimacy reporting – that is, as compared with the coverage of parochial registration.[20] It is difficult to see how that can be demonstrated until a much larger series of parish register analyses has been completed. And even then the situation may not be clear, given the fact that ecclesiastical registration was defective and may well have been particularly defective for illegitimate births. Moreover, when the coverage of vital registration in general is incomplete variations in the numbers of illegitimate births may reflect other factors than the fre-

Table 2: Great Britain: Illegitimate live births per 1000 unmarried women aged 15-44 years

| Period | England & Wales | | Scotland | Period |
	Official rates	'Minimally corrected' rates	Official rates	
1851-60	18·3	19·1	–	–
1861-70	18·2	18·6	23·2	1860-62
1871-75	15·9	16·1	24·5	1870-72
1876-80	14·4	14·5	21·4	1880-82
1881-90	12·6	12·6	17·1	1890-92
1891-1900	9·6	9·6	13·8	1900-02

Sources: *Registrar General's Statistical Review of England and Wales* for 1969, Part II, Tables, Population, London 1971, p.14; *Annual Report of the Registrar General for Scotland* for 1969, Part II, Edinburgh 1971, p.84. For the 'minimally corrected' rates for England and Wales, see discussion in this Appendix.

---

quency of extra-marital intercourse – changes in Poor Law administration, for example, in the conditions for acquiring a settlement, or in the grounds for applying for affiliation orders against putative fathers. The nineteenth century not only saw changes in the vital registration system but also in the law relating to bastardy; and the first major change in the latter almost coincided with the change in the former.[21] The interpretation of apparent differences between eighteenth- and nineteenth-century levels of illegitimacy will have to await more detailed studies of the circumstances which might have affected reporting.

There is little doubt, however, that illegitimacy was under-reported in the early period of civil vital registration. As Farr explained – and as Shorter pointed out – 'no specific reference is made to illegitimate children in the Registration Act; and, as it is not stated on the face of the Register of Births, whether the children registered are or are not born in wedlock, the attempt to determine this point cannot always be successful; but great care has been taken in framing this Abstract, and in every doubtful case the child being classed as legitimate, I am confident that the Abstract now submitted to you cannot in any view be conceived to overstate the number of illegitimate children born in England.'[22] The difficulty, as Farr stated many years later in his evidence to the Select Committee on Protection of Infant Life, was that illegitimacy was only detected if the name and surname of the father were not given at birth registration, or if the father's surname was different from that of the mother. The mother was not asked whether or when she was married. The only safeguard was that giving a false name constituted perjury.[23] But in 'populous districts', in the earlier years at least, there were ways of concealing births, and a woman might with impunity 'suppose that she can assume a name, or give the name of a father...'[24] Hence the statistics of illegitimate births must be regarded as an understatement. But how much of an understatement?

First, so far as prior ecclesiastical registration is concerned, Rickman's returns for 1830, based on replies to a questionnaire circulated at the time of the 1831 census, were also derived primarily from the parochial system. According to these returns the total number of births in England and Wales in 1830 was 399,324. (382,060 baptisms, plus an annual average of 17,124 unentered baptisms, plus 140 births estimated for places which did not send in returns), and the reported number of illegitimate children born in 1830 was 20,039, an illegitimacy ratio of 5·02 per cent.[25] For 1842 the registration statistics gave a ratio of 6·7 per cent, which does not suggest a less complete coverage than was achieved by Rickman's inquiry.[26] Both sets of data were deficient,[27] and Farr, in his subsequent evidence to the Select Committee on Protection of Infant Life, reiterated his belief that the civil registration net was still not fully effective. 'I proposed myself, a more complete registration', he said, 'and took the trouble of trying it in several parts of London, and by the additional questions which I asked, I ascertained that many of the cases that would otherwise have escaped observation were really cases of illegitimate births.' But it is very doubtful if by the term 'many' he meant a large number for the country as a whole, as may be seen from his reply to a member of the Committee Mr Charley. 'In an inquiry carefully conducted', Charley stated, 'it was found that out of 165 illegitimate children 49 were not registered, equal to 30 per cent; this would raise the London rate of illegitimacy from 4·2 to 5·6 per cent, and applied to the whole of England, would show that 18,719 illegitimate children were not registered; do you think that that is correct?' Farr's answer was: 'I think that would be an overstatement as applied to all England, because the cases are not parallel; but it might apply to London.'[28] And for England and Wales as a whole it is probably true that by the 1870s there was no longer a gross concealment or mis-reporting of illegitimate births. Had there been, and especially if there was a large-scale misreporting of illegitimate children who died in early infancy (by burying them as stillbirths), it might have been expected that the 1874 Act would have been followed by a rise in the illegtimacy rate. But that was not the case, on the contrary, the rate was lower in 1876-80 than in any previous period covered by Table 2.

The evidence suggests that the under-registration or concealment of illegitimate births was greater in the earlier part of the period covered by Table 2. Making a minimal allowance for this – by assuming that the overall 'correction factors' apply equally to illegitimate and legitimate births – the rates given in the second column of the table are obtained. But these are minimal corrections, and a more realistic adjustment, if the necessary data were available, would almost certainly produce considerably higher rates for the 1850s and 1860s and slightly higher rates for the 1870s. It is clear that, whatever may have been the trend between the eighteenth and early nineteenth centuries, that from the mid-nineteenth century was downwards. Illegitimate fertility thus began to fall much earlier than legitimate fertility, the latter falling only from 1876-80.

Given the possible errors in the statistics of illegitimacy, it is likely that the published analyses of regional and local variations, especially for the earlier periods, need careful scrutiny and reassessment. The registration coverage probably varied more for illegitimate than for legitimate births. In addition, the search for anonymity, coupled with the fact that births were not transferred back to place of usual residence, must have introduced a larger element of artificiality in the illegitimacy rates for a number of areas. As for the social significance of the rates, Farr himself was sceptical. He wrote: 'Indeed, neither the Returns of illegitimacy, nor the Criminal Returns, can be taken as tests of the state of morals; and, in employing them at all with this view – to avoid gross fallacies, – a great variety of circumstances, besides the bare facts, must be considered.'[29] This is, of course, even more important in international than in inter-regional comparisons. There is obviously a great attraction in constructing broad, cross-national generalizations and some of them – such as the secular decline both of marital and of extra-marital fertility – are certainly supported by the facts, which suggest a uniformity powerful enough to overcome historico-cultural differences. But underneath that uniformity there are still variations in level, related to specific historical and cultural circumstances. For example, the high levels of illegitimacy in some of the German states and in Austria in the nineteenth century cannot be understood without reference to the attempts to prevent the poor from marrying.[30] In France, on the other hand, the high levels in some areas may have been related to the development of wet-nursing as an important field of female employment.[31] By contrast, it has been suggested that the unusually low level of illegitimacy in Ireland is explained in part by the particularly strong and persistent drive by the Roman Catholic priesthood to protect morals in a society which, as a reaction to the famine of 1845, had spontaneously adopted, as a means of population control, a rise in the age at and a reduction in the probability of marriage, complementing massive and continuing emigration.[32] The increase in illegitimacy in Sweden between the mid-eighteenth and the nineteenth centuries, on the other hand, was attributed by Sundbärg to the excessive consumption of spirits which, according to him, probably reached its peak in the period 1821-30.[33] Even when illegitimacy rates are believed to be 'correct' or have been suitably 'corrected', other circumstances of the kinds mentioned need to be taken into account in intepreting their significance.[34]

Although, as Farr claimed, the statistics of deaths were, from the beginning of civil registration, more comprehensive in coverage than those of births, other limitations need to be taken into account. Even today, death statistics are imperfect. Diagnosis is not always certain – not even when there has been an autopsy. The immediate cause of death may not be the basic cause, and this may be especially important in the study of occupational and social class mortality rates. Treated with care, however, modern death statistics are of the greatest importance and form the indispensable basis of socio-medical policy. Nineteenth-century death statistics, too, when used by medical statisticians like Farr, were of very great value. But additional factors need to be taken into account in handling them.

First, ages at death cannot be regarded as fully reliable. They are proxy statements and their accuracy will depend upon the informant's knowledge, which in turn will be related to the existence of a birth or baptismal certificate, the custom of celebrating birthdays and other circumstances. Some of these circumstances apply today. But the present combination of complete birth registration, comprehensive social security, compulsory education and high literacy greatly reduces the likelihood of serious involuntary errors. In the nineteenth century substantial numbers of the older people would not have had either baptismal or birth certificates and literacy was much lower – even among the marriages contracted in 1869-78 in England and Wales, 17·9 per cent of the grooms and 24·4 per cent of the brides signed the register with marks, instead of with their full names.[35] At the youngest ages there were transfers of children between age-groups, while the oldest ages often tended to be overstated. This was also the case in the census returns, and it is therefore not surprising that, in many countries, the proportions of centenarians fell as census-taking, vital registration and literacy improved.[36] There are techniques for dealing with age mis-statements, though they need to be applied with consideration for the kinds of errors most likely to occur in the particular society.[37]

Secondly, errors arose in connection with the certification of cause of death. As was mentioned earlier, there was the general problem of the identification of disease, dependent upon the progress of medicine, and especially upon advances in pathology and the development of bacteriology. But, in addition, there was the question of how far deaths were certified by qualified persons.

The 1836 Act did not make medical certification compulsory; that was left for the 1874 Act. In fact, however, there was from the start a very helpful response from the medical profession, so that the coverage of medical certification was much more extensive than might have been feared. A special tabulation of the deaths in the three months ending 31 March 1858 in England and Wales showed that, of a total of 125,519 deaths, 79 per cent were certified (as to cause) by medical attendants, 4 per cent by coroners, 6 per cent had no certificate because there had been no medical attendant and 11 per cent were not certified. Again, there was considerable regional variation. London had the best record: 92 per cent of deaths were certified by medical attendants and 5 per cent by coroners. By contrast, the poorest coverage was in Monmouthshire and Wales, where only 61 per cent of the deaths were certified by medical attendants or coroners.[38] With the 1874 Act the system was tightened up. When the Select Committee on Death Certification was taking evidence it was told that in the period 1882-92 only 3·3 per cent of deaths were uncertified in England and Wales; the position was not quite as satisfactory in Scotland, but even there only 5·8 per cent of the deaths in 1880 were uncertified. There were still pockets of resistance, so to speak; North Wales with 8·5 per cent and South Wales with 7·0 per cent; and, in Scotland, Edinburgh with 7·6 per cent. But the overall response was very good and the poorer areas were improving.[39]

Even in the 1890s, however, the data were not quite as satisfactory as these statistics might suggest. Apart from the imperfections of diagnosis, some medical certification was, in effect, fraudulent – the patient had not been seen for some time before his death and in some cases the death certificate was given by the doctor while the patient was still alive. Nor were coroners' inquests always helpful. Dr Ogle of the General Register Office gave examples. In Norwich, in 1882, there had been inquiries into fifty-five deaths; in forty-two cases the coroner's verdict was simply 'died from natural causes'. Perhaps the most absurd verdict was: 'Child, three months old, found dead, but no evidence whether born alive.'[40] The situation was worse in earlier years, when large numbers of informants were both unqualified and illiterate. An inquiry in eleven districts or sub-districts in England and Wales in 1864, covering 3196 deaths, classified the informants (excluding coroners and informants in institutions) by sex and literacy. There were 1208 men, of whom 26 per cent signed the register with marks; and there were 1988 women, of whom 62 per cent signed with marks. Farr's comment was: 'Why should a majority of the informants of some districts be ignorant women who sign the registers with marks, and cannot read and check the entry to which their signature is attached in the national records? The medical certificate is indispensable under such circumstances.[41]

It was claimed in the earlier discussion that, in spite of their limitations, nineteenth-century death statistics are still extremely valuable. Their use by Logan,[42] together with statistics for the present day, illuminates the decline in mortality in England and Wales during the past hundred years and provides an essential basis for going back further into the past. It might almost be argued that the evident crudeness of the mid-nineteenth century cause mortality data are a help in that connection – in the sense that, as a result, they are relatively near in spirit to the even more crude data of the London Bills of Mortality of the seventeenth and eighteenth centuries. It would take up too much space to discuss that in detail here.[43] But it may be of interest to show the proportionate mortality from main groups of cause at several points of time, though it is important to remember that proportionate mortality gives no idea of the level of mortality rates. The data in Table 3 do no more than reveal the changing *pattern* of mortality, influenced not only by changes in the chances of death from various diseases, but also by the modification of the age-composition of the population, affected primarily by the fall in fertility since the 1870s. Even so, the table provides information on what happened when England was transformed from an underdeveloped society, with high fertility, a young population, widespread poverty and inadequate sanitation and housing, to a fully industrialized society, massively urbanized, with a markedly lower level of fertility, an older population, extensive social, medical and public health provisions and relative affluence.

Sections A and B of the table offer a tentative comparison of proportionate cause mortality in London at three points of time – the Bills of Mortality being drawn upon for the first two and the Registrar General's official statistics for the third. In addition to the gross statistical deficiencies of the Bills – their incomplete coverage – they also suffer from the inexpert diagnosis of the 'searchers', an inadequate classification system and disease names which are now not easy to identify.[44] However, I have tried to select all those diseases which would qualify as 'infectious' in the sense used subsequently.[45] Tuberculosis has been shown separately – though it was later included in the category of infectious diseases – because of its special importance in both the eighteenth and nineteenth centuries, associated with poverty and overcrowding.[46] One important cause has been omitted from the list of specified diseases, namely convulsions, about which there was some controversy in the past. In the Registrar General's classification convulsions were included among nervous diseases. But in the nineteenth century, and almost certainly in the eighteenth century too, convulsions were primarily a cause of infant deaths (they were not a cause, but rather a condition of the infants in the terminal stages). In 1845, in London, 82 per cent of deaths from convulsions occurred under one year of age, and it is likely that they were associated with infantile diarrhoea, in turn heavily influenced by hot summer infections. They accounted for 27·3 per cent of all deaths in London 1706-10, 21·2 per cent in 1806-10 and 5 per cent in 1845, when together with diarrhoea they were responsible for 25 per cent of all infant deaths. Even in 1870, in England and Wales, those two causes accounted for almost 30 per cent of all infant deaths.

Table 3: Cause mortality in London and England & Wales: Proportionate mortality; deaths from specified causes per 1000 deaths from all causes

		A	
	Source	Bills of Mortality	
	Place	London	London
	Period	1706-10	1806-10
Cause		Persons	Persons
Infectious disease (excluding tuberculosis)		272	199
Tuberculosis (all forms)		153	269
Cancer (neoplasms)		3	4
Diseases of the nervous system			
Diseases of the circulatory system			
Diseases of the respiratory system			
Diseases of the digestive system			
Diseases of the genito-urinary system			
Violence		10	17
Sub-total		438	489
All causes		1000	1000

Sources: London 1706-10 & 1806-10: British Museum collection of Bills of Mortality (abortives and stillborn havebeen excluded); London, 1845: *Fourth Annual Report of the Registrar General*, London 1848, pp.cxxx-cxxxii; England & Wales, 1848-72: W. P. D. Logan, *op. cit.*; England & Wales, 1965: *Registrar General's*

In spite of the many defects of the Bills of Mortality,[47] there is sufficient 'sense' in them, and sufficient continuity with subsequent mortality statistics, to make it clear that infectious diseases and tuberculosis were the main killers in London in the eighteenth and early nineteenth centuries and continued to be so both in London and in England and Wales as a whole through the middle of the nineteenth century. In periods of epidemics their impact was still greater. In London in 1849, for example, when cholera alone killed more than 14,000 people, infectious diseases and tuberculosis together accounted for over 50 per cent of all deaths.

This Appendix has examined only a few of the problems involved in using nine-teenth-century British vital statistics. Some other problems were not discussed because, though they continued to apply until the implementation of the 1938 Population (Statistics) Act, they were relatively marginal. For example, until the 1938 reform in our vital statistics, birth statistics were statistics of registrations and not of occurrences. Since a delay of up to forty-two days was allowed for birth registration, time series of births contain a doubtful element which might itself vary with such outside factors as rationing. The difference in delay in registering births and deaths would also affect the calculation of infant mortality rates. But reasonable allowances can be made for these elements.

Other problems are much more important, but would require substantial studies to deal with them. One example relates to marriage statistics. English marriage

B Registrar General London 1845			**C** Registrar General England & Wales 1848-72		1965	
Persons	Males	Females	Males	Females	Males	Females
197	194	200	175	183	4	4
143	151	134	146	155	6	2
15	7	23	9	22	206	186
161	169	152	129	117	122	186
36	36	35	53	63	376	374
164	174	153	148	134	142	100
79	77	81	83	85	26	28
22	16	29	14	6	19	15
28	37	18	49	18	50	38
845	861	825	806	783	951	933
1000	1000	1000	1000	1000	1000	1000

Statistical Review (for 1965), Part 1, Tables, Medical, London 1967, table 7)
Note : It should be emphasized that between the nineteenth century and the present day there were considerable changes in cause-mortality classification.

statistics, as was pointed out earlier, are largely organized through the churches, and ministers are not necessarily effective registrars. In the past, at least, they did not appear to take sufficient trouble to avoid ambiguities in the occupational statements entered in the marriage register. Unstated ages – other than 'full age' – were also a problem in the mid-nineteenth century. Nevertheless, the marriage registers are a valuable source of information, not so far sufficiently used by the Registrars General. Thus the only official tabulation I have seen age at marriage by groom's occupation for England and Wales was for 1884-85.[48] Analyses of proportions married and age at marriage have been produced on the basis of census returns. But they do not have the same meaning, for the census occupations are those held at the time of the census and not when the marriages took place. There have been tabulations of two samples drawn from the central marriage certificate files. My colleagues and I designed, and were able to have extracted by the General Register Office, nationally representative samples of the marriages of 1871 and 1951. Table 4 displays some of the results, namely the mean ages at first marriage (that is, bachelor-spinster marriages) by the socio-economic position of the grooms at the time of the marriage. The table is included here for illustrative purposes only. There is no reason why similar samples should not be drawn for other years, so as to yield a picture of the history of age at marriage from the middle of the nineteenth century to the present day.[49]

Table 4: England & Wales, 1871 & 1951: Age at marriage of grooms and brides (first marriages of both), by the socio-economic position of the grooms at the time of marriage

		Mean age at marriage (years)			
		1871		*1951*	
		Grooms	*Brides*	*Grooms*	*Brides*
1	Farmers	26·92	24·80	26·61	23·35
2	Agricultural workers	25·65	24·39	25·32	22·97
3	High administrative, professional & managerial*	29·61	24·38	27·62	24·67
4	Intermediate, administrative professional & managerial	25·97	23·72	26·90	24·23
5	Shopkeepers	26·93	23·78	28·96	25·03
6	Clerical workers	25·54	23·02	26·49	23·70
7	Shop assistants	25·98	23·65	25·64	22·92
8	Personal service	26·24	25·20	26·02	23·57
9	Foremen	23·30	22·39	27·03	24·58
10	Skilled manual workers	23·99	22·53	25·52	22·85
11	Semi-skilled manual workers	24·05	22·53	26·26	23·26
12	Unskilled manual workers	24·69	22·87	25·42	22·88
13	Armed forces (other ranks)	25·93	22·74	22·45	21·19

*Including gentlemen

Notes: Sample size 1871: Total sample 4040; number with age stated – 2865 grooms, 2925 brides; no information on groom's occupation – 3
1951: Total sample 4141; number with age stated – 4111 grooms, 4109 brides; no information on groom's occupation – 34
Source: Unpublished data of Population Investigation Committee, derived from samples drawn from General Register Office marriage certificate files. The tabulations were carried out by my colleague, Dr Savitri Thapar.

Table 5: England & Wales: The previous marital status of men and women marrying in 1872, 1931 & 1965 (percentages)

Previous	*Men*			*Women*		
marital status	*1872*	*1931*	*1965*	*1872*	*1931*	*1965*
1 Bachelors or spinsters	86·3	91·7	88·5	90·1	94·3	89·3
2 Widowers of widows	13·7	7·6	4·9	9·9	5·0	4·3
3 Divorcés or divorcées	0·0*	0·7	6·6	0·0*	0·7	6·4
Total	100·0	100·0	100·0	100·0	100·0	100·0

*Less than 0·1 per cent

Source: The relevant issues of the Registrar General's *Annual Reports* and *Statistical Reviews*

We need more studies of this kind. In the past there was some tendency to consider that the data on births and deaths were almost the only data of importance in demographic analysis – perhaps because marriage did not appear to be a significant, independent variable in respect of the long-term decline in fertility. But events since the 1930s have shown that changes in marriage patterns can be substantial: the changes in Britain between the 1930s and the 1960s were greater than any experienced in the previous two or three centuries. In addition, marriage still generally marks the establishment of a household and provides the context for the socialization of children and, to a considerable extent, the perpetuation of the system of social stratification. It is unfortunate that the reforms of the 1938 Population (Statistics) Act did not cover marriage statistics; a great deal of relevant knowledge would be gained if the recording of occupations (of bride and groom, bride's father and groom's father) were in line with that used in the census and if the entries in the marriage register were extended to include places of birth of bride and groom and blood relationship. Even with the present limited and not fully satisfactory information, however, the retabulation of samples of marriage certificates would provide, at the national level, information otherwise unobtainable on the background of marriage and of the role of marriage in the system of social stratification.

Divorce statistics, too, have until recently been treated in too superficial a fashion. Divorce has now taken over from death in breaking marriages before the end of the reproductive period. And as Table 5 shows, the remarriages of divorced men and women have substantially taken over from the remarriages of widowers and widows. Since World War II more attention has been given to divorce statistics and divorce petition files have been retabulated on lines similar to those followed in connection with the analysis of marriage certificates. The results of two unofficial retabulations for 1871 and 1951 are compared, in Table 6, with the Registrar General's analysis for 1966. The change in the social class composition of divorcing couples is striking.[50] It would be of interest to have comparable analyses for years following major changes in divorce legislation and/or in the provisions for financial aid to petitioners.

The most laborious of possible further studies would be those designed to yield new information on marital fertility levels and trends during the nineteenth century. The published vital statistics are not very illuminating on those matters, and until the 1938 Act few questions were asked at birth registration. But in principle there is no reason why 'family reconstitution', originally designed to deal with parish registers, should not be attempted on the basis of the civil documents of local registrars, provided that the necessary co-operation can be obtained from the registrars. The reconstitution would have to be done at the local level, for there are no linkage references in the central files at the General Register Office. Many problems would be involved, but the advantages, as compared with parish register reconstitution, are that civil registration was more nearly complete and that the necessary civil documents – marriage, birth and death certificates – provide much more information to facilitate matching. Social class differences as well as overall levels could be looked at. But the work would be time-consuming and in order to yield the most useful results it would be essential to have a suitably designed sample of districts which would serve as the target either for a research team or for co-operating indi-

Table 6: England and Wales: Divorces in 1871, 1951 & 1966 — socio-economic status of husbands at the time of the divorces (percentages)

Husband's socio-economic status	1871	1951	1966		Married males in 1961 census	
1 Professional & managerial*	41·4	11·4	2·3		3·6	
2 Intermediate	19·0	14·3	7·2		16·2	
3 Skilled manual				(45·5)		(48·5)
4 Semi-skilled manual	16·8	58·5	72·4	(17·1)	75·4	(19·4)
5 Unskilled manual				(9·8)		(7·5)
6 Armed forces†			16·2		1·1	
7 Not stated or not classifiable‡	22·8	15·8	1·9		3·6	
	100·0	100·0	100·0		99·9	

*For 1871 this category includes 'gentlemen' and 'independent means'

†For 1871 and 1951 these have been allocated to the other socio-economic categories which appeared most appropriate

‡The evidence suggests that in 1871 most of these husbands probably belonged to category 1, while in 1951 they were probably in the manual categories

Sources: 1871 & 1951: G. Rowntree & N. H. Carrier, 'The Resort to Divorce in England and Wales, 1858-1957', *Population Studies*, March 1958. The 1871 cases represent a 100 per cent coverage – only 285 cases. The 1951 cases represent a random sample of 1813 divorces, the petitions for which were lodged in 1951.

1966: *Registrar General's Statistical Review for England and Wales* (for 1967), Part III, Commentary, London 1971, p.32. A 10·6 per cent random sample (4152 cases) of dissolutions made absolute (and annulments granted) in 1966. The 1961 census data on married men are also cited from this source.

---

vidual research workers. This is not to suggest that the published nineteenth-century materials should be discarded. On the contrary, a thorough search of the literature would be highly desirable (on this and other demographic questions). There is a great mass of nineteenth-century materials, official and unofficial, and there is no reason to doubt that valuable data would be rediscovered.[51] But those data are likely to be unsystematic. A valid overall view could only be obtained by properly organized retabulations of the basic vital registration documents.[52]

NOTES

1 In implementing the 1874 Act, administrative improvements made it easier to register births and deaths.

2 The 2 per cent deficiency was in accordance with the assumption of the Registrar General (*Second Annual Report*, London 1840, p.7). The stricter requirements in respect of death registration would support Farr's view that few deaths escaped registration (W. Farr, *Vital Statistics*, ed. N. A. Humphreys, London 1885, pp.523 & 525).

3 P. E. Razzell has used this technique to estimate completeness of birth registration in England and Wales in the late eighteenth and early nineteenth centuries. A paper by him on the subject was published in *Population Studies* in March 1972. Various problems are involved in applying the technique and there is always the question of whether the sample of areas selected is fully representative. In fact, of course, no technique – not even a direct birth registration test of the kind used in the USA – can deal with cases of infants who have died and whose birth and death were totally concealed.

4 It was believed that stillbirths amounted to about 4 per cent of all births (Farr, *op. cit.*, p.107). Presumably this belief was based upon some collation of the various local estimates made by doctors and statisticians. For example, Dr A. B. Granville's data for London working-class women – for 1825 and earlier years (probably 1818-25) – indicated a stillbirth rate of 4·4 per cent (*Report from the Select Committee on the Laws Respecting Friendly Societies*, London 1825, pp.134-135). But in a subsequent publication covering a longer period – 1818-28 for one lying-in institution and 1821-28 for another – only 2·2 per cent of stillbirths were reported for a total of 12,478 singleton births (A. B. Granville, 'On Certain Phenomena, Facts and Calculations incidental to or connected with the Power and Act of Propagation in Females of the Industrial Classes in the Metropolis', *Transactions of the Obstetrical Society of London*, 1860, 2, pp.139-196. This paper appears to be identical with the item by Granville listed in the British Museum catalogue and reported as destroyed by a bomb during World War II; no copy of the item has been found in any other library and it seems very probable that Granville presented the Museum with a bound offprint of his paper). Other estimates include those for Glasgow by James Cleland, Superintendent of Public Works for the City of Glasgow. For 1821 Cleland reported 5031 baptisms (including 2370 unregistered) and 247 stillbirths in Glasgow and its suburbs, giving a stillbirth ratio of 4·7 per cent; for 1830 the comparable figures were 6397 baptisms (including 3172 unregistered) and 471 stillbirths, giving a ratio of 6·9 per cent (see J. Cleland, *Enumeration of the Inhabitants of the City of Glasgow and County of Lanark*, Glasgow 1831, pp.11-19).

Subsequently – after Farr had written – an official attempt was made to estimate the numbers of stillbirths by collecting statistics from Burial Board cemeteries of interments in 1890. These cemeteries reported the interment of 17,335 stillbirths and 239,950 other burials. For England and Wales as a whole the number of deaths in 1890 amounted to 564,248, and if the stillbirths were 'grossed up' in the same proportion, the national total would amount to 40,772. Adding these to the 869,937 live births registered in England and Wales in 1890, the resultant stillbirth ratio would be 4·7 per cent. (The statistics of stillbirths and other interments in

Burial Board cemetries are given in *Still-Birth Interments*, House of Commons Paper, 352/1891, B.P.P. 1890-91, Vol.LXVIII.)

For Europe the longest available series of stillbirth rates is that for Sweden. The rate for 1756-60 was 2·5 per cent; for 1801-10, 2·5 per cent; for 1851-60, 3·2 per cent, after which the rates began to fall, slowly and irregularly, reaching 1·2 per cent in 1961-65 (the increase in the mid-nineteenth century may be partly a reflection of improved registration). The comparable rate for England and Wales in 1961-65 was 1·7 per cent and for Scotland 1·9 per cent.

5 W. Acton, 'Observations on Illegitimacy in the London Parishes of St. Marylebone, St. Pancras, and St. George's, Southwark, during the year 1857', *J.R.S.S.*, Vol.22, 1859, pp.491-505.

6 It was not rare for the police to find the abandoned bodies of dead infants in the cities. Evidence on this was given to the Select Committee on Protection of Infant Life. For example, the Metropolitan and City Police reported that the bodies of 396 infants had been found in London during 1870 (*Report from the Select Committee on Protection of Infant Life*, July 1871, B.P.P. 1871, Vol.7, p.123). These deaths would have been recorded, but we do not know how many of the infants had been registered at birth. In addition, there were no doubt cases of infants whose birth and death had been concealed from the registrars and the police. (The Committee's Report cites a smaller figure for infants found dead in London in 1870-276 cases.)

7 These statistics were cited incorrectly in the *Report* of the Select Committee.

8 This had also been the recommendation, twenty years before, of the Infant Mortality Committee appointed by the London Obstetrical Society (see *Trans. Obst. Soc. London*, 1870, Vol.12, pp.388-403). But one of the expert witnesses to the Select Committee on Death Certification – Dr William Ogle, in charge of vital statistics at the General Register Office – while agreeing with the importance of information on stillbirths, regarded stillbirth registration as impracticable (*Report*, pp.xxiii & 227).

9 Since stillbirths were not registered, the Committee had little evidence on the comparative incidence of stillbirths among illegitimate and legitimate births in England and Wales. It had evidence (already cited) of the considerable percentage of uncertified stillbirths and also statistics for Glasgow for 1886-90, showing the higher proportion of uncertified deaths among illegitimate than among legitimate infants and children under five years of age (*Report*, p.269). However, the statistics for Sweden in the mid-nineteenth century revealed a substantial disparity between the legitimate and illegitimate stillbirth proportions. In 1841-50 the stillbirth rates were 5·16 per cent among illegitimate births and 2·92 per cent among legitimate births. The disparity decreased subsequently, and in 1961-65 the proportions for illegitimate and legitimate births were 1·29 and 1·15 per cent respectively (*Historisk Statistik*, p.108). In England and Wales, 1961-65, the stillbirth rates were 2·16 per cent for illegitimate and 1·72 per cent for legitimate births. Stillbirth rates, like infant mortality rates, are strongly influenced by socio-economic circumstances, and differences in such circumstances between married and unmarried mothers would certainly have affected the stillbirth rates in the mid-nineteenth century. Nevertheless, deliberate action no doubt also played a part.

10 See the references in the *Report* of the Committee on Death Certification, p.iv. Farr (*op. cit.*, p.222) noted that in twenty-nine years only four Registrars had been

found guilty of inventing 'fictitious entries of deaths which never occurred. They invented all the particulars of hundreds of deaths.' These Registrars were convicted and presumably their records were corrected. Fraud by 'outsiders' is likely to have been more important than fraud by officials.

11 Farr, after the passage of the 1874 Act, wrote: 'Formerly [before the 1874 Act] many births annually escaped being recorded in the civil registers, more particularly illegitimate births in large towns. It may be hoped that this *compulsory* clause may reduce the numbers omitted, although the birth registration is not as yet quite complete.' And 'with respect to deaths, very few escaped civil registration, and the chief defect was the want of accuracy in the information supplied for record by persons "present at death", and "in attendance" during fatal illness' (*Thirty-Eighth Annual Report of the Registrar General* – Farr, *op. cit.*, p.527).

12 Coale and Demeny, using techniques derived from stable population theory, have produced estimates of the crude birth rate in the years preceding the 1881 census of England and Wales, and their estimates are similar to mine. But that does not constitute an entirely independent check, partly because their estimates involve assumptions regarding under-registration of births. At the same time, the margin of indeterminacy in their estimates would allow them to fit either the uncorrected or the corrected birth rates. (A. J. Coale & P. Demeny, *Regional Model Life Tables and Stable Populations*, Princeton 1966, pp.35-37.)

13 The literature on mid-nineteenth century urban slums is vast – including, of course, the famous Chadwick Report (*Report... on an Inquiry into the Sanitary Condition of the Labouring Population of Great Britain*, London 1842). But as a single example of the contemporary, statistical investigations, it is worth referring to the inquiry undertaken by the London (subsequently Royal) Statistical Society in 1847 in one street in London. See 'Report of a Committee... to investigate the State of the Inhabitants and their Dwellings in Church Lane, St. Giles's', *J.R.S.S.*, Vol.11, March 1848. For annotated references on urban conditions in nineteenth-century Britain, see Ruth Glass, 'Urban Sociology in Britain, a Trend Report', *Current Sociology*, Vol.4, No.4, 1955. On London, see H. J. Dyos, 'The Slums of Victorian London', *Victorian Studies*, Vol.11, No.1, September 1967; and G. S. Jones, *Outcast London*, Oxford 1971.

14 This is certainly the case at present. An analysis of the 1966 census data on the birth places of the population in England and Wales shows that 84 per cent of the males and 83 per cent of the females born in the various regions were enumerated in the region of their birth (a detailed analysis will be included in a forthcoming study of internal migration, with particular reference to London).

15 Farr, *op. cit.*, pp.197-199. The *Report* also presented comparable rates for Glasgow, 1873-75, showing a ratio of slightly under 2 to 1. At present I can see no way of estimating the 'true' infant mortality rate for illegitimate births in England and Wales. Recourse may again be had to Swedish statistics in order to obtain a comparative picture for a country with more reliable data. Infant mortality rates for legitimate births were 144 and 137 per 1000 in 1841-50 and 1851-60 respectively; for illegitimate births the rates were 248 and 232, the ratio of illegitimate to legitimate being 1·72 and 1·69. In 1961-65 the rates were 14 and 22, the ratio being 1·57 – a small reduction in the ratio though a great reduction in the absolute levels of both rates (*Historisk Statistik*, p.115). The situation in England and Wales, how-

-ever, is rather different. In 1906-10, from which period serial data on legitimate and illegitimate infant mortality are available, the rates were 113 and 224 per 1000, a ratio of nearly 2 to 1; in 1961-65 the rates were 20 and 26, a ratio of 1·30 to 1. In Scotland the 1961-65 rates were 24 and 36, a ratio of 1·50 to 1. The mortality of illegitimate infants in England and Wales was also understated as a result of the determination of the illegitimacy of infants who died from the information recorded at death. In 1969 this was changed, information on illegitimacy being thereafter obtained from the birth records. The mortality rate of illegitimate infants, having fallen to 23 per 1000, then rose to 26 in 1969 and 1970 (*Registrar General's Statistical Review of England and Wales* for 1970, Part 1, Tables, Medical, London 1972, pp.vi & 5).

16 For example, E. van de Walle, E. Shorter & J. Knodel, 'The Decline of Non-Marital Fertility in Europe, 1880-1940', *Population Studies*, November 1971.

17 See in particular E. Shorter, 'Illegitimacy, Sexual Revolution, and Social Change in Modern Europe', *Journal of Interdisciplinary History*, Autumn 1971; and P. E. H. Hair, 'Bridal Pregnancy in Earlier Rural England further Examined', *Population Studies*, March 1970.

18 G. Sundbärg, *Bevölkerungsstatistik Schwedens 1750-1900*, reprint, Stockholm 1970, p.117.

19 Marital condition was not ascertained in the censuses of England and Wales until 1851. Hence illegitimacy before that year can only be measured by ratios – that is, illegitimate births as a percentage of all live births. But the ratio is an unsatisfactory index, since it is affected not only by the probability of unmarried women having illegitimate births, but also by the proportion of unmarried women and the level of marital fertility.

20 *Op. cit.*, p.260.

21 See, for example, U. R. Q. Henriques, 'Bastardy and the New Poor Law', *Past and Present*, No.37, July 1967. There were important legal changes in 1834, 1844 and 1872. See also W. G. Lumley, 'Observations on the Statistics of Illegitimacy', *J.R.S.S.*, Vol.25, June 1862, esp. pp.245-256.

22 *Sixth Annual Report of the Registrar General*, London 1845, p.xxxi.

23 *Report*, pp.165-166.

24 *Sixth Annual Report of the Registrar General*, p.xxxi. Farr added: 'The attention of the Registrars has been specially directed to these points, and they are required to acquaint every informant that any false statement wilfully made by her respecting any particular to be recorded in the register, will render her liable to the pains and penalties of perjury; they are also instructed to discourage the entry of the names of putative fathers in the Register Books of Births.'

25 1831 census, England and Wales, *Parish Register Abstract*, London 1833, p.486. The question addressed to the clergy (to all officiating ministers of churches and chapels in England and Wales) was: 'What number of illegitimate children may have been born in your parish or chapelry during the year 1830, according to the best information you possess or can obtain; and distinguishing male and female children?' (1831 census, *Enumeration Abstract*, Part I, London 1833, p.xxv).

26 *Sixth Annual Report of the Registrar General*, p.xxxii. Although the results were not available when Farr wrote, a second questionnaire on illegitimate births had been circulated in connection with the 1841 census. The results (including supplemen-

tary returns and allowances for no returns) gave a total of 386,752 baptisms in 1840, those for illegitimate children being 22,312, an illegitimacy ratio of 5·77 per cent. This, too, is lower than Farr's ratio for 1842 (and the absolute numbers in the census return are considerably lower than the numbers of registered births – 386,752 baptisms in 1840 as compared with 502,303 registered births in 1840 and 517,739 in 1842: once civil registration began, baptisms fell). The census report itself referred to the 'supposed numbers of baptisms of illegitimate children' and noted that the baptismal returns in general 'cannot include the numbers unbaptized or still-born, which latter class may be supposed to comprise a large proportion of illegitimate children' (1841 census, England and Wales, *Parish Register Abstract*, London 1845, pp.v. & vii).

27 There were at least two other official attempts – both partial – to estimate the number of illegitimate births. First, there was the return to the House of Lords in 1839, (cited by Lumley, *op. cit.*, pp.222-223), reporting the illegitimate children baptized in ten counties in two successive three-year periods, 1832-34 and 1835-37 inclusive. The returns are given separately for each parish, but without corresponding returns for legitimate births, and it is clear that some of the children baptized were not newborn (one parish reported that in 1834-37 'half the illegitimate persons were adults'). Some of the parish comments are of interest. Thus several of the illegitimate children were born to married women whose husbands had been in Australia or elsewhere for more than a year. For one parish, in reporting an illegitimate child, it was stated to be the first in fifty years; the incumbent of another, however (Aldershot, Southampton), believed that 'not one half the illegitimate children are brought to baptism'. Some of the children returned were not illegitimate, but were conceived before marriage. Finally, returns from two parishes comment on the role of the law. Blackmore (Essex) commented that 'previous to 1836, many marriages took place previous to the birth of a child, from intimidation or compulsion, but do not under the new law'. The other parish (Wye, Kent) noted that many legitimate children were conceived before marriage, 'so that these returns prove nothing as to the improved morality of the parishes. In this parish improvident marriages have been fewer within the last two years; but the alteration of the Poor Law has effected no improvement in the moral conduct of the females.' (*Abstract of the Returns of the Number of Illegitimate Children Registered* . . . , June 1839, House of Lords Library, *State Papers*, 1839, Vol.16.)

The second attempt was in a return to the House of Commons, covering the illegitimate children whose baptisms were registered in 1831-33 and 1839-41 inclusive in five counties (*Illegitimate Children. Abstract Return of Illegitimate Children Registered in the Several Parishes of Lancashire, West Riding of Yorkshire, Norfolk, Surrey and Herefordshire, 1831-1833, and 1839-1841,* London 1842, House of Commons Paper 1843-86, *B.P.P.*, 1843, Vol.45). The returns are given for each year as well as in aggregate, and it is therefore possible to compare them fairly closely with the 1831 and 1841 census returns and with the civil vital statistics for 1842, as in the table overleaf.

It is clear from this table that, in general, the census returns yielded larger numbers than the parish returns sent directly to to the House of Commons for the same or nearest equivalent years, and that the civil vital statistics yielded still larger numbers than either of the returns based on parochial registration. For England

Statistics of illegitimate births for five counties

1831 census returns for:	House of Commons returns for:				
	1830	1831	1832	1833	1839
Lancaster	2930	1739	1833	1818	1988
Yorkshire, West Riding	1534	1087	1145	1150	1135
Norfolk	648	697	650	681	787
Surrey	309	342	285	332	326
Herefordshire	234	235	220	265	224
Totals	5655	4100	4133	4246	4460

Parish Register Abstract, tables (a), p.ix, & (k), p.xxiii. Because of the changes associated with the creation of registration districts in 1837, the census provided an analysis both by geographical counties and (approximate) registration counties. The county statistics do not include the supplementary returns and other allowances, but they amounted to only 222 illegitimate children for England and Wales.

---

and Wales as a whole, the civil vital statistics registered 34,796 illegitimate births in 1842, as compared with 22,312 returned for 1840 in the 1841 parish register abstract.

28 *Report*, pp.166 & 174-175. I have not been able to find a full account of the inquiry referred to by Charley. The very low reported illegitimacy ratio for London puzzled many contemporary writers. The official view was that registration of illegitimate births was particularly deficient in London, but also that in London and such other large towns as Birmingham, Liverpool and Manchester 'the unrestrained passions which in other districts result in illegitimate offspring are in these large towns diverted into the channel of barren prostitution' (extract from *Forty-Second Annual Report of the Registrar General*, cited in *J.R.S.S.*, Vol.44, June 1881, p.397).

29 *Sixth Annual Report of the Registrar General*, p.xxxv. For a contemporary analysis of national differences in illegitimacy rates, see J. Bertillon, 'Les naissances illégitimes en France et dans quelques pays de l'Europe', *Sixth International Congress of Hygiene and Demography*, Vienna 1887. *Proceedings*, Vol.29. Bertillon's paper also covers stillbirths and concludes that the higher stillbirth rate among illegitimate births was the result of the miserable condition of the mothers rather than of criminal action on their part.

30 See my paper on Germany and Ireland in D. V. Glass (ed.), *Introduction to Malthus*, London 1953; and J. Knodel, 'Law, Marriage and Illegitimacy in Nineteenth-Century Germany', *Population Studies*, March 1967.

31 There are references in the article on 'Nourrice' in *Dictionnaire encyclopédique de sciences médicales*, Ser.2, Vol.13, Paris 1879, p.395; and A. Armengaud, 'Les nourrices de Morvan au XIXe siècle', *Études et chroniques de démographie historique*, No.1, Paris 1964, p.138. Acton, *op. cit.*, p.504, claimed that in England, too, unmarried mothers were employed as wet-nurses and advocated that, if controlled by a public institu-

1840	1841	1841 census returns for 1840*		Civil vital statistics for 1842†
		Geographical counties	Registration counties	
2045	2129	2773	2872	5592
1125	1122	1549	1454	2842
805	830	973	962	1214
364	376	423	427‡	657‡
229	228	229	188	292
4568	4685	5947	5903	10597

†*Sixth Annual Report of the Registrar General*, p.40
‡Surrey here consists of both the county outside of London and of the Surrey section of Metropolitan London – the two being equivalent to the former geographical county

tion, 'a good proportion of the mothers might be found situations as wet-nurses . . .
32 A full account is given in the study by R. E. Kennedy, *Irish Emigration, Marriage and Fertility, 1841-1966*, Berkeley 1973.
33 Sundbärg, *op. cit.*, pp.52-53.
34 More light might be thrown on the background of illegitimacy in nineteenth-century Britain by retabulating samples of the birth certificates. Acton (*op. cit.*) did this for the occupations of the mothers of 339 infants who died in 1857 in the London parishes of Marylebone, St Pancras and St George's, Southwark (194 were domestic servants and 33 dressmakers), and he also collected data on the occupations of the fathers of 180 illegitimate children born in Marylebone workhouse. Apart from this, the only other nineteenth-century British study I have seen which lists the occupation of the mothers is that by A. Leffingwell (*Illegitimacy and the Influence of Seasons upon Conduct*, London 1892). Leffingwell quotes (p.68) an analysis undertaken by the Registrar General of Scotland in 1883 of the occupations of 10,010 mothers of illegitimate children – 4706 were domestic servants and 2442 were factory workers. The detailed statistics are given in the *Twenty-Ninth Detailed Annual Report of the Registrar-General*, Edinburgh 1886, pp.xi-xviii. The highest illegitimacy rates were for the mainland rural districts – Banff county had a rate of 36·4 per 1000 unmarried women aged 15-44 and Wigtown county 37·8 – and for Glasgow (with 23·8 per 1000). The table below summarizes, for the main types of area, the occupations of the mothers of illegitimate births (percentage distribution). It would not be difficult to extract a series of national samples from the central files of birth certificates. It would be far more difficult, however, to carry out an inquiry comparable to that organized by the Registrar General of England and Wales in connection with the 1961 census – that is, to link a sample of illegitimate births occurring shortly before a census with the relevant census schedules in order to see what fraction of the births had apparently been the product of *de facto* unions.

Occupations of mothers (percentages)

Type of district	Domestic servant	Agricultural servant	Seam-stress	Factory worker	Profes-sional*	Non-pro-fessional†	Not stated	All
Principal towns	34·0	2·6	10·0	38·2	1·0	10·3	4·0	100·1
Large towns	36·9	8·9	4·6	38·3	0·4	6·3	4·5	99·9
Small towns	49·3	14·2	4·4	20·6	0·3	6·3	4·9	100·0
Mainland rural	65·0	17·1	2·4	5·2	0·1	7·4	2·8	100·0
Inland rural	69·1	10·3	5·1	0·6	1·1	12·0	1·7	99·9
Scotland	47·0	9·8	6·1	24·4	0·5	8·3	3·8	99·9

*No occupation – daughters of non-professional men
†No occupation – daughters of professional men

---

35 *J.R.S.S.*, Vol.44, June 1881, p.395 – cited from *Annual Report of the Registrar General* (for 1879).

36 On centenarians and the inquiries undertaken in connection with various nineteenth-century censuses, see E. Levasseur, *La population française*, Vol.2., Paris 1891, pp.326-333. Errors in age statements make it necessary to use special techniques for studying mortality at the oldest ages. See P. E. Vincent, 'La morta-lité des vieillards', *Population*, Vol.6, April-June 1951; and G. T. Humphrey, 'Mortality at the Oldest Ages', *Journal of the Institute of Actuaries*, Vol.96, Part 1, 1970.

37 See N. Carrier & J. Hobcraft, *Demographic Estimation for Developing Societies*, London 1971.

It is probably true that, in many Western societies in the nineteenth century, people had a more accurate idea of their ages than is often the case in developing societies today. As was mentioned earlier, ecclesiastical registration, for all its defects, covered the bulk of the population.

38 Farr, *op. cit.*, p.263.

39 *Report*, pp.vii, 286 & 298. By no means all medical statisticians or public health specialists were satisfied with the 1874 Act. See, for example, the preface to H. W. Rumsey, *Essays and Papers on Some Fallacies of Statistics*, London 1875.

40 *Report*, p.viii.

41 Farr, *op. cit.*, p.227. It was not infrequently suggested that the use of burial clubs or life assurance in connection with infants tended to encourage neglect of those infants and occasionally their murder. A recommendation made to the Select Committee on Protection of Infant Life (*Report*, p.vii) urged 'That no infant or very young person should be entered in a burial club, or become the subject of life insurance' (the committee did not accept the recommendation, which was outside the scope of its inquiry). It seems likely, however, that in general high infant mortality was so visible, especially in urban working class districts, that parents simply took the precaution of providing funds for a strongly probable even-tuality. After all, with an expectation of life at birth of some forty years – as was the case for England and Wales in the mid-nineteenth century – the probability of

a newborn infant dying by his fifth birthday was over 25 per cent. In the towns the probability of death would have been still greater, especially for working-class children.

42 W. D. P. Logan, 'Mortality in England and Wales from 1848 to 1947', *Population Studies*, September 1950.

43 Mortality trends in England and Wales in the eighteenth and early nineteenth centuries are the subject of a separate study, now in progress.

44 T. R. Forbes (*Chronical from Aldgate*, Newhaven & London, 1971, esp. pp.102-118) has identified many of the causes, by using ninteenth-century dictionaries of obsolete words and eighteenth-century medical texts, and his glossary has been very helpful. His list could no doubt be extended. But for a fuller understanding of the diseases named, a rather more thorough study would be needed, on lines similar to those discussed by N. D. Grmek ('Préliminaires d'une étude historique des maladies', *Annales : Économies, Sociétés, Civilisations*, November-December 1969 and J.-P. Peter 'Une enquete de la Société Royale de Médecine (1774-1794): malades et maladies a la fin du XVIII- siècle', *ibid.*, July-August 1967).

45 I have included among infectious diseases agues and fevers, fevers, fluxes and bloody fluxes, flox and smallpox, French pox, griping in the guts and dysentery, leprosy, measles, swinepox and chickenpox, quinsy and sore throat (in 1845 quinsy was included in the respiratory category but was later transferred to infectious diseases), influenza, chincough (whooping cough) and cough and whooping cough. I have not allowed for any share of 'infants', though some of those would certainly have died from infectious diseases. 'Inflamation' has not been included.

46 Tuberculosis in this analysis covers consumption, tissick, scrofula or King's evil and rising of the lights (believed to be a pulmonary infection). It is the first two terms which account for the vast bulk of the entries. On cause mortality in eighteenth-century London, a pioneer analysis will be found in J. Brownlee, 'The Health of London in the Eighteenth Century', *Proc. Royal Soc. Med.*, Vol.18, 1924-25, Epidemiology Section, pp.73-85. Brownlee also dealt with tuberculosis in a separate monograph – *An Investigation into the Epidemiology of Phthisis in Great Britain and Ireland* (National Health Insurance: Medical Research Committee, Special Report No.18), London 1917, pp.38-44. On tuberculosis mortality in England from the mid-nineteenth century, see P. D'Arcy Hart & G. Payling Wright, *Tuberculosis and Social Conditions in England*, London 1939.

One of the problems in connection with the London Bills of Mortality is the varying specificity of disease names from year to year. One bill, for example, may attribute some deaths to 'hectic fever' (which might be equated with 'Hectika' and 'Hectika fever' in the eighteenth-century Vienna Bills, included by S. Peller among tuberculosis cases – S. Peller, 'Zur Kenntnis der städtischen Mortalität in 18 Jahrhundert...', *Zeitschrift für Hygiene und Infektkr.*, Vol.90, 1920, p.253), but in another bill this may not be shown separately. Nor can we tell how many other 'fevers' were of a 'hectic' kind. But that tuberculosis was a major cause is confirmed by contemporaries. Thus Robert Willan (cited by Brownlee, pp.40-41), who was very careful in his diagnosis, reported that, among 4500 persons admitted under his care in 1795 and 1796, 245 died, and 77 of these (31 per cent) from pulmonary consumption.

It is of some interest to compare the London bills with the results of present day attempts in India to use para-medical personnel to classify causes of death, taking as the universe the populations of 714 Primary Health Centre villages. In 1967, when cholera mortality was negligible and smallpox mortality very low, the classification yielded the following percentage distribution of causes (both sexes, all ages):

Diarrhoeas	8·8
Broncho-pneumonia, pneumonia and bronchitis	14·2
Tuberculosis (all forms)	5·6
Specified infectious diseases (malaria, smallpox, measles, typhoid)	8·0
Unclassified fevers	10·5
Total specified causes	47·1
All causes	100·0

Even with large-scale BCG campaigns and with modern treatment, tuberculosis was evidently still an important cause of death; in the age groups 35-54 years it accounted for almost 17 per cent of all deaths (*Report on Survey of Cause of Death 1966 and 1967*, Office of the Registrar General, New Delhi 1970).

47 Another defect arises in connection with deaths from violence (which here cover drowning, murder, accidents, overlaid, poison, stabbing, strangling, suffocation, suicide and execution). William Black, the eighteenth-century medical statistician, believed that the bills grossly understated the number of executions. He could find no records in London for the years prior to 1754, but made what he considered a 'reasonable estimate' for the period 1762-77, during which time he believed there had been about 1020 executions, 19 out of 20 being males and predominantly between eighteen and forty years of age (W. Black, *An Arithmetical and Medical Analysis of the Diseases and Mortality of the Human Species*, London 1789).

48 *Forty-eighth Annual Report of the Registrar General*, London 1886, pp.viii-x.

49 The full results of the tabulations of the two samples will be published in a symposium on demographic aspects of marriage and the family in Britain since 1871. The analyses include ages at marriage by socio-economic status, inter- and intra-class marriage frequencies and distances between bride's and groom's place of residence at the time of the marriage. Naturally, changes in age at marriage cannot be interpreted solely in terms of the means reported in Table 4. Apart from sampling errors, it would be necessary to examine medians and modes and also to take into account the kinds of bias produced by the very large number of marriages in 1871 in which age was not recorded (other than 'full age'). There is also the question of the influence on overall mean age at marriage of changes in occupational composition between 1871 and 1951.

50 Both the academic and the official tabulations provide information on other relevant characteristics – duration of marriage and number of children, for example.

51 A most unusual collection of information on fertility was gathered by a committee of the London Statistical Society in an investigation of the 'poorer classes' in East London in 1845 ('Report... from a Committee... Appointed to make an

Investigation of the Poorer Classes in St. George's in the East...' *J.R.S.S.*, Vol.11, August 1848). Unfortunately, the data were not published in a form which would permit retabulation on lines more compatible with present-day fertility analysis. Nevertheless, some of the results are extremely interesting, not least the short table reproduced below, showing for fertile married women the mean numbers of children born per woman by age at marriage and number of years since the birth of the first child (p.223).

Years since birth of first child	Age at marriage 16-20	21-25	26-30	31-35
10	5·05	4·51	4·42	3·44
20	7·68	7·01	6·43	3·00
30	8·41	7·89	6·80	7·00
40	10·85	8·24	5·00	4·00

Married women (including the childless) aged 45-49 years at the time of the survey had borne an average of 6·8 children, of whom 3·2 had died, a mortality loss of 47 per cent. The mean age at first birth of the women aged 45-49 was 23·1 years. 52 In the past, wide use has been made of the fertility data collected at the 1911 censuses of Great Britain and Ireland, and justifiably so, for those censuses were pioneers in the investigation of fertility. Unfortunately, the data are biased in at least two respects. First, the marriages of very long duration, reflecting the patterns of fertility of the 1870s and earlier years, are inevitably over-weighted by young ages at marriage. This can be corrected to some extent by reweighting. The second bias derives from the definition of the universe covered by the fertility questions – namely currently married couples, with husband present. But 'currently married' excludes couples whose marriage remained unbroken until the end of the wife's reproductive period and became broken (primarily by death of the husband) thereafter. Given both level of mortality and sex differential in the death rates, this means that the women married in, say, the 1870s and 1860s and included in the fertility census represented only a fraction of those women who were still alive in 1911 – about 52 per cent of the women married in 1871-75 and 32 per cent of the women married in 1861-65 and alive in 1911 (D. V. Glass & E. Grebenik, *The Trend and Pattern of Fertility in Britain*, Part 1, London 1954, pp.68-70).